KiTCHEN COACH
FAMILY MEALS

KITCHEN COACH

FAMILY MEALS

JENNIFER BUSHMAN
and SALLIE WILLIAMS

WILEY

Wiley Publishing, Inc.

Library of Congress Cataloging-in-Publication Data:

Bushman, Jennifer, 1967-
    Kitchen coach family meals / Jennifer Bushman and Sallie Williams.
        p. cm.
    Includes index.
    ISBN 13 978-07645-4312-8 (pbk.)
    ISBN 10 0-7645-4312-1 (pbk.)
1. Cookery. I. Williams, Sallie Y. II. Title.
    TX714.B878 2006
    641.5—dc22
                                2005032325

Printed in the United States of America
10 9 8 7 6 5 4 3 2 1

Contents

Acknowledgments   vi

Introduction   vii

Why Cook for Your Family?   1

Is Your Kitchen Ready?   9

Appealing Appetizers   20

Satisfying Soups   33

Substantial Salads   42

Incredible Eggs   52

Fish and Shellfish   65

Perfect Poultry   77

Poultry Encores   88

Beef, Pork, Veal, and Lamb   100

Beef, Pork, Veal, and Lamb Encores   112

Vegetables for Everyone   121

Ready and Waiting: Slow Food   130

Make Aheads for the Freezer   142

One-Dish Meals   151

Bountiful Breads   161

Delectable Desserts   170

Drink to the Good Life   179

Lip-Smacking Snacks   188

Cooking with Kids   196

Index   205

Pantry Checklist   215

Metric Conversion Guide   216

Acknowledgments

For Sallie and me, our families are the foundation upon which we have built our lives. The caring way that they have shared our journey by allowing us to feed them has made this book possible. These families, both immediate and extended, need to be acknowledged. First of all, I thank my editor Linda Ingroia and assistant editor Rachel Bartlett for their invaluable assistance. I also appreciate the efforts of other dedicated Wiley staff including Shannon Egan, the production editor; Jeff Faust and Holly Wittenberg, the cover and interior designers; and Gypsy Lovett, in publicity and Todd Fries and Michael Friedberg in marketing. Thank you, Jeffrey Dow, for your great photographs that bring my food to life. To my dear family of friends at Nothing to It! and beyond for tasting and attending every chance they could to support my mission. To Lara Ritchie and Barbara Mills for their unwavering commitment. To my mother, for without her quiet understanding and strength I would have never sat still long enough to cook. Finally, to Matt, your presence has defined the true meaning of our Family Meals.

Jennifer Bushman

There is no way I can ever thank Jennifer enough for the sheer continuing pleasure of knowing and working with her. It has been a wonderful experience. I would, however, also like to thank those true friends and family who gamely continue to come when invited "to taste"—all the while never knowing what they are going to confront—and who still remain honest and candid in their comments, most especially Peter, Whit, Courtney, and Allegra (whose opinion should be invaluable as soon as she is able to express it).

Sallie Y. Williams

Introduction

Here's the truth: I love to cook and my favorite times in the kitchen are when I am making something for my family. Of course, it's very simple to pick up some ready-cooked foods or go out to eat, but instead, I remind myself of why I love to cook and why it often simply makes good sense to cook.

The sights, smells, and sounds of cooking can be a source of true pleasure. The methodic rituals of food preparation—chopping, stirring, and sautéing—are soothing to me, allowing me to put life in perspective and slow down my normal hectic pace. Cooking also offers a creative challenge. I often start by thinking, "What can I create with what's already in my kitchen?" Other times I sit down and plan something, taking the time to make a list and go to the store for ingredients that aren't on hand. When it turns out that with a little effort I've actually outdone my own expectations, I get an enormous kick out of how simply roasting super-fresh fish in olive oil, or tossing together a sizzling stir-fry can make me feel as accomplished as a four-star chef. It makes me glad I cooked at all—and it pleases the whole family.

I bring my love for food—and sense of fun with it—to all the cooking classes I teach. I have found that sharing how to master versatile techniques and adaptable recipes can truly make anyone a comfortable, efficient, confident cook. As their "kitchen coach," I go one step further: I inspire and motivate them to want to cook—to enjoy the process of cooking, not just the results. In *Kitchen Coach: Family Meals,* I aim to let you in on the fun, too. In this book, I bring you recipes for cooking for and with the family, when you need or want ideas on how to eat or feed your family creatively.

This book is meant to help slow down your brain taxed by the nonstop whirl of daily life and let you focus on both the real as well as the less tangible benefits of family cooking. There's no getting around the fact that preparing a meal normally takes more time than you spend eating it. The usual family cooking goal is getting food on the plate and then on the table as quickly as possible. But family cooking offers an opportunity to develop different tastes, different ideas for eating, and more creative ways to put more homemade meals before the family. This process can help create a sense of pleasure, often taking the "chore" factor out of cooking. The biggest change will be the sense of achievement that comes from feeding yourself and your family well—sometimes with the simplest recipes.

I have found that people usually don't hate cooking; they hate wasting time in the kitchen. You'll find I emphasize time management and organization. Even though this sounds like following unpleasantly rigid practices, in fact, organization just boils down to some simple principles, beginning with the French culinary concept of *"mise en place"* or "everything in its place." While it may sound intimidating, this practice actually simplifies preparing a meal. Simpler means less stressful, which means more enjoyable. By organizing your ingredients, equipment, and utensils at the start, and properly anticipating the time a task will take, you set the mental boundaries needed to focus on the experience to its fullest.

Cooking can also be more manageable and fun when you target your cooking to your specific needs of the day. Throughout the week you are tired and overscheduled. In this cookbook, you will find family foods that fit the different schedules you have in your life. Sometimes your family will need to eat at different times of the evening, a stew might be perfect for that. Other times your family simply wants a favorite dish, like pizza—again; or, at yet another time your kids and spouse have crazy sports or activity schedules and you need food that can travel, or that will keep, or that can be easily reheated—there are dishes here to fill all those needs.

In the chapter "Why Cook for Your Family?," you'll find a simple chart to help you decide what to prepare for a meal. I'll give you several suggestions for types of dishes or meals—like slow-cook foods, soups, or chicken—and you decide what will work for your family, and, quite frankly will work with what you're in the mood to cook. (And isn't that truly what happens? Sometimes you really love the idea of a quick but delicious steak dinner; sometimes you just want to take home a rotisserie chicken and turn it into a meal-sized chicken salad.) You might refer to this quiz a few times, but soon it will become an automatic trigger, an easy checklist, to help you plan any meal, or series of meals. It takes the pressure off and gets you on the right path.

Kitchen Coach: Family Meals will be your guide to family cooking success. Success might mean you get a round of applause from the family because you outdid yourself, or maybe it just means that everybody's eating together at the same table, taking time to discuss the day or laugh at the dog's latest crazy antic. Cooking isn't magic, but it does give you an opportunity to exercise your creativity, all the while bringing your family a little closer together. In this book, I'll give you the tools and the ideas you need to get the most out of cooking no matter what your family's schedule is like. These recipes will let you stretch your culinary experience to include some truly memorable dishes. So, grab your apron, pick out a recipe, and enjoy!

Why Cook for Your Family?

Any day of the week, cooking for your family is a challenge. With changing schedules, homework, soccer practice, and meetings always getting in the way, you often may feel that cooking is something you have to squeeze in or avoid in order to make everything else happen. The easier choices are to go out to a restaurant, go to the drive-through, buy a takeout dinner from the supermarket, or have something delivered. Your family can get by just fine—takeout gives you and your family proper nutrition. Or does it?

Studies have shown that families eat up to 75 percent less fruits and vegetables when they eat on the run. Children are less likely to try new things when left to their own choices, sticking to just a few beloved favorites. Foods that are store-bought or from takeout are usually higher in calories, fat, and sodium than home-cooked foods—not to mention the fact that servings are often double or triple what is appropriate for one meal. If health reasons aren't enough, we know that family time around the dinner table provides every member with the stability and interaction they need to meet life's problems together—or at least as a more cohesive whole.

Why do it? Well, cooking even just a couple of times a week for your family will make a difference. I see the proof every day during the course of my work teaching people how to cook, and in cooking for my own family.

Ask yourself a few questions:

1. Could you get more out of your food budget by eating out less?

2. Would you prefer to spend more time with your family?

3. Could you and your family be eating better-quality and more healthful food than you are at present?

4. Do you dread the time spent in the kitchen?

5. Do you feel you alone are bearing the brunt of preparing the family meals?

If you answered yes to any of these questions, this book is for you. Cooking for your family and with your family shouldn't have to be an unpleasant chore; it can provide you with a tremendous amount of satisfaction in your life.

How? Here's a scenario: It's the weekend and you are planning the foods you will need for the next few days. We know that most Americans shop for groceries on the weekend. We also know that you will be in the grocery store at least once more to pick up things on the way home. You can save time by planning out at least three meals per week. These meals might include something that is quick to prepare, something that is simmered in the slow cooker, and finally something made from a leftover chicken or beef dish from the weekend—I call those made from leftovers "encore" meals.

The week you plan looks like this: Over the weekend you do your regular grocery shopping. You also will choose some specific recipes and buy the special ingredients to make them. For example:

(continues on page 3)

A Week of Recipes

Herb-Crusted Lamb Chops (page 107) • Quick and Easy Chicken Pot Pie (page 94) • Lamb and Brown Rice Salad (page 119) • Classic Roasted Chicken (page 78) • Hands-Off Pasta Sauce (page 139)

Shopping Lists

	Pantry Staples		Needed from the Supermarket	

Herb-Crusted Lamb Chops	Dried basil
	Dried thyme
	Sweet paprika
	Dry mustard
	Onion powder
	Garlic Powder
		Black pepper
		Cayenne pepper
		Salt
		Lemons (for zest)
		Olive oil
			Dried dill
			Lamb chops–12, each
			  1¼ to 1½ inches
			  thick	

Quick and Easy Chicken Pot Pie	Olive oil
	Chicken–in the freezer,
	  or leftover from Classic
	  Roasted Chicken
	Butter
	Flour
	Chicken broth
		Milk
		Salt
		Black pepper
		Dry Sherry
		Frozen peas
		Frozen pie crust
			White onion
			Carrots
				Celery
				Italian flat-leaf parsley

Lamb and Brown Rice Salad	Extra-virgin olive oil
	Brown rice
	Salt
	Black pepper
		Cooked lamb–in the
		  freezer, or leftover from
		  Herb-Crusted Lamb
		  Chops
			Garbanzo beans–1 can
			Tomatoes–2
			Italian flat-leaf parsley
			Green onions–3 bunches
				Lemons–8 (more than
				  normally kept on hand)
				Fresh mint
				Butter leaf lettuce–1 head

Classic Roasted Chicken	Olive oil Garlic Lemon Salt	Black pepper Chicken broth Flour	Roasting chicken– 7 pounds	Fresh thyme Marsala wine

Hands-Off Pasta Sauce	Olive oil
	Salt
	Garlic
	Bay leaf
	White wine
		Chicken broth
		Tomatoes–canned whole
		Parmigiano-Reggiano
		  cheese
		Kalamata olives
			Onion
			Fresh oregano
			Fresh rosemary
			Tomato sauce–
			  28-ounce can
				Capers–in vinegar
				  or salted
				Italian flat-leaf parsley

During the weekend you can make the Classic Roasted Chicken (page 78) for a traditional Sunday dinner. In my home if I think about roasting one bird, I usually roast two. It only takes about 20 percent more time to double a recipe when you are already making one.

On a busy Monday, you might throw together the Hands-Off Pasta Sauce (page 139), which can be doubled and the leftovers frozen to bring out in a week or two for a quick pasta or pizza.

On Tuesday night, the leftover roasted chicken can be cut into pieces and used for the Quick and Easy Chicken Pot Pie (page 94). Did you know that leftover chicken can be frozen? You might have even more leftovers if you roasted two chickens over the weekend. Just shred or dice the chicken and freeze it in tightly resealable plastic bags. Then, you can have a chicken quesadilla or a chicken salad any time you don't know what to make for dinner.

On Wednesday, you may have a free night and decide to make Herb-Crusted Lamb Chops (page 107). Cook extra lamb chops to use for an encore recipe for Thursday like the Lamb and Brown Rice Salad (page 119).

On Friday you can either let someone else in your family cook the meal of his or her choice or you can all go out and have some fun!

Before you know it, you've served your family almost a full week's worth of wholesome, tasty meals, and have stocked the freezer with chicken and pasta sauce for later. Okay, so maybe dinner at your house won't be like that every week, but it's a goal worth striving for. Take some satisfaction in accomplishing the smaller, mostly unacknowledged, steps of cooking, from which you and your whole family benefit. Even a quick tasty meal will be highly appreciated.

For many people, including me, cooking is also part of "the good life." So don't cheat yourself of this rewarding aspect of cooking, even if you are single or a two-person household. You are not alone—more than 65 percent of American households are now made up of one or two people. Besides enjoyment, the health benefits you gain by cooking for yourself are considerable as you have control over the quality and quantity of ingredients, the cooking method, as well as the serving size. Treat yourself to a great meal and freeze the leftovers to enjoy later. Many of these recipes provide you with freezing instructions. No matter what the size of your family, it's worthwhile for you to cook.

The time we put into cooking is valuable time, not wasted time. Many cooking and eating experiences last well beyond the food and flavors of the moment. Every time you cook what you bought, how you cooked it, and how you and your family responded to it, register in your mind and accumulate, giving you a bank of ideas for future reference about how to cook more efficiently, more creatively, and more precisely.

Good food and enjoyable family meals become lasting memories. I was lucky enough to have my mother's and grandmother's recipes and treasure memories of them cooking in the kitchen and serving wonderful meals. But even if your own family didn't cook much when you were growing up, you can work with a few recipes to make them your own. You may want to take the Rotisserie Chicken and Matzo Ball Soup (page 38) recipe from my grandmother and turn it into one of your own creations. You can also improvise with the recipes from the Poultry Encores chapter (page 88) and use rotisserie chicken from the supermarket or deli if you don't want to roast one yourself. Or if you want to cook the more sophisticated dishes associated with restaurant dining (but much more simply) take on the Chicken Enchiladas with Tomatillo Sauce (page 97). You can make them quickly, take all the credit, and satisfy the entire family.

Knowing there's something to look forward to at the end of the day makes life's ride a little easier, whether you are thinking about the grilled chicken you're going to make for dinner at 3 pm because your stomach is grumbling, or because you are anticipating your child's reaction when you make her/his favorite treat. To me, the good life is about pleasurable experiences. The more of these experiences you create in the kitchen, the happier you and your family will be.

Enjoying the Journey

You have likely heard the expression "Life is about the journey, not the destination." In the same way, you could also say, "Cooking is about the process too, not just what's on the plate." My guess is, if you've picked up this book and are still reading, you probably do love food, or can imagine that you might, if only you could figure out a way to keep family meals interesting but manageable in the midst of demanding schedules. To help you enjoy the process of cooking, first you have to get out of that frenetic weekday mode and slow down in order to appreciate what's happening when you cook. Enjoy the sound of the onions cooking in the pan, the scent of breakfast bacon, the aroma of something roasting in the oven. Making other sensory connections to food and cooking means paying attention, being curious, and being adventurous. You will find yourself sorting through the lettuce bin to pick the freshest, heaviest head; searching out the best local vegetables; tasting the cheese before adding it to a dish.

Actually, tasting, in particular, is an essential step all through your cooking. Tasting tells you if your cooking is going in a direction you like or if alternative action is needed. And if it is good, you'll be quite pleased with yourself!

Fitting Cooking into Your Life

In my years of working with home cooks, I've heard just about every reason for not cooking, including no time, hectic schedules, fussy eaters, the ease of having restaurants on every street corner, and the availability of takeout and delivered meals.

First, let me be clear that I am not an overzealous proponent of cooking every single meal. It's fun to get out and try new restaurants or head right for your family's regular booth at your neighborhood favorite. And if you want or need to bring home takeout on occasion or to have something delivered to the door, do. But because there are so many benefits from cooking, the scale should be tipped well in favor of cooking for and with your family—often.

I've found that teaching someone how to cook is not the tricky part. It's helping them learn to fit cooking into their daily lives that isn't easy, especially on busy weeknights. That concept often takes a little outside-the-box thinking and creativity. Fitting cooking into your life is really no different from fitting in other things that you want and need to do. You just have to want to do it enough to make the time. The way that I look at it, you have to eat, sometimes you even have to cook, so why not enjoy the process?

Try not to fall into a rut of thinking that you have "no time" every week. Obviously, your family's schedule will vary each week. Some weeks you might not have any time at all to cook. That's when you pull something out of the freezer that you have made ahead. It doesn't mean

that you won't have something great to eat, it just means that this is the time when you make a withdrawal from the freezer or pantry "bank" you have built up ahead of time. Other weeks, when you have time, make extra or freeze the leftovers as an investment in future meals. Look at the upcoming weeknights: which nights might you have an hour or so to cook? Most of the people of whom I ask that question are surprised when they realize that they have more nights available than they might originally imagine. If cooking is a priority, typically, the time appears somehow. So take a good look at your calendar.

Once you find the time, you need to think about planning the details. Spend 10 to 15 minutes planning the shopping. Plan some extra time to build your pantry; build it up a little each week. Your pantry includes your freezer, refrigerator, and dry goods cabinets. Some people even have extra storage in a garage or basement for canned goods. Look at the space that you have and plan around it. Build a pantry you can truly cook from (so don't just stock it with drinks, snacks, and paper products). I have found that most people use their pantries for dead storage. A pantry by most definitions seems to be a place to put nonperishable foods that are leftover, like an extra can of tomatoes or foods that were bought for a specific recipe then not used. Even though the pantry is full, you are often left with the feeling that there is nothing to eat, unless you have specifically shopped for it. That extra can of tomatoes (and the boullion cubes, tin of sardines, and various spices) languishes unremembered for months or even years.

To use the contents of your pantry more efficiently, make up two shopping lists. One is for pantry items you know you can use in a pinch, any time. I only shop for these things once a month. That's the time to go to a bulk food store, a specialty store, or a butcher shop—places you don't have time for most of the month. You may only have a small amount of space, so use it wisely. Buy two cans of tomatoes, olive oil, ground beef for the freezer, an extra roasted chicken to shred or dice and freeze. Every time you run out of one of these items, buy a replacement. These items are your answer to your family's question, "What's for dinner?"—and don't be surprised if, once you begin cooking more often at home, you hear this quite frequently.

The other shopping list is your weekly list. Items on this list include your family favorites: vegetables, fruits, milk, cheese, yogurt, and lunch items. Don't forget to include family breakfast ideas. Most of us eat some type of cereal, fruit, or yogurt. How about making a batch of hearty steel-cut oatmeal? These unprocessed oat groats are much higher in fiber, vitamin C, and protein than rolled or instant oats. The longer cooking time takes them out of the instant breakfast category, but the result is wonderfully chewy oatmeal filled with the natural nutty flavor of the original grain. With a little forethought, it only takes about 40 minutes to cook on the back of the stove the night before you want to serve it, requiring just an occasional stir while the family is cooking dinner. Refrigerate it, then each family member can warm up a bowl of oatmeal in the microwave in the morning. Add some fruit and milk, and they will have a satisfying, whole-grain breakfast in no time—turning a long-cook dish into a very healthy instant meal.

The key to good cooking lies in a simple equation: Good Ingredients + Good Techniques = Good Food. It's really that simple.

So, let's get started.

Cooking with Your Family

One of my favorite passions is spending time with my family. The other passion that I have is cooking. Why not bring those two forces together? Cooking together gives you so much more than just a meal. It is an experience, a journey that helps you get to know one another in a way that you may not have yet discovered.

When my grandfather used to come home at the end of a long hard day, he would loosen his tie, and sit down at the dinner table. Within minutes of his sitting down, my grandmother would give him a plate of whatever she had cooked for dinner. The process that she went through to get dinner ready was one that he missed entirely during the 55 years that they were married. Don't let your family fall into that rut—make meals a real family affair. Even four-year-olds can set the table and feel important. Invite your children to join you in the kitchen for more family time together. Teach them simple techniques and tasks that will contribute to the overall meal, take some of the pressure off you, and give them a sense of responsibility for the well-being of the whole group. Trade off cooking nights with your spouse to share the responsibility, and the reward, of getting a home-cooked meal on the table. Or, learn to cook together.

As I have said before, I firmly believe that cooking can be a way to bring a family together. One of the greatest compliments that I ever received was from a couple whom I had taught to cook together. It gave them something fascinating and new to talk about. The discussions that they had went beyond the problems of the day, the issues with kids, or work. In the kitchen, those issues melted away for this couple. They thanked me for giving them an interesting hobby that brought them together as friends again.

I have also had experiences with families that really needed help just working together in the kitchen. I can remember one instance where we needed to split the couple up because they were fighting over who should do what in a recipe. Once we worked through the different cooking styles, and gave them each a recipe to prepare, each one had a great time. Cooking can still be a family affair even if family members don't work together side by side, but each concentrates on his or her own element of a meal.

Cooking is different for each person. If you are the part of the couple who likes everything neat and organized, you might have trouble cooking with a significant other who trashes the kitchen. Alternating meals might be an answer. All of these issues can be worked out. Everyone can find his or her passion in the kitchen.

Here are some ideas to help your family find its cooking style:

- Talk about what you like to cook. Most of us—even children—have an opinion about what they would like or not like to do in the kitchen. You may love to put together desserts; your spouse grills like mad; your daughter prefers fixing foods for special breakfasts; cookies are the younger children's idea of cooking. Explore the types of cooking that you want to do, so that each of you gets the chance to make things that excite you.

- Get together and choose recipes all of you are interested in (or ask each person individually to select recipes he or she likes, then pool them to see where there are similarities or conflicts). Make the shopping lists, and then head to the store for some additional couple or family time. It makes the job a lot easier if two of you go to the store together. It can be fun exploring places like the grocery store, wine shop, or gourmet shop when you are not alone and rushing to beat the clock.

- Once the shopping is done, let the family help organize everything in the refrigerator, clean the vegetables, and put everything away. They'll know where everything is and feel more comfortable preparing something spontaneously or following your directions if you are running late and need someone to start the meal for you. This can be done several days before you're ready to use them.

- Now, you and your family are ready to cook. The time has come to get ready for a dinner, family baking, or a party for friends. Start out by carefully reading the recipe, getting all of the ingredients ready, and figuring out how you will divide the work. Some of us prefer to let one person be the executive chef and the other the sous chef. My son is always the one who slices, dices, and chops while I put the recipes together.

  If you want to cook together, there are two different ways you can divide up the recipes. The first option is to work on the recipe together. Things will go very quickly if you both want to work this way. It also gives you a chance to work together and learn new things. Your child or spouse might never think to put a whole meal together alone, but with your help and guidance on one dish at a time, he or she will be a cook in no time. Creating foods together can help avoid mistakes. The best part is that you get to work together, the drawback is that you have to work together—that old catch-22.

  The second option is to divide the recipes up and each work on a different dish. One of you can make the salad, while the other works on the main course. Just the process of creating a meal together and spending time in the kitchen can be really satisfying, rather than the decision of who does what.

- Usually, in every family, one person ends up doing the majority of the cleanup. Talk about this before you start. When will the dishes get done? How will the responsibilities be divided? You may have to compromise if you usually do the dishes at the end of the cooking process because it is hard to keep a kitchen organized with all of the dirty dishes piling up. Remember, most professional cooks clean up as they go along, leaving little to do except the table dishes once the meal is over. It's a good habit to get into.

Defining and Dealing with Cooking Challenges

There are 160 recipes and lots of cooking information in this book and you can use what's here any way you like. Pick your three favorite recipes and make only those until they are your specialty. Or, look in the index for an ingredient you have in the kitchen to make a spur-of-the-moment meal. Or, try all the recipes one at a time. They are all simple great family ideas.

Here are some other ways to get yourself in gear for family cooking:

- Make a list of things you and your family like to eat. If you like, make a computer file with the list, so you can print it out and use it as a shopping list, adding to it the things you might need for particular recipes.

- Add a heading to your list for "Foods to Try" and on a regular basis jot down one or two items like arugula, artichokes, or panko bread crumbs—so you remember to look for them in the supermarket or figure out where there's a specialty food store nearby that might carry them. Adding a new food from time to time will keep cooking interesting and creative. For a family, trying new foods should be very important, and can be a kind of shared adventure.

- Remember, your family may turn away a new food, but it is very important that you continue to introduce that ingredient again—and again, and again. It might take being introduced to a new food up to 15 times, gently, creatively, before a child will try it—but once he does, the effort is well worth it.

- Next, and most important, make a list of things that you consider challenges to your making dinner on a regular basis. I've done this for myself and with cooking students and we have found it helpful in making cooking regularly more manageable.

Maybe you are stressed from work, or too tired to cook, or your kids are picky eaters. It's possible that there are several challenges at the same time, even so try to figure out what is the primary issue for you on a given day. Then, look for recipes in this book that will satisfy your needs. Keep checking back here to figure out where to start, then keep the categories in mind when thinking about dinner or food shopping. Here are a number of situations you might recognize and some of my suggestions.

The Situation	Type of Recipe Needed	Recipe Suggestions
1. Chicken is on special at the supermarket, but you are sick of the old stand-by recipes.	You need a new chicken recipe to get your menus out of a rut.	Perk up your menu with Chicken with Feta Cheese and Tomatoes (page 82), or try Chicken and Yogurt Pitas (page 89), or, a personal favorite, Chicken and Rice—with Variations (page 80).
2. The remains of Sunday's roast beef are languishing in the refrigerator.	You need a new way to serve beef to the family.	They will love Lentils with Shredded Beef and Feta Cheese (page 120), or Roasted Beef or Lamb with Gnocchi and Sherry Cream Sauce (page 115), or even Stuffed Eggplant Mediterranean (page 118).
3. The kids are getting finicky about what they will eat.	You need a new dish or two to inspire your family to eat their vegetables.	Try Baked Onions (page 126), Oven Ratatouille (page 127), or Mixed Vegetables and Quinoa (page 122).
4. Fish is going to be a regular part of your family's fare from now on.	You need a few appealing recipes to get started.	Pick out anything from the Fish and Shellfish chapter (page 65) and they will ask for more, or give them Shrimp and Pesto Pasta Salad (page 50), or even Asian Broiled Salmon Salad (page 48).
5. Friends are invited for winter Saturday night dinner after a day of sports together.	You need something ready to put on the table as soon as you return.	Spicy Scalloped Ham and Potatoes (page 155), Baked Cannelloni with Meatballs (page 152), or even Chicken Provençal (page 147) are all perfect.
6. You miss the aroma of freshly baked bread, but don't have time to start from scratch.	You need a quick but satisfying solution.	Use refrigerated dough and make our Poppy Seed Bread Sticks (page 166), or Tabasco Cheddar Cheese Bread (page 163), or make Quick and Easy Cinnamon Pull-Apart Loaf (page 202).
7. The holidays mean a dessert party to bring close friends together, but you are at a loss for what to serve.	You need a few ideas that will appeal to everyone.	Anything or everything from the Delectable Desserts chapter (page 170) would be perfect. Or try Chocolate Chip Cookie Pizza (page 203) from Cooking with Kids.
8. The temperature outside has hit 90°F and you just cannot bear the thought of fixing a hot meal.	You need something special that won't heat up the kitchen.	Light up the grill for a quick outdoor cooking session and try Broiled New York Strip Steaks with Baby Greens (page 46), or Mediterranean Seared Tuna Salad (page 49), or Butter Leaf Salad with Glazed Scallops (page 51).
9. A business trip means two nights away from your family.	You need dinners ready and waiting in the freezer for them to pop in the oven.	Stuffed Flank Steak with Roasted Peppers and Feta Cheese (page 144), Turkey and Green Chile Enchilada Pie (page 150), or Grandma's Baked Spaghetti (page 154) should fill the bill.
10. It is your turn to bring the snacks to the neighborhood's monthly drinks get-together.	You need several new recipes to awe the guests.	Choose three or four dishes from the Appealing Appetizers chapter (page 20) such as Hot and Spicy Spinach Crab Dip (page 21), Herbed Cheddar Cheese Spirals (page 24), or Crusty Pizza Rolls with Tomato Dipping Sauce (page 30), and your reputation will be made.

Other tools you might find useful in choosing recipes are the symbols next to the recipe titles, highlighting dishes that offer certain benefits, such as:

Easy Preparation (for when you don't have the energy to do much chopping and washing and the like); No Cooking Needed (for time-strapped or just plain hot nights); Take-Along (for foods you and your family can take with you on busy nights, or to the next potluck occasion); Make-Ahead (so you can finish it off right before you need to eat); Freezer-Ready (for when you want something that you can make and freeze to eat a few days or even a few weeks later); Ready and Waiting (for something that you have roasting or simmering while you are out); Something Special (for when you need or want to make something with a little extra effort for yourself, your family, or guests).

This isn't a cooking bible with thousands of recipes, but a source of ideas based on situations I know many cooks are faced with. Some days you want to cook like a chef on TV; other days your kids only want to eat peanut butter. Cooking naturally ebbs and flows this way. Even the most refined chefs have secret fetishes for junk food—I sometimes use prepared seasonings and bottled condiments or ready-cooked foods in my meals one night, then feel inspired to bake a quiche from scratch the next. An award-winning chef might long for a late dinner of scrambled eggs or a pizza from the local pizza delivery.

I know some people might think it is sacrilegious to serve French toast for dinner or wouldn't call making salads cooking, but you know that the demands and challenges you face every day could keep you out of the kitchen altogether if you let them. If you are the cook, you make the call about what's right for you and your family. As long as you keep an eye on nutrition, and aim for variety, go with the type of cooking you know your family will eat and enjoy, and that will make you glad you cooked.

Is Your Kitchen Ready?

Let's face it—maintaining a family kitchen is a hard job. When I go grocery shopping, often within two days my son and his friends have eaten everything I bought. Growth spurts, changing schedules, and even the seasons will affect how efficient you are at anticipating daily food needs. The one thing for certain is that your kitchen is in a constant state of flux. You will frequently need to adjust your food and equipment supplies based on your family's situation, but preparation is key to making it less difficult to keep up.

In order to enjoy cooking regularly and not find it a bore or a chore, get yourself and your kitchen into gear—literally and figuratively. Spend some time organizing your kitchen so it is well stocked and arranged in a way that makes it comfortable and safe to work in. Clean out your pantry, make sure you have the right cooking equipment and pans, and plan food shopping excursions to provide a balance of fresh, seasonal foods.

A Well-Stocked Pantry

To keep shopping time to a minimum, you will need to maintain a properly stocked pantry—and properly stocked may mean different things to different cooks at different times. Certainly, the family pantry provides us with different challenges than a pantry for entertaining, or simple everyday cooking. There is a set list of items well worth everyone having on hand, but then your additional supplies will be based on what you like

to cook and what your family eats. Before you take a look into your cupboards, try a little exercise: make a list of ingredients that you think should be on hand. Base it on what you like to cook with or what you know is on your shelves. Then, go have a look at your pantry and equipment and start getting your kitchen into shape.

A Trip Through Your Pantry

Approximate Time: As much time as you need to get rid of the old, organize the new, and make a pantry that works for you.

Setting the Scene

Put on your work clothes and plan to spend some time. Get out a few trash bags, and don't be reluctant to fill them. It's quite possible you have been shopping for food for years, but have never thought to clean out the old stuff. So let's begin with a few guidelines.

A Guide to Organizing Your Pantry

Everyone needs more space in the kitchen; use it wisely. Here are some tips:

1. Make a Map of Your Kitchen—I used to organize my cooking students' kitchens. It amazed me how many people gave little thought to where they stored things in relation to the work surfaces where they would be used. For instance: You should be able to reach the

cabinets where you store the glasses and plates while standing close to the stove or refrigerator, and not far from the dishwasher. Where are yours stored?

To help resolve problems like this, I would draw them a map of their kitchen. And you can do the same for your own kitchen. Think about the following:

- What are your cooking and food preparation patterns? If you have your pans stored more than five feet away from the stove, it's too far to make cooking quick, efficient work.

- Keep knives in a drawer rack or upright rack right next to the chopping board.

- Store your wooden spoons and rubber spatulas in a container right next to the stove so you won't have to move to pick up one and stir a bubbling sauce.

- What about your spices? They should be near your food preparation area (but not near the heat or the quality will quickly deteriorate).

- Keep lunch-making food supplies such as peanut butter, jam, sandwich bags, waxed paper, ready-made snack servings, etc. in one place. That way fixing school lunches won't be a series of search forays into the pantry.

- Make one shelf the after-school snack shelf. Kids will know what they can and cannot have when hunger strikes. Teach them how to use the microwave so they can even make hot snacks for themselves.

- Keep the "just-in-case" canned and boxed food on one of the higher or lower shelves, so the eye-level shelves can be used for often used foods.

2. Make Better Use of the Space You Have—If you have kitchen equipment, like an ice cream machine that you only use in the summer, try to find an out-of-the-way spot for it. It's amazing how few things we actually use on a daily, even weekly basis. I keep my special equipment in a cabinet in the garage.

3. Keep a Pantry List—There are some staples your family needs or likes to eat—pastas, canned goods, cereals, ketchup, mayonnaise—but many times when shopping, you may buy these standard items over and over out of habit because you don't know if you have them and don't want to have to make another trip to the store. So, on the inside door of your pantry, keep a list of the items inside, then mark them off as you use them. Use the computer to develop the list, as well as a standard shopping list. A new copy can be printed any time you need it.

The "pantry" list should also include other food items, even those that are stored in your refrigerator and freezer. It's really a guide for all your shopping needs, and will help you make food storage efficient, too.

4. Have a Logic to Your Food Storage—Keep similar pastas, condiments, and canned goods in the cupboard and frozen vegetables, leftovers, and other items in the freezer together with some sense of order, not wherever there's a space when you're rushing to empty your grocery packages or put food away after a meal. Otherwise, you'll find that when you do inspect your kitchen you have multiples of things and too many outdated items. If you have duplicates, say of chicken broth or brown sugar, place them all together in a row so you know how many and what kinds you have. Just a little investment of time when putting away groceries gives back a large amount of time saved when the moment arrives to prepare dinner and everything is where you expect it to be.

Case in point, as a wedding gift, I cleaned out my brother and sister-in-law's newly combined pantry. There, among other things, I found four bottles of maple syrup—three of which were open and taking up space. Hense, condensing can save you a huge amount of space. Moral: Better to collect and conquer. It will save you space.

5. Put Your Senses to Work—Inspect your food from time to time to make sure it is still usable—does it look right, smell good or fresh, taste like it should? If it doesn't look, smell, or taste right, it won't magically become good in a recipe.

Learn how long food lasts:

- Dried herbs last one year; dried spices last one to one and a half years. That is all! So if you still have Grandma's spices from when you cleaned out her kitchen five years ago, throw them away! The natural oils dry up when they get much older.

- Beans and grains are best used within one and a half years. Once a box or package is opened, shelf-life decreases more rapidly even if you store the contents in a tightly sealed container.

- Oils last one year; vinegar, vanilla, and other extracts last two years. Some oils, such as walnut oil or other nut oils, are very fragile and have shorter shelf-lives. Because of the additional organic elements in them, such as garlic or chiles, flavored oils have a very short shelf-life once opened—usually not more than a few days in the refrigerator.

Exposure to changing elements decreases the usable life of foods. In general, keep fresh or dry foods away from heat, light, air, and moisture and they should stay fresher longer. The one exception to this rule—cereals usually stay crisp longer if stored in the cabinet over the stove.

Now here's my suggested list of what to keep on hand for a family kitchen. Your list will probably be different, based on your family's needs, likes, and dislikes—but this one provides a good starting point.

Dried Herbs and Spices

Mark your dried herbs and spices with the date that you bought them. Store them in an airtight container away from heat and light. The herbs should last one year, the spices 18 months.

____ Allspice

____ Basil

____ Bay leaves

____ Cayenne pepper (ground red chile pepper)

____ Chili powder, preferably a pure chili powder such as ancho or pasilla

____ Cinnamon, ground

____ Crushed red pepper

____ Cumin, ground

____ Curry powder, several strengths if you like

____ Garlic powder

____ Ginger, ground and crystallized

____ Mustard, dried powder

____ Nutmeg, whole

____ Old Bay Seasoning (spicy seasoning mix with great pepper flavor)

____ Onion powder

____ Oregano

____ Paprika, sweet Hungarian

____ Peppercorns, black and white (and a grinder)

____ Poppy seeds

____ Rosemary

____ Sage

____ Salt (if possible, sea salt, ground and coarse)

____ Seasoned pepper (such as Mrs. Dash, for quick effective seasoning of everyday foods)

____ Sesame seeds

____ Tarragon

____ Thyme

Other Seasonings and Flavorings

____ Anchovy fillets in olive oil

____ Baking powder, double acting

____ Baking soda

_____ Beans, white, great northern, and black, in cans and dried

_____ Bouillon, cubes and powder (to use in a pinch if you have no broth or stock)

_____ Brandy

_____ Bread crumbs, unseasoned and panko (Japanese bread crumbs)

_____ Chicken broth, low-sodium, canned or boxed

_____ Chocolate, unsweetened and semisweet morsels

_____ Cocoa, unsweetened baking

_____ Cornmeal, yellow

_____ Cornstarch

_____ Flour, unbleached all-purpose

_____ Honey

_____ Horseradish, jarred

_____ Jam, seedless apricot, raspberry, or other favorite

_____ Ketchup

_____ Lentils

_____ Mandarin oranges, canned

_____ Mustard, Dijon, yellow, and your favorite flavored varieties (I have at least 5 in my refrigerator so that a quick mustard marinade is only moments away)

_____ Oil, olive (regular and extra-virgin), vegetable, peanut, Asian sesame, and walnut

_____ Olives

_____ Peanut butter, chunky and/or creamy

_____ Pineapple chunks, canned

_____ Roasted red bell peppers, jarred

_____ Sherry, dry

_____ Soy sauce, light and, if you like, a low-sodium one as well

_____ Sugar, granulated white and dark brown

_____ Tabasco sauce

_____ Tomatoes, whole plum, diced, tomato paste, tomato puree, and sun-dried

_____ Vanilla extract, pure

_____ Vinegar, white wine, red wine, cider, rice wine, and balsamic

_____ Wine, at least Chardonnay and Cabernet (_not_ the commercial product sold as cooking wine)

_____ Worcestershire sauce

_____ Yeast, dry active

Pasta and Grains

_____ Arborio rice (for risotto)

_____ Bulgur

_____ Couscous

_____ Cut pastas (small shells and other shapes)

_____ Thin pastas (linguine, spaghettini, or angel hair)

_____ Rice, white long-grain, basmati, and brown

Fresh Basics

We all obviously stock our refrigerators with our own favorite fresh foods. But at the very minimum, having these items on hand will help you be creative and flexible when making satisfying family dinners.

_____ Butter, unsalted—or salted if you prefer—except for baking

_____ Cheddar cheese

_____ Eggs, grade A large (unless otherwise noted, all recipes call for large eggs)

_____ Garlic, fresh cloves, or finely chopped in oil (to use in a pinch)

_____ Goat cheese, or another soft cheese such as ricotta or cream cheese

_____ Lemons

_____ Margarine

_____ Mayonnaise

_____ Milk, whole and fat-free

_____ Parmigiano-Reggiano cheese

_____ Yogurt, plain nonfat

Freezer Basics

The freezer is an important part of a family kitchen. Try keeping a few of these items in the freezer so that you can make snacks and dinners that will please your family without stressing you.

_____ Berries of all kinds (Spread out on a cookie sheet in a layer 1 berry deep and freeze until solid. Pour into heavy resealable freezer bags and store flat. Frozen berries last 2 to 3 months and are especially good for pies, crumbles, and sauces.)

_____ Bread, sourdough, ciabatta, and whole wheat (Cut the bread into pieces that are about what your family will eat in one meal. Store in the freezer wrapped in plastic wrap and placed in a resealable freezer bag. It will last 2 months. Thaw in the bag, slice and toast on the grill to serve, or just reheat in the oven as a whole piece.)

_____ Bread dough, store-bought (to make pizzas, breads, and crusts)

_____ Chicken, shredded and cubed (make some extra to freeze next time the grill is hot)

_____ Chocolate wafers and graham cracker crumbs (great for topping dessert or making a quick crust for a fresh fruit pie)

_____ Corn, yellow and/or white kernels

_____ Green beans, preferably the small haricot verts, or extra-thin beans that you can buy flash-frozen

_____ Nuts and seeds, pecans, almonds, pine nuts, poppy seeds, and sesame seeds (stored in the freezer they will last twice as long)

_____ Peaches

_____ Peas

_____ Pesto, store-bought or homemade

_____ Pie crusts, store-bought, folded or rolled, not prefitted into pans

_____ Tomato sauce (make some one night and freeze the extra in 2-cup containers)

_____ Tortillas, corn and flour (Thaw them in the refrigerator and use them toasted for quesadillas or in enchiladas. Do not try and use them for tacos or fajitas, because they will taste stale. Frozen corn tortillas can be made into great chips; see the Appealing Appetizers chapter.)

_____ Vanilla ice cream (This is basically frozen custard sauce. So you can serve it scooped, or softened for a sauce.)

Premade Mixes and Other Items

_____ Barbecue rubs (As long as they are not high in salt or sugar, they are perfect to cook with in a pinch. Make your own and store for up to 6 months.)

_____ Barbecue sauce, 1 or 2 really good commercial ones (for quick grills)

_____ Bread mixes (I have a bread mix that I use to make rosemary focaccia in about an hour and a half. Quick mixes like this save time and can help add that special touch to a dinner even when you are in a hurry.)

_____ Brownie mixes and cake mixes (My grandmother's Harvey Wallbanger cake, a delicious liqueur-laden yellow bundt cake with a citrus glaze, is one of the best cakes I have ever tasted, and the base is a yellow cake mix. When you are desperate for dessert in a hurry, turn to a mix.)

_____ Chutneys, tapenades, and specialty jams

_____ Crackers (Specialty companies are making healthy low-fat and lower-sodium alternatives for snack crackers. Shelf life is usually long, say 6 months, and you will go through them in that amount of time.)

_____ Granola (great for breakfast, but more important to top cobblers, and other fresh fruit desserts)

Kitchen Equipment

Good equipment is essential for a well-stocked kitchen. It is easier and more enjoyable to cook when you have good sharp knives and the best pans that you can afford. Just as new or high-quality running shoes or sports gear make sports more enjoyable, good equipment makes you want to get going in the kitchen, and can help make cooking fun. The list may seem long, but add to your selection a little at a time.

How to Outfit a Family Kitchen

Knives

Knives are your most important kitchen tools. If you can, invest in high-quality knives. (I prefer nonserrated knives. Although serrated don't need to be sharpened, their edges aren't suitable for all foods and can make your work more difficult, often shredding rather than cutting cleanly.) Keep all knives sharp (read directions and talk with a knife seller) and carefully stored in a butcher block, on a magnetic rack, or with the blades covered. Never just throw knives in a drawer as they will become quickly dull and can develop nicks and scratches when they touch each other. Remember, dull knives are dangerous—far more so than very sharp ones.

Knives should be professionally sharpened every six months or at least once a year. Ask the meat cutter in your supermarket where you can get your knives sharpened, or look in the telephone book for a sharpening service that will come to your home. Hone the knife on the steel every two to three times you use it. And never put a knife in the sink—ever—even if there is no water in it. Wash knives separately, dry them, and put them away as you use them. Always leave knives in plain sight when you put them down and never drop a cloth or towel on top of one.

_____ 3-inch paring knife (for all those small cutting jobs, very useful for people with small hands)

_____ 5- or 7-inch Santoku knife (the perfect knife for slicing; the special indentations or "kullens" in the surface of the blade keep foods such as tomatoes, cheese, and cold meats from sticking to the blade, and it chops well, too; it is rapidly becoming my favorite knife.)

_____ 8- or 9-inch chef's knife (the workhorse knife, for slicing, dicing, and most other cutting jobs)

_____ Bread knife

_____ 10-inch slicing/carving knife (a very useful blade for slicing roast meats, ham, etc., or for carving poultry)

_____ Sharpening steel, diamond edge (an everyday tool used for bringing back a fine edge, though it cannot sharpen a very dull knife)

Equipment and Utensils

_____ Set of 11 glass nesting mixing bowls

_____ Set of measuring spoons consisting of ¼ teaspoon, ½ teaspoon, 1 teaspoon, and 1 tablespoon measures

_____ 2 sets of measuring cups, one for dry foods, one for liquids. Liquid measures are glass or plastic and are available in 1-, 2-, and 4-cup sizes. Dry measures come in sets of four: ¼ cup, ⅓ cup, ½ cup, and 1 cup.

_____ Instant-read meat thermometer and a frying thermometer

_____ Oven thermometer (Oven temperature controls are not always accurate, use a separate thermometer to be sure.)

_____ Wooden spoons for stirring foods or serving, at least 2 (perhaps one with a long handle and one with a short handle)

_____ Stainless steel slotted spoon (a long-handled spoon useful for removing foods from liquids)

____ Stainless steel cook's spoon (the same as the slotted spoon without holes, used for basting, mixing liquids, and removing foods from pots and pans)

____ Large strainer/colander

____ Fine-mesh strainer

____ Whisks, a large balloon whisk and a small whisk, or, if you can have only one, a medium whisk

____ 2 rubber spatulas

____ Flat metal spatula (for transferring and serving food)

____ Ladle

____ Cook's fork (a three-tined or two-tined fork used for moving foods around while cooking, and for holding meats and poultry steady while carving)

____ Tongs (spring action are extremely useful for moving meat and poultry in and out of pans, off and on the grill, or for turning without piercing the exterior and releasing essential juices)

____ Grater, box or flat, stainless steel (so it can go in the dishwasher)

____ Bulb baster (essential in the kitchen)

____ Heavy can opener (one also fitted with a bottle opener)

____ Vegetable peeler

____ Citrus zester (my favorite is the Microplane zester)

____ Wine opener

Pots and Pans

____ Heavy ovenproof Dutch oven or 4-quart heavy casserole with lid

____ 1-quart, 2½-quart, and 3-quart saucepans, with lids

____ 4-quart soup kettle with lid

____ 8-quart stock pot with lid

____ 10- or 12-inch slope-sided skillet with ovenproof handle

____ 12-inch straight-sided skillet with ovenproof handle (sauté pan)

____ 8-inch skillet, nonstick preferred, with an ovenproof handle

____ Roasting pan with rack

____ Heavy-duty ridged grill pan, preferably with an ovenproof handle

Baking Equipment

____ Rolling pin

____ 10-inch springform pan

____ 8- or 9-inch loose-bottom tart tin

____ 2 cookie sheets, heavy stainless steel

____ 2 baking sheets with raised edges (half-sheets)

____ Two 8-inch cake pans

____ Two 9- × 5- × 3-inch loaf pans

____ 9-inch glass pie plate

____ 2 muffin tins, a 12-cup and a 24-cup miniature muffin pan

____ 9- × 13- × 2-inch ovenproof glass dish

____ Flour sifter

____ Wire cooling rack

____ Pastry brush

Machines

These items can be expensive but worth every penny. With proper care they can last a lifetime. Because these are big purchases, I offer my favorite brands, which have stood the tests of use and time.

_____ Food processor, preferably one with a large capacity (My preference is for the 11-cup Kitchen Aid for versatility and power. It has a mini chopper built in that is so convenient.)

_____ Stand mixer, preferably the 6-quart Kitchen Aid if you make a lot of bread, though a 4½-quart mixer should be fine for most uses (My grandmother's big Kitchen Aid has been working since 1943. Now that's a great investment.)

_____ Heavy-duty blender, 40-ounce capacity (My preference is Waring though Oster is another good brand. I have Gram's Waring from 1942 and it works better than most new ones.)

_____ Digital kitchen scale, a spring-action scale with a digital read-out (useful for weighing ingredients and for portion control)

_____ Immersion blender (A very useful appliance for mixing and pureeing in the same container in which the food is being prepared. Wonderful for pureeing soups, for quickly beating eggs, for making homemade mayonnaise, and for whipping drinks such as milk shakes and smoothies. Saves cleanup and the mess of transferring food from one container to another.)

_____ Electric ice cream maker (optional but great to have)

Grilling Equipment

You don't need to have multiple grills for great grilling (although we know quite a few grilling fans who have several). Below is a review of the benefits of the different types available, along with other tools that will help you make grilling a frequent method of cooking in your home.

_____ Small hibachi grill, tabletop charcoal grill (Adequate for 2 or 3 servings, it uses a small amount of charcoal and is convenient to store.)

_____ Kettle grill, covered charcoal grill, available in several sizes (Good in windy situations and can be used in light rain or snow, it also serves as a high-heat oven. It uses charcoal and/or wood chips, which burn hotter and give more flavor to foods than gas grills.)

_____ Large, rectangular or drop-in charcoal grill (A covered grill with a very large grilling surface for families with a great love for barbecue. It functions just the same as a kettle grill.)

_____ Gas-fired grill, a covered grill that uses propane gas instead of charcoal (Requires no fire starter, no long preheating time, and grilling temperatures are easy to control. It can be small, or as large as a kitchen range.)

_____ Electric grill, open or covered grill great for using indoors or outdoors where space or regulations prohibit using an open flame.

_____ Vegetable grate or basket, a grid with small holes that allows grilling vegetables without losing them to the coals below

_____ Fish basket or fine grill, a fine-meshed cooking grill for grilling fish

_____ Electric rotisserie (Useful for roasting chicken or other whole poultry, roasts, or even racks of ribs. Sometimes it is included with a gas grill, but often is an easy to add on accessory.)

_____ Large turner or spatula (essential for turning fish or other fragile foods)

_____ Flashlight or battery lamp (very useful for grilling in the dark)

Making the Most of the Market

Once your kitchen is in order, learning to shop well is the next step. The core principle of good cooking is: use the best available ingredients. I don't mean excessively expensive or exotic vegetables and condiments. I mean searching local markets for the most vibrantly fresh, brightly colored fruits and vegetables, quality condiments, freshly butchered meats and poultry, and just-out-of-the-water fish and shellfish. A perfectly fresh piece of white cod grilled with olive oil and garlic alongside grilled vegetables is both nutritionally and gastronomically superior to a heavily sauced portion of Fettuccine Alfredo.

Today, the range of foods accessible to us across this country is truly incredible. While cities and sophisticated urban areas may offer a wider selection than smaller communities, a variety of fruits, vegetables, and other fine edibles is within reach for more Americans than ever before. Consumers are demanding more choice and better quality in fresh foods. Gradually supply has begun to catch up with demand.

At farmers' markets, green markets, and well-stocked supermarkets everywhere, we are being exposed to a new fruit or vegetable nearly each week. Old, familiar vegetables are reappearing in new guises. Tiny yellow, pear-shaped tomatoes are offered as well as several varieties of the customary cherry tomatoes. Typically, red and green bell peppers are seen in company with varieties of orange, purple, black, and white ones.

Even sizes of fresh produce are changing. Petite culinary gems are pushing out the old bigger-is-better prizewinners. Small and toothsome seem to be desirable qualities in today's vegetables. Tiny, crisp carrots, pencil-slim leeks, and miniature ears of corn are just a few of the varieties available.

Convenience has become the working family's mantra. Readily available in stores now are cleaned and pared vegetables, washed and dried greens, even boned meats and fishes, portioned and often already marinated or stuffed. When time or energy is short, you can take advantage of the fact that some of the kitchen work has already been done, and put more interesting food on the table in a short period of time. Of course, all this convenience comes at a cost, though you can still produce an excellent meal that is less expensive and better quality than one at a low-end restaurant.

It shouldn't be long before eating well does not mean eating expensively, but knowing how to buy fresh foods at the peak of their quality, how to store them, how to prepare them, and, ultimately, how to cook them appropriately so that they retain the best of their flavor. And that is where I come in. Here are a few tips for a successful trip to the market to speed you on your way to better meals at home:

- Choose ingredients that are in full season, while they are at the peak of quality, full of flavor, and capable of being prepared with a minimum of effort.

- Leafy vegetables should be bright or richly green—no yellow patches. Leaves must be crisp and sound, not limp, slimy, brown, or full of holes.

- Root vegetables must be plump and firm, not floppy or limp, with no shiny, soft, or damp patches, or other surface damage such as nicks and cuts. Look for potatoes with few if any eyes, and no greenish tint.

- Tomatoes and peppers should have taut, shiny skins, full of bright color—no bruises or soft spots.

- Herbs must be vibrantly colored, with strong scent and flavor. Avoid any that are wilted, yellowed, or showing signs of rot. Trim the stems and store them, stems down, in a jar of water in the refrigerator. If you like, cover with a plastic bag to protect other foods from their strong scents.

- Plan to use items from the farmers' market within two days of purchase—at the very most. All vegetables are more nutritious if they are at their freshest when you use them, ideally the same day picked or purchased. In fact, most fresh produce, with a few notable exceptions, is best within hours of being harvested. There is an old country tradition that says one should have the kettle boiling before one picks the corn for dinner. That is really last-minute freshness!

- Ask local growers or purveyors about the foods they are selling. Usually they take great pride in what they produce, and often they can and will provide a wealth of information on how to prepare what they sell. Ask to sample things you haven't tried before. Often, you will enjoy the new flavor or food, and may decide to introduce it to your family.

- While bringing a list helps you to shop efficiently, don't consider it written in stone when you are in fresh food markets or aisles of the supermarket selling produce, meats, and fish. Decide what appeals to you and looks freshest, then form your menus around what you have bought, just as many great chefs do. This may take a little more time, but is really sometimes more rewarding than following your list or a recipe which calls for food not at the peak of quality, or even in season.

So, you have a well-stocked kitchen and pantry; now for the working rules.

Kitchen Safety

Safety in the kitchen is mostly common sense, though there are definitely things to remember. Here are just a few:

Equipment

Knives

- Keep out of reach of children. If possible, always store them with the blades covered. If using one of the magnetic racks, store with the sharp edge away from you.

- Never put a knife in the sink, whether it is full of water or not.

- Never cut with the sharp edge toward you, always cut away from you.

Pots and Pans

Always turn handles away from the front edge of the stove so children cannot pull pots down on themselves or spill hot liquids, and so you don't accidentally hit a handle and spill the contents.

Always use dry cloths or potholders to take hot pans from the oven—a wet or damp cloth will transfer the heat quickly to your hand and burn you.

Always drain liquids by pouring from the side away from you so the steam will not burn your face.

Be very careful of noninsulated pot and skillet handles. While they are wonderful for going directly into the oven, they become quite hot. One chef I knew sprinkled the handle with flour the minute he took a pan out of the oven to remind him the handle was extremely hot.

Do not wear dangling jewelry, long scarves, or long or loose sleeves when cooking as they may catch on pot handles and lead to spills or burns.

Appliances

Check all cords to be sure they are not frayed and are plugged in correctly, without too many appliances on one circuit.

Be sure appliance cords are not tangled, which could make an appliance fall or spill when you move it.

Hold the covers on blenders and food processors with your hand to keep them from splashing liquid—especially hot liquid. Use a potholder or folded towel to prevent accidental burns if a hot liquid should leak.

Kitchen

Always have a small kitchen fire extinguisher readily available—not in the broom closet or under the sink—just in case there is a flare-up in a pan or in the oven. Learn how to use it.

Anchor any mats or rugs to the floor so you do not slip while holding a knife or a pot full of hot food. Wipe all spills as soon as they happen for the same reason, and take particular care if you spill oil or fat of any kind.

Basic Food Safety

Shopping

- Buy the freshest foods possible. Check expiration dates. Buy the freshest of the lot. And don't buy anything you don't think you can use before the expiration date—it is a waste of money.

- Do not buy dented cans, or cans that have a bulge in the top or bottom; the contents risk being contaminated.

- Do not buy meat if the wrapping has been cut or torn; the contents risk being contaminated.

- Do not buy food in plastic bottles or packages if they are dented or cracked; the contents risk being contaminated.

- Arrange your trip around the supermarket to buy the most perishable things last. Dairy products, juice, eggs, and frozen food products should go in last and come out first at home.

- Do not refreeze ice cream or frozen products that have melted on your way home.

- Keep a cooler in the back of your car or truck and transfer the refrigerated and frozen foods to it for the trip home.

- Go through the refrigerator regularly and discard anything that is over its expiration date, or has been cooked and then left for more than two or three days. It's best to throw it away, in a tightly closed container where pets and animals cannot get to it. The old adage still holds true: When in doubt, throw it out!

Preparation

- Wash your hands frequently before, during, and after food preparation and cooking—especially after handling anything raw, particularly meat, poultry, and fish.

- Use plastic cutting boards for meat, poultry, and fish and wash thoroughly between uses. Do not cut meat on a board that has been used for poultry or fish without thoroughly washing it with hot soapy water first.

- A good rule of thumb, if you can follow it, is to cut fruit first, then vegetables, then the meat, poultry, or fish you will be using. If that isn't possible, wash the board thoroughly with hot soapy water before cutting fresh produce on it.

- To help prevent contaminating food, buy several cutting boards in order to be sure you will always have a clean one at hand for each different type of food. The new colored boards are very convenient: use red for meat, yellow for poultry, blue for fish, and green for produce, for example.

- Don't leave raw eggs, meat, poultry or fish out of the refrigerator for more than about 20 minutes—or the length of time to warm to room temperature—before cooking or re-refrigerating.

- Throw away marinades that have been used on raw meat, poultry, or fish. If you want to use some for basting, reserve a quantity in a separate container before you add the rest to the meat, etc. The only exception is when the food is actually cooked thoroughly in the marinating liquid.

- Wash any plate that has held raw meat, poultry, or fish in hot soapy water before using again, and get out a clean platter for cooked food.

Appealing Appetizers

In my family, it is often the appetizer that motivates the meal, because we try to have fun or be adventurous—trying new foods or mixing and matching smaller dishes such as a combination of dips and dippers, little bites, quesadillas, and small sandwiches, to create a whole meal. (I take this idea from restaurants, which often feature more intriguing tastes and dishes in smaller portions at the top of the menu as starters.)

Small dishes fit into our family meals in many different ways. Little nibbles can serve as snacks, delicious eats for a late afternoon ball game, and even a nosh in front of the television while watching a movie on a Saturday night. I keep dips and vegetables in my refrigerator all of the time. This way I can have something in the afternoon for the family to snack on—something fresh, and so much better for us than fat-filled crackers or chips.

Speaking of chips, many of these recipes are kid friendly and kid approved. A rainy afternoon is the perfect time to prepare home-baked tortilla chips with your children. Serve them with a quick fresh salsa and you have a healthy alternative to the fattening snacks that most kids request. In addition, having your kids help make them is a great opportunity for "together" time. Even "noncooking" spouses can find their culinary niche by perfecting one or two of these simple snacks.

With some thought, you can combine several appetizers to make a meal at home or expand on these ideas to make main courses. For example, fix the Layered Cheese–Avocado Bean Dip (page 27) and include chicken to make it more substantial. Vegetables can be added to quesadillas for more fun and nutrition. Children love to have a picnic in the living room or family room even if you serve nothing more than fresh vegetable sticks and a homemade dip, and a wedge or two of quesadilla. So take an extra half hour and prepare one or two of these easy, but special dishes that will give your family a treat.

Some of these recipes can be prepared ahead of time and kept on hand in the freezer. When you need them, take them out to finish off in a hurry when unexpected or impromptu guests arrive. The Herbed Cheddar Cheese Spirals (page 24) can be adjusted to suit any taste and they freeze beautifully. There are others that can be made early in the day, leaving you free of the need to be in the kitchen when others are enjoying themselves elsewhere.

Hot and Spicy Spinach Crab Dip

MAKES 6 SERVINGS

✓ *SOMETHING SPECIAL*   ✓ *TAKE-ALONG*

A great dip offers instant gratification. With its smooth texture the flavor hits your taste buds right away and because you dunk in crunchy foods like chips and vegetables, you get sensations of flavor and texture in every bite. I sometimes serve dips like this one to my family as an afternoon snack. If I need something delicious for a party, this substantial snack comes together quickly, can be heated before I leave the house, and is delicious served cold or at room temperature if it has to sit for any length of time. Use canned lump crabmeat to save money. In this dip, no one will be able to tell the difference.

★ TIP: Grilling bread adds flavor without adding a lot of fat. Preheat your grill pan or grill to medium-high heat and toast the bread until golden on each side, turning only once. Watch closely as grilled or toasted bread seems to burn the minute you turn your back.

One 8-ounce package cream cheese, softened

2 tablespoons half and half

¾ cup mayonnaise

2 tablespoons finely chopped shallots (from about 4 medium cloves)

1 teaspoon creamed horseradish

1 teaspoon Dijon mustard

½ teaspoon cayenne pepper

½ teaspoon white wine vinegar

¼ teaspoon freshly ground pepper

½ teaspoon salt

One 10-ounce package frozen chopped spinach, thawed and squeezed as dry as possible

Two 6-ounce cans crabmeat, drained

½ cup grated Parmigiano-Reggiano cheese (from 2 ounces)

One thin French bread baguette, thinly sliced

¼ cup olive oil

1. Preheat the oven to 375°F.

2. In a food processor, fitted with the metal blade, blend the cream cheese, half and half, mayonnaise, shallots, horseradish, mustard, cayenne, vinegar, pepper, salt, and spinach. Scrape the mixture into a medium bowl and fold in the crabmeat. Spread the combined mixture in the bottom of a 9-inch square baking dish or a 1-quart casserole dish. Sprinkle the cheese over the top.

3. Bake for 20 to 25 minutes, until heated through.

4. While the crab dip is baking, brush the bread rounds with olive oil and season with salt and pepper. Bake or grill 2 to 3 minutes on each side, until light brown. ★

5. Serve the bubbling hot crabmeat mixture with the toast rounds for dipping.

Jalapeño Poppers with Chili Mayonnaise

✓ *SOMETHING SPECIAL*   ✓ *MAKE-AHEAD*

The first time I served these was almost eight years ago, when I began my cooking school. I had invited my first famous guest chef to Reno and was entertaining him at dinner. I carefully prepared the chiles, and fried them ten minutes before he was due to arrive. To save the poppers, I placed them on paper towels to drain. An hour and a half later he finally got to my house. Once he arrived, I put them on a cookie sheet and reheated them at 425°F in the oven. They were great, and I learned a new trick. You can fry these poppers up to two hours ahead, leave them at room temperature, then just pop the "poppers" in the oven to recrisp. Whew! It saved the day.

★ TIP: Protect your hands when working with chiles. If you know that your skin is sensitive, wear rubber kitchen gloves while you are doing this work. Do not touch your eyes or your face, because the oils from the chiles will create a painful burning sensation.

3 cups vegetable oil

20 medium fresh jalapeño chiles

3 cups ice water

1 teaspoon salt

2 cups white vinegar

One 8-ounce package cream cheese, softened

2 tablespoons fresh thyme leaves

1/2 teaspoon freshly ground pepper

1/2 teaspoon chili powder

1/2 cup all-purpose flour

1 large egg, slightly beaten with a fork just until combined

1/2 cup grated Parmigiano-Reggiano cheese (from 2 ounces)

1/2 cup fresh salsa

1 cup mayonnaise

1. At least 6 hours, or as long as 24 hours, before serving, heat 1 cup of the oil in a frying pan over high heat until it reaches 375°F. Add the chiles, in 4 or 5 batches, to the oil and fry each batch until the skins are well blistered. Using a slotted spoon, transfer the chiles to a bowl of cold water.

2. With the chiles in the cold water, gently remove the skin with your fingers. ★

3. Using a small paring knife, carefully make a thin slit lengthwise on one side of the chile. Do not cut the chile in half. Gently open the slit and remove any seeds or vein. Drain the water from the chile. In a small bowl, combine the cleaned chiles, the ice water, the salt, and the vinegar. Allow them to marinate for at least 6 hours or up to 24 hours.

4. When you are ready to stuff the chiles, drain them and run them under cold water. Pat the chiles dry.

5. In a small bowl, mix together the cream cheese, thyme, black pepper, and chili powder. Use a teaspoon to carefully stuff each of the chiles with the cheese mixture.

6. Place the flour, egg, and grated cheese in separate small bowls. Dip the stuffed chiles into the flour, then the egg, then roll them in the cheese. Repeat until all of the chiles are done. Lay the coated chiles on a rack until ready to fry them.

7. In a small bowl, combine the salsa and the mayonnaise.

8. Pour the remaining 2 cups of vegetable oil in a large skillet. Heat the oil to 350°F over medium-high heat. When the oil is hot, add the chiles a few at a time and fry for 2 to 3 minutes until golden brown and crusty. Transfer the chiles to a paper towel to drain.

9. Serve the poppers warm with the salsa mayonnaise on the side for dipping.

Herbed Cheddar Cheese Spirals

✓ EASY PREPARATION   ✓ MAKE-AHEAD   ✓ TAKE-ALONG

These little appetizers are the perfect way to turn ordinary store-bought puff pastry into a great appetizer. You can serve them in a basket on their own, as a quick snack in the afternoon, or as part of the main meal with the salad. Have a package of puff pastry in the freezer all the time and these will come together easily with a minimal amount of effort. Or, make them ahead of time and freeze them for a quick fix for unexpected company.

★ TIP: An easy way to twist the cheese spirals is to hold one end on the work surface and twist the other end two revolutions.

One 17-ounce package frozen puff pastry dough, defrosted

1 tablespoon all-purpose flour

1 large egg, blended with
1 tablespoon of water

1 cup grated Parmigiano-Reggiano or Asiago cheese (from 4 ounces)

1/2 cup grated cheddar cheese (from 2 ounces)

1 teaspoon dried oregano

1/4 teaspoon crushed red pepper

1/4 teaspoon salt

1/4 teaspoon freshly ground pepper

1. Place the sheet of puff pastry on a lightly floured cutting board and roll out to a 20- × 10-inch rectangle. Cut in half to make two 10-inch squares. Note: some brands of puff pastry will already be in 2 pieces just roll each into a 10-inch square.

2. Lightly brush both of the squares on one side with the egg and water wash.

3. Sprinkle the first square with the cheese, oregano, and crushed red pepper. Season lightly with salt and pepper. Roll the rolling pin lightly over the cheese to press the topping into the surface of the puff pastry. Place the second square, egg-side down, on the top of the cheese. Roll the 2-layer square into a 20- × 12-inch rectangle.

4. Transfer the dough to a parchment-lined cookie sheet and refrigerate until it is firm, about 20 minutes.

5. Preheat the oven to 425°F.

6. Remove the puff pastry from the refrigerator and put the pastry back onto the cutting board. Trim 1 inch off all sides of the pastry rectangle and discard the edges.

7. Cut the pastry in half lengthwise. You will have 2 pieces that are roughly 18 × 5 inches. Cut each piece across into eighteen 1- × 5-inch strips. Twist each strip to form a long spiral. ★

8. Place the twists, 1 inch apart, on an ungreased baking sheet. Press each end down firmly on the sheet so that they do not untwist. Refrigerate the cookie sheet for 20 minutes.

9. Bake 8 to 10 minutes, until lightly brown. Allow to cool and serve warm or at room temperature.

Deep-Fried Cheese Bites with Curry Mayonnaise

MAKES 8 SERVINGS

I know that when I want a quick snack on the weekend or an appetizer to serve as guests are arriving, I can whip up these cheese bites in no time. Use any combination of melting cheese and dry cheese that you happen to have on hand.

1 cup Curry Mayonnaise (next page)

4 large egg whites, at room temperature

3 cups grated medium or sharp cheddar cheese (from 12 ounces)

1 cup grated Parmigiano-Reggiano cheese (from 4 ounces)

1 teaspoon dried oregano

1/2 teaspoon freshly ground pepper

1/2 teaspoon ground nutmeg

4 cups peanut or vegetable oil for frying

1. Make the curry mayonnaise.

2. Place the egg whites in a medium bowl and beat them lightly. Add the grated cheeses, oregano, pepper, and nutmeg. Work these ingredients together lightly with a spoon until a soft mixture is formed.

3. Scoop up a teaspoonful of the cheese mixture and roll it between your palms into a 1-inch ball. Form the balls as needed, while you are frying the first ones you made.

4. Pour the oil into a deep-fat fryer or a heavy saucepan. Heat the oil to 350°F. *

5. Carefully slip the cheese balls, a few at a time, into the oil and cook them until they are golden brown, about 2 minutes. Do not allow the balls to touch or they will stick together like melted cheese does. Use your slotted spoon to keep them from touching while frying. With a slotted spoon remove the cheese balls from the oil and place them on paper towels to drain.

6. Repeat with the remaining cheese balls, arrange on a serving plate, and serve warm with the curry mayonnaise as a dip.

＊TIP: The secret to **perfect frying** is getting the oil temperature right. Use a deep-fry or candy thermometer (often one and the same) to measure the temperature. Look for one that reads up to 400°F. These cheese bites should be fried once the oil reaches 350°F and is no hotter than 375°F. The cheese will brown quickly on the outside while being creamy and melted inside.

(continues on page 26)

Curry Mayonnaise

1 cup mayonnaise

2 teaspoons curry powder, mild or hot to taste

2 teaspoons grated lime zest

¼ cup fresh lime juice

½ teaspoon salt

Combine all the ingredients in a small bowl. Chill and serve with the cheese bites.

Layered Cheese–Avocado Bean Dip

✓ *MAKE-AHEAD*   ✓ *TAKE-ALONG*   ✓ *EASY PREPARATION*

You're hanging out with friends and family to watch a game; in need of a great dip to take to a party; want to watch movies and enjoy a casual dinner—whatever your need, this layered dip fits all of those occasions and many more. I can't tell you how many times I have thrown this together when we were just lounging around on the weekend and wanted a snack. If there is time, the Tomatillo Sauce (page 97) from the Poultry Encores chapter works well in this dip. But store-bought salsa is fine in a pinch.

Two 16-ounce cans vegetarian refried beans

1¼ cups freshly prepared salsa

3 tablespoons drained chopped mild green chiles (from 4-ounce can)

2 teaspoons hot sauce

1 cup sour cream (½ pint)

1 cup mayonnaise

2 tablespoons fresh lemon juice

2 large, ripe Haas avocados, seeded, peeled, and sliced

2 cups grated medium sharp cheddar cheese (from 8 ounces)

1 cup grated Monterey Jack cheese (from 4 ounces)

2 tablespoons chopped black olives

¼ cup thinly sliced green onions (from about 4 whole green onions)

1. Preheat the oven to 375°F.

2. In a medium bowl, combine the refried beans, ¼ cup of the salsa, the green chiles, and hot sauce. Spoon the mixture into a 13- × 9-inch glass baking dish and spread it evenly into the dish.

3. In a small bowl, combine the sour cream, mayonnaise, and lemon juice. Pour the mixture evenly over the beans.

4. Arrange the avocado slices evenly in one layer on the sour cream mixture. Pour the remaining 1 cup salsa over the avocado. ∗

5. Spread the cheddar and the Monterey Jack cheese on top of the salsa.

6. Sprinkle with the olives and the green onions. Bake for 40 minutes or until hot and bubbly. Serve with the Crispy No-Fry Tortilla Chips (page 28) or regular store-bought tortilla chips. The dip can be prepared up to 24 hours in advance, refrigerated, then brought to room temperature and baked when ready to serve.

∗ TIP: If you find that your own or store-bought **fresh salsa** is watery, pour the salsa into a fine mesh strainer set over a bowl. Drain for 15 minutes. Use the chopped tomato mixture in the salsa and reserve the liquid to flavor another recipe.

Crispy No-Fry Tortilla Chips

✓ *EASY PREPARATION*   ✓ *MAKE-AHEAD*   ✓ *TAKE-ALONG*

Buy the freshest yellow or white corn tortillas that you can find, or for a twist, try making these with flour tortillas. These chips can be used to garnish soups, salads, and even cheese dip. I use them to make quick nachos for my son, Matthew. I just follow this recipe, then sprinkle with grated cheese and salsa, and bake five minutes more.

Twelve 8-inch corn or flour tortillas

Nonstick cooking spray ✱

Salt, to taste

1. Preheat the oven to 400°F.

2. Cut the tortillas into quarters. Place as many as you can in a single layer on a cookie sheet. Spray lightly with nonstick cooking spray.

3. Bake for 3 minutes or until golden brown, and then turn the chips over. Lightly spray the second side of the chips and bake 3 minutes more or until crisp and golden. ✱

4. Sprinkle with salt and serve.

✱ **TIP:** **For added flavor,** try the olive oil–flavored cooking spray, but note that these flavored sprays won't last very long on the shelf. If you have it more than a few weeks, do a quick flavor check before using for your meal.

✱ **TIP:** These **tortilla quarters** are also delicious grilled. Just spray the whole tortillas with nonstick cooking spray and grill on a hot grill pan or grill until golden brown. Cut into quarters while still warm from the grill and serve.

Crispy Fried Tortilla Chips

✓ *EASY PREPARATION*   ✓ *MAKE-AHEAD*   ✓ *TAKE-ALONG*

Homemade fried tortilla chips are a real treat. Originally this preparation was to give life and flavor to leftover tortillas. You can make these at least two days in advance—just store them loosely wrapped on a cookie sheet so that they will stay crisp. If you want to serve them warm, reheat in the oven for three minutes at 425°F.

Twelve 8-inch corn or flour tortillas

2 cups vegetable or peanut oil

Salt, to taste

1. Cut the tortillas into quarters.

2. In a large skillet, heat the vegetable oil to 350°F. Add as many of the tortilla quarters as will fit in a single layer in the skillet. Fry until golden, drain on paper towels and sprinkle with salt to taste. Repeat with the remaining tortilla quarters and serve.

Crusty Pizza Rolls with Tomato Dipping Sauce

MAKES 24 BITES

✓ SOMETHING SPECIAL   ✓ MAKE-AHEAD   ✓ FREEZER READY   ✓ TAKE-ALONG

These Greek-inspired, Italian-flavored snacks are wonderful to have on hand in the freezer, especially when impromptu entertaining calls for something special to serve with drinks. And children love them, especially as after-school snacks. These little stuffed phyllo rolls can be made ahead of time and baked at the last minute; just be sure to cool them slightly before serving, as the filling is very hot when they first come out of the oven.

Tomato Dipping Sauce (next page)

¼ cup chopped sun-dried tomatoes

¾ cup shredded mozzarella (from 3 ounces)

½ cup chopped pepperoni (from 2 ounces or about ¼ of an 8-ounce package sliced pepperoni)

1 tablespoon chopped fresh oregano

2 tablespoons storebought pizza sauce

Salt and freshly ground pepper, to taste

6 sheets frozen phyllo pastry (about 4 ounces), thawed and covered with a damp towel

½ cup butter, melted (1 stick)

1. Make the tomato dipping sauce.

2. Preheat the oven to 350°F. In a medium bowl, combine the sun-dried tomatoes, mozzarella, pepperoni, and oregano. Season lightly with salt and pepper. Stir in the pizza sauce and set aside.

3. Lay out the phyllo pastry and cut crosswise into 4 equal strips, each 4 inches wide by 12 inches long. Turn strips until the short ends face you. Brush 1 strip with melted butter. *

4. Place 1 teaspoon of filling at the center of the short end of the buttered pastry strip. Begin at the short end and roll the filling in the pastry like a cigar, stopping after rolling up about one-third of the pastry. Fold the sides over the filling and then continue to roll to the end. The final result will look like a mini spring roll. Place finished rolls, seam side down, on a greased, rimmed baking sheet and brush the surface with more melted butter. Repeat with the remaining phyllo. *

5. Bake 15 to 20 minutes, until golden brown.

*TIP: Cover unused phyllo pastry with a damp towel until you are ready for it. Uncovered pastry dries out very quickly and becomes too brittle to handle, but not so quickly that you can't work with it. With just a little practice, however, you will find phyllo very easy to work with.

*TIP: To freeze these pizza snacks, place the finished rolls on their tray in the freezer until frozen solid (the length of time for this to happen depends on the temperature in your freezer). Transfer the frozen rolls to a tightly covered plastic container and store in the freezer. When ready to use, bake them still frozen, increasing the time by about 5 minutes. No need to thaw them.

Tomato Dipping Sauce

✓ *EASY PREPARATION*

1 cup storebought pizza sauce

3 tablespoons chopped fresh cilantro

2 tablespoons butter

½ teaspoon balsamic vinegar

1 teaspoon hot sauce (such as Tabasco) or more, to taste

In a small saucepan over medium heat, combine the sauce, cilantro, and butter. Stir until the butter is melted and thoroughly blended. Remove from the heat. Stir in the vinegar and Tabasco. Serve warm.

Grilled Vegetable Quesadillas

✓ *EASY PREPARATION*   ✓ *MAKE-AHEAD*

The smoky flavor of the grilled vegetables and cheese makes them especially satisfying as accompaniments for drinks. Make them whenever you already have the grill fired up for dinner. Kids love them, too, and this is a great way to get them to eat extra vegetables.

¼ cup olive oil

2 cloves garlic, peeled and crushed

1 small zucchini, sliced very thinly lengthwise

1 small eggplant, sliced very thinly lengthwise

2 large green bell peppers, cored, seeded, and cut into eighths

1 large red onion, peeled and sliced into ¼-inch-thick slices

Eight 8-inch flour tortillas

Salt and freshly ground pepper, to taste

2 cups grated Monterey Jack cheese (from 8 ounces)

One 4-ounce can sliced green chiles—I like hot, but use mild or medium hot if you prefer

2 tablespoons chopped fresh oregano

1 pint sour cream

1. Preheat the grill, or a grill pan, on medium-high for 5 minutes.

2. Combine the olive oil and garlic in a small bowl and let stand for 10 minutes.

3. Brush the zucchini, eggplant, green bell peppers, and onion slices with the garlic-flavored oil. Arrange on a vegetable screen for the outdoor grill or directly on the grill pan. Grill 2 to 3 minutes until slightly charred on the underside. Turn and grill 1 minute more. Remove from the grill.

4. Lay 4 of the tortillas on the counter. Divide the roasted vegetables equally among the tortillas. Season with salt and pepper. Sprinkle each with ⅓ to ½ cup cheese. Add 1 tablespoon chiles and ½ tablespoon oregano to each. Cover with the remaining tortillas. *

5. Lay the filled quesadillas on the grill for 1 minute. Using a large spatula, turn the quesadillas over, pressing down to seal them. Grill 1 to 2 minutes more until the cheese is melted.

6. Remove the quesadillas from the grill, cut into quarters, and serve hot with sour cream on the side.

SERVING SUGGESTION

Bowls of thinly sliced green onions, guacamole, and freshly made salsa are also delicious accompaniments to these quesadillas.

★TIP: The **quesadillas can be prepared to this point,** wrapped tightly in plastic wrap, stacked, and refrigerated up to 8 hours. Bring to room temperature for about 20 minutes before grilling.

Satisfying Soups

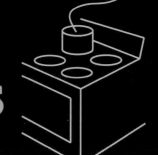

Whether or not science can prove it, soup must have healing powers; witness the curative effect of chicken soup, especially when nothing else appeals or when someone in the family is sick. Even when we are in robust health, soup restores our spirit and symbolizes a real home-cooked meal, which can satisfy everyone in the family.

In the past, people often made soups when they wanted to cook for their families but had nothing left but scraps of vegetables or meats. Today, soups are often a top-of-the-mind dish that people look forward to and some even consider them their favorite food to eat and make—even from scratch. Soups are unique because they follow a recipe less rigidly than baking, and allow greater flexibility with ingredients. Soup can be made with virtually anything but the kitchen sink. And soups can be eaten fairly fresh—requiring only a little cooking—or if allowed to cook slowly, they mellow and develop richer flavors over time. Here are a few soup-making hints:

- Keep low-salt broth on hand and soup can be ready for any meal in short order.

- Leftover chicken, beef, or other meats can be cut into small cubes and added after the broth has cooked a bit but at least 20 minutes before the end of the cooking, to allow the meat flavor to enhance the soup.

- Noodles, rice, potatoes, or vegetables can add heartiness to a soup, not only because of the added bulk of the ingredients but also because they release starches that thicken the liquid.

- A can of seasoned diced tomatoes or drained canned beans are perfect ways to stretch a pot of soup.

- Strips of leftover tortillas are a nice addition to chicken-based soups.

Homemade soup does not need to be a whole-day effort. Most do not need to be cooked for hours, just 30 minutes or a little longer. If all the preparation has been done ahead of time, soup can be a quick, worknight meal; some of these may even be finished a day or two ahead of time and reheated. Some will freeze quite well, too, making them your ace in the hole for last-minute special meals.

One of the great things about soup is that the preparation can include every family member. It's a good thing for kids to help with because they usually don't need to have a precise result, so there's more of a chance for them to feel successful, as long as it tastes good. From the time my son could break up a vegetable, tear herbs, or even stir a pot, he has helped me make soup. Soups were his first "secret" recipes. I would let him make hot dog soup or tortilla soup. Letting him take on the job helped him explore his creativity and gave me great hope that he would continue to enjoy his time in the kitchen. Soups can mean the same for you and everyone in your family!

Creamy Roasted Tomato Soup

✓ *SOMETHING SPECIAL*   ✓ *MAKE-AHEAD*

Roasting the tomatoes adds a wonderful flavor to this old favorite. If you cannot find good-quality tomatoes, you have two good options: use Roma or plum tomatoes, which are smaller but can usually be found year-round, or use canned roasted tomatoes, which are available at many supermarkets. This soup is comfort food at its very best.

* TIP: If you like a little **more texture** in your bowl, puree only two-thirds of the soup, leaving some of the vegetable pieces whole.

2 pounds vine-ripened tomatoes

About 2 tablespoons olive oil

3 tablespoons butter

1/2 cup finely chopped shallots (from about 16 medium cloves)

2 medium carrots, finely chopped (about 1 cup)

1/2 cup diced celery

1/2 cup diced fennel

2 cups vegetable or chicken broth

1 tablespoon chopped fresh tarragon

1 tablespoon chopped fresh curly-leaf parsley

Salt and freshly ground pepper, to taste

1 cup heavy cream or evaporated skim milk

1. Preheat the oven to 425°F.

2. Cut the tomatoes in half, seed them, and lightly coat with olive oil. Arrange the tomatoes cut side down in a shallow baking dish and bake for 30 minutes, turning at least once, until the skins begin to darken and blister. Remove from the oven and let cool. Remove the skins, coarsely chop the pulp, and reserve with all the juices.

3. Melt the butter in a medium saucepan over medium heat, add the shallots, carrots, celery, and fennel, and cook, stirring from time to time, until they are very soft. Add the stock and herbs and simmer for 30 minutes. Add the tomato pulp and reserved tomato juices.

4. Puree the soup in batches in a blender or food processor, or all at once with an immersion blender. Season with salt and pepper. *

5. Add the cream or evaporated skim milk and heat until warm. Ladle into bowls and serve very hot.

SERVING SUGGESTION

A dollop of sour cream and a sprinkle of finely chopped fresh tarragon in the middle of each serving add a company touch.

Cheesy Potato Soup

✓ SOMETHING SPECIAL   ✓ MAKE-AHEAD

When it's raining and miserably cold outside, this hearty soup will not only warm up chilled bodies, but will raise frozen spirits as well. Cheese lovers will especially love the hearty cheddar flavor, and the creamy texture is eminently comforting.

2 tablespoons butter

2 cups well-cleaned thinly sliced leeks, white and light green parts (from 2 large leeks)

2 medium yellow onions, halved and sliced (about 3 cups)

2 teaspoons finely chopped garlic (from 2 medium cloves)

6 cups peeled and ½-inch diced potatoes (from 4 medium potatoes)

4 cups chicken broth

Salt and freshly ground pepper, to taste

1 cup half and half

¼ teaspoon Tabasco sauce, or more to taste (optional)

2 cups shredded cheddar cheese (from 8 ounces)

2 tablespoons chopped fresh curly leaf parsley, for garnish

1. Melt the butter in a 4-quart stock pot over medium heat. Add the leeks and onions and cook, stirring, until just tender but not browned, about 5 minutes. Add the garlic and stir 1 minute more. Stir in the potatoes and chicken broth. Season with salt and pepper.

2. Cover and simmer for 45 minutes, until the potatoes are very tender.

3. Using an immersion stick blender, puree the soup, being careful not to overmix. *

4. Stir the half and half and Tabasco into the soup and simmer until heated through, for 3 minutes. Add the cheese and stir until melted and smooth—be careful not to boil once the cheese has been added.

5. Garnish each serving with parsley.

VARIATION

Add one 14-ounce can diced tomatoes and the juice to the chicken broth before adding to the soup. Puree the tomatoes along with the rest of the soup.

✱ TIP: For the best texture, **don't overmix the soup** at this point or the potatoes may become slightly gluey. Puree just until smooth.

Vegetable and Bean Soup

✓ MAKE-AHEAD ✓ FREEZER READY ✓ TAKE-ALONG

Here is a real, old-fashioned meal in a bowl. It is comfort food of the first kind. Add or subtract vegetables according to the season and your whim, and substitute pork, lamb, duck, or chicken for the ham hocks to make it your very own special soup. But potatoes, onions, and carrots are essential. Like many other country soups, this one is not only better the day after it is made, but it freezes very well. This is an excellent dinner choice for a cold night when busy schedules don't permit eating as a family. Everyone can heat up his/her serving when they have time.

★TIP: If you like **hot and spicy soups**, add Tabasco to taste.

½ pound dried navy or great northern white beans

1 pound salt pork, side meat, or streak-of-lean in one piece, or 1 pound smoked ham, cut in ½-inch dice

3 tablespoons chicken fat or olive oil

2 medium yellow onions, chopped (about 2 cups)

6 medium cloves garlic, peeled and crushed

3 large carrots, chopped (about 1½ cups)

1½ cups well-washed sliced leeks, white and light green parts (from 2 small leeks)

1½ quarts water (6 cups)

3 cups coarsely chopped cabbage (from ½ medium head)

1 smoked ham hock

½ teaspoon crushed red pepper

1 whole hot red pepper (serrano)

3½ cups ½-inch diced potatoes (from 3 medium potatoes)

Salt and freshly ground pepper, to taste

1 tablespoon fresh thyme leaves

2 tablespoons chopped fresh Italian flat-leaf parsley, for garnish

1. Place the beans in a heavy 2-quart saucepan. Add enough water to cover them by more than 1 inch. Bring to a boil, and cook for 2 minutes. Remove the pot from the heat and cool completely in the cooking water. Drain.

2. Place the salt pork in another 2-quart saucepan. Add water to cover, bring to a boil over high heat, and simmer for 10 minutes. Drain completely, rinse well, and cut the meat into ½-inch dice.

3. Heat the chicken fat or oil in a 4-quart kettle over medium-high heat. Stir in the onions, garlic, carrots, and leeks. Cook, stirring, for 5 minutes. Add the water, beans, cabbage, salt pork, ham hock, crushed red pepper, and whole red pepper. Simmer for 1 hour, stirring from time to time.

4. Add the potatoes. Season very well with salt, pepper, and thyme. Simmer 45 to 60 minutes more, until the potatoes are very tender, but not falling apart.

5. Remove the hot pepper and the ham hock from the soup. Discard the hot pepper. Pull the meat from the hock, return it to the soup, and discard the bone.

6. Serve in flat bowls and garnish with chopped parsley. The soup should be very thick with the vegetables—almost like a stew. ★

Spicy Peanut Soup

You might never have thought of using peanut butter as a base for soup, but give this luscious, creamy soup with a spicy bite just one taste and you will be hooked. It's a classic Virginia favorite and has been around in one form or another since before the Revolution. Experiment with both smooth and chunky peanut butter, and see which one you like best. Children especially seem to love this delicious soup.

✻ TIP: Immersion blenders are invaluable for pureeing soups, sauces, and gravies. The cleanup is very simple and there is no need to transfer hot liquids from pot to blender or food processor, which can be messy and even dangerous.

3 tablespoons butter

2 ribs celery, chopped (about 1 cup)

1 cup sliced yellow onion

2 teaspoons finely chopped garlic
(from 2 medium cloves)

1 teaspoon cayenne pepper,
or more to taste

2 tablespoons all-purpose flour

2 cups chicken broth

2 cups milk

1/2 cup heavy cream

1 1/2 cups smooth peanut butter
(12 ounces)

Salt and freshly ground pepper,
to taste

2 tablespoons chopped fresh curly
leaf parsley

1/2 cup chopped roasted peanuts,
for garnish

1. Melt the butter in a 3-quart saucepan over medium heat. Add the celery and onion, and cook until tender, about 7 minutes. Add the garlic and cayenne. Stir, and cook for 1 minute more. Sprinkle with flour and stir to combine completely. Cook, stirring, for 2 minutes, but do not brown.

2. Stir in the chicken broth, and simmer 30 minutes.

3. Puree the soup with an immersion blender, or in an upright blender. ✻

4. Return the puree to the saucepan. Stir in the milk, heavy cream, and peanut butter until smooth. Season with the salt, pepper, and parsley. Cook over low heat for 1 to 2 minutes.

5. Serve very hot and garnish each serving with 1 tablespoon chopped peanuts.

Rotisserie Chicken and Wild Rice Soup

✓ *EASY PREPARATION*   ✓ *MAKE-AHEAD*

This quick chicken soup is perfect with wild rice. But just imagine, you can also use a cup of leftover rice, or leftover noodles, or even a few extra pieces of chicken that may have eluded your hungry clan and have been stashed in the refrigerator. Soup is conducive to mixing and matching flavors; try using white onion instead of green onion, or adding a few cubes of cooked potato, or whatever your family prefers. It's all up to you.

✱ TIP: For a little more flavor in this soup, try cooking about $1/2$ cup diced fennel with the onion and garlic. When the soup is finished, add some tarragon instead of the parsley. The final soup will have a lovely delicate anise flavor.

2 tablespoons butter

1 teaspoon minced garlic

3/4 cup sliced green onions (from about 12 whole green onions)

3/4 cup sliced mushrooms (from about 10 mushrooms)

1 cup chopped tomato (from about 1 large tomato)

5 cups low-salt chicken broth

2 cups shredded rotisserie chicken or other cooked chicken (from a 3-pound chicken)

2 cups cooked wild rice

1/4 cup dry white wine

1 tablespoon lemon juice

1 tablespoon chopped fresh Italian flat-leaf parsley

Salt and freshly ground pepper, to taste

1. Melt the butter in a large saucepan over medium-high heat. Add the garlic and the green onions. Cook, stirring, for about 2 minutes. ✱

2. Add the mushrooms and tomato and cook about 2 minutes more.

3. Add the chicken broth, shredded chicken, wild rice, white wine, and lemon juice.

4. Simmer for 15 minutes. Add the parsley. Adjust the seasonings and serve.

Rotisserie Chicken and Matzo Ball Soup

✓ *SOMETHING SPECIAL*   ✓ *MAKE-AHEAD*

My grandmother made the most amazing matzo ball soup, and she always used a shortcut. She took store-bought low-salt or no-salt chicken broth, added carrots, onions, and celery, and simmered it for 50 minutes. Then she drained the broth off the vegetables and used the broth for her chicken soup. Try it! This trick gives the store-bought broth a great homemade flavor. This recipe uses another shortcut, making use of a deli or supermarket roast chicken.

4 quarts low-salt chicken broth

1 cup finely diced yellow onion

4 medium carrots, finely diced (about 2 cups)

5 or 6 large ribs celery, finely diced (about 2 cups)

½ teaspoon freshly ground pepper, plus more to taste

¼ cup vegetable oil

4 large eggs, room temperature, separated

1 cup matzo meal

2 cups shredded rotisserie chicken meat (from a 3-pound chicken)

1 tablespoon chopped Italian flat-leaf parsley

Sea salt, to taste

1. Bring the chicken broth to a boil in a large stock pot, over medium-high heat. Add the onion, 1 cup of the carrots, and 1 cup of the celery. Simmer for 50 minutes. Strain the broth, pressing on the vegetables to remove as much broth as possible and return the broth to the pot. Discard the vegetables. Add the remaining 1 cup carrots and 1 cup celery to the strained broth. Season with ½ teaspoon pepper. Cook until tender, about 10 minutes.

2. In a medium bowl, beat together the vegetable oil and egg yolks. Add the matzo meal. The mixture will appear very dry.

3. In an electric mixer fitted with the beater or whisk attachment, beat the egg whites until soft peaks form.

4. Fold the egg whites into the matzo meal mixture—the mixture should be very light. Let the mixture rest in the refrigerator for at least 15 minutes.

5. Once the mixture is firm and the soup has come to a simmer, wet your hands. Gently scoop about 2 tablespoons of the matzo mixture into your hands. Form into small ball. ∗

Add the ball to the simmering soup. Repeat with the rest of the matzo meal mixture.

6. Cover the pot, lower the heat to a very slow simmer, and allow the matzo balls to cook 20 minutes or until fluffy and tender. ∗

7. Stir in the chicken and parsley. Season well with salt and pepper. Serve. ∗

∗ **TIP:** When shaping the **matzo balls,** a form of dumpling, keep in mind that they will swell quite a lot while they are cooking in the broth. I like them fairly large—generally serving one in each bowl of soup—but make them smaller if you prefer several matzo balls per bowl.

∗ **TIP:** Be sure to **reduce the heat to low.** You want the liquid at a constant light simmer, but do not let it boil as the matzo balls are tender and can break apart when they first begin to cook. When cooked gently, the result will be beautifully swollen, light, and tender dumplings.

∗ **TIP:** I find that **chicken that has been precooked before being added to a soup** at the end of the cooking process **tastes better** and is more tender than when adding raw chicken early to cook slowly with the other ingredients. The chicken can be grilled, roasted, or store-bought. It should be cut into cubes or shredded and then added to the soup just in time to warm it through.

Mom's Beef and Beer Chili

✓ EASY PREPARATION ✓ MAKE-AHEAD ✓ FREEZER READY

My mom has been making this chili for as long as I can remember. The addition of a good dark beer gives it a satisfying but subtly rich flavor. Mom always begins with a lean ground beef the way we do here, but for a healthier choice you can use ground chicken or turkey. This is a favorite dish in our house when all the men are glued to a game on television. Why not get the host into the kitchen to help before the game begins so the food tastes just the way he likes it?

2 tablespoons olive oil

2 cups chopped white onion

2 tablespoons chopped pickled jalapeño

2 tablespoons chopped garlic (from about 6 medium cloves)

2½ pounds lean ground beef

¼ cup ancho chili powder

2 tablespoons ground cumin

1 teaspoon paprika

½ teaspoon cayenne pepper

One 28-ounce can chopped tomatoes with the liquid

One 15-ounce can kidney beans, rinsed and drained

1 cup dark beer or ale

One 14-ounce can low-salt beef broth

Sour cream, chopped green onion, black olives, fresh cilantro, for garnish

1. Heat a 4-quart stock pot over medium-high heat. Add the olive oil, chopped onion, jalapeño, and garlic; cook until the onion is softened but not changing color, about 4 minutes.

2. Add the ground beef to the pot. Cook until lightly browned, turning frequently, breaking up the meat as it cooks, about 5 minutes.

3. Once the meat has browned a little and is cooked through, add the chili powder, cumin, paprika, and cayenne to the pot, stir to mix well, and cook over medium heat for about 1 minute more.

4. Add the tomatoes, kidney beans, beer, and broth to the pot. Lower the heat to a simmer and cook the chili for about 45 minutes. Serve in deep bowls with the garnishes. ✴

✴ **TIP:** When using canned beans, pour the beans into a colander and run cold water through them until the foam dissipates. The beans will have better texture and flavor if they are rinsed, and some of the added sodium will be removed.

Shrimp and Coconut Soup

✓ *SOMETHING SPECIAL*

A Thai-style noodle soup, this delicious dish combines many of the wondrous flavors of Asia, including ginger, garlic, chili paste, and coconut milk. The shrimp are the ultimate touch. Together they all add up to a delightful, satisfying starter or Sunday supper. If you cannot find the Asian garlic chili paste, garlic-chili sauce can be substituted.

1 tablespoon peanut oil

2 cloves garlic, peeled and lightly crushed

1½ tablespoons finely chopped fresh ginger

1 teaspoon Asian garlic chili paste, or more to taste

½ teaspoon crushed black peppercorns

1 teaspoon ground cumin

4 cups chicken broth

2 ounces dried rice noodles or rice sticks

1½ cups unsweetened coconut milk

½ pound small (36–45 per pound) shrimp, peeled and deveined

1 tablespoon fresh lime juice

3 tablespoons chopped fresh cilantro

3 tablespoons thinly sliced green onions, white and up to 1 inch dark green (from 3 green onions), for garnish

1. In a 3-quart saucepan, heat the oil over medium heat. Add the garlic, ginger, garlic chili paste, peppercorns, and cumin. Cook, stirring, to release the flavor and fragrance of the spices, for 1 minute. Stir in the chicken broth and simmer for 20 minutes. Remove and discard the garlic.

2. Pour boiling water over the rice noodles in a bowl and soak until they are soft and pliable, for 15 minutes.

3. Stir the coconut milk into the broth and simmer 5 minutes.

4. Drain the noodles and add to the soup. Add the shrimp, lime juice, and cilantro. Cook just until the shrimp are pink and the noodles are heated through, 2 to 3 minutes more. ✱

5. Serve very hot in deep bowls, garnished with the sliced green onions.

✱ TIP: For perfectly cooked **shrimp**, it is important to add them in the last 2 to 3 minutes, just before serving, or they will be overcooked. If you make the soup ahead of time, leave the noodles and shrimp out until everyone is seated.

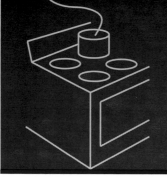

Substantial Salads

For many years in America, the term *salad* simply meant a wedge of iceberg or plain greens tossed with vinegar and oil. Well, say goodbye to bland "rabbit food" and hello to today's creative choices. Salads can range from a hearty Chunky Sour Cream and Basil Chicken Salad (page 43) to a salad you might concoct of greens, fruit, and chiles with Asian seasonings. Today, your choice of salads is limited only by your imagination, and your family's preferences. Substantial salads can be the star course of a meal, especially in warm weather. Toss together combinations of vegetables and greens along with a nourishing addition of cheese or meat or a selection of succulent fruits, with dressings as light as a little olive oil or as filling as homemade ranch. Main course salads are good dishes for young cooks. With no actual cooking necessary, they can make a whole meal with little effort. Just be sure to have all the ingredients ready and waiting for them in the refrigerator.

Salad Tips:

- Be ready to make great salads at home, anytime, by always putting several different types of greens in your weekly shopping cart, even if you don't know up front exactly how you want to use them. If they are ready in the fridge, you will use them.

- Once you bring home salad greens, rinse them well. Soak the greens in cold or better yet, ice, water for at least 20 minutes to maximize their crispness, and then dry them well. Use a salad spinner for drying and it can be accomplished in a jiffy. Cleaned and dried, stored in the refrigerator wrapped in paper towels and sealed in a plastic bag, they will last at least seven days. These greens can now be used for many different dishes throughout the week.

- When you serve your family salads often, and children are raised eating them, it is much easier to make a salad the main dish of the meal. But if salads are a sometime thing for your family, begin by incorporating familiar ingredients. Fresh arugula, torn into a bowl of pasta and grilled chicken served cold with a thick vinaigrette dressing, is a great main dish salad to begin with.

- Keep in mind that many leftovers can be turned into main dish salads. You might make the chicken and pasta dish I just mentioned on a night when you have some extra cooked chicken. Imagine the possibilities: You roast a chicken for dinner, and you might add extra potatoes to make a roasted potato salad for dinner tomorrow night. I have even tossed chicken or roast beef into the potato salad to make it heartier and then served it over the fresh greens. Strips of roasted peppers can be tossed with fresh greens to make a fantastic base for cooked meats. The possibilities are endless! Have the pantry items, such as good mustard, vinegar, and oil, on hand and you are on your way to creating great salads.

Chunky Sour Cream and Basil Chicken Salad

MAKES 4 TO 6 SERVINGS

✓ EASY PREPARATION   ✓ MAKE-AHEAD   ✓ TAKE-ALONG

This refreshing chicken salad is ideal for that sultry summer evening when everyone is hot and tired and dinner on the deck is a must. Serve it with a platter of sliced tomatoes, a big wedge of Brie, and a loaf of crusty whole-grain bread.

1 quart chicken broth

2 cloves garlic, peeled and crushed

One 3-pound chicken, cut up, back discarded, skinned

1 cup red onion, peeled, quartered, and thinly sliced

1/2 English cucumber, washed, halved, seeded, and thickly sliced *

1/2 cup coarsely chopped celery

1/2 cup sour cream

1/2 cup mayonnaise

1/2 teaspoon seasoned pepper, such as Mrs. Dash

2 tablespoons Dijon mustard

1/3 cup freshly chopped basil (5 tablespoons)

Salt, to taste

3 cups fresh mixed salad greens (about 4 1/2 ounces)

1. In a large 4-quart saucepan over medium-high heat, combine the broth and garlic. Bring to a simmer. Add the chicken pieces and simmer gently until tender, for 30 minutes. Cool in the broth for 15 minutes. Drain well, reserving the broth for another use.

2. Remove the chicken from the bone and cut into bite-sized pieces.

3. In a large bowl, toss together the chicken, onion, cucumber, and celery. Refrigerate, covered, for about 30 minutes. *

4. In a small bowl, beat together the sour cream, mayonnaise, pepper, and mustard. Pour two-thirds of the dressing over the chilled chicken and mix well. Add a little more dressing if the salad seems dry. Toss with the basil and season with salt to taste. Chill several hours to develop the flavors.

5. Serve on a bed of salad greens, or stuff into tomatoes cut into wedges.

✱TIP: English cucumbers are the long, dark green, shrink-wrapped cucumbers found in the supermarket produce section. They can be eaten skin and all as they are not waxed to preserve them. These cucumbers have many fewer and smaller seeds than the more common waxed variety and therefore do not cause as much indigestion. To seed them completely, cut the cucumbers in half lengthwise and drag the tip of a sharp spoon down the center of the flesh, removing the seeds.

✱TIP: Cool the chicken completely before adding the dressing, otherwise the chicken has a tendency to shred and the salad becomes mushy rather than chunky.

Grilled Chicken Salad with Black Beans and Barbecue Ranch Dressing

✓ *SOMETHING SPECIAL*

Every summer I visit friends in Crested Butte, Colorado. The first thing we do is head over to a restaurant called The Steep for lime margaritas and the barbecued chicken salad. This recipe is inspired by that salad, and now I can serve it whenever I want. If you are taking the salad to a potluck or dinner party, get everything ready, then heat the chicken when you arrive. Pass this dressing on the side.

2 cups peeled, seeded, and sliced cucumber (from about 2 medium cucumbers)

1/4 cup white wine vinegar

1/4 teaspoon salt

1/4 teaspoon freshly ground pepper

BEANS

One 15-ounce can black beans, drained and rinsed well

1/4 cup stemmed, seeded, deveined, and diced red bell pepper

1/4 cup stemmed, seeded, deveined, and diced yellow bell pepper

1/4 cup stemmed, seeded, deveined, and diced orange bell pepper

1/4 cup diced red onion

1/4 cup chopped fresh Italian flat-leaf parsley

1/4 cup fresh lime juice (from 2 medium limes)

1/4 cup extra-virgin olive oil

1/2 tablespoon dried oregano

1/2 tablespoon honey

1/2 tablespoon ground cumin

BARBECUE RANCH DRESSING

1/3 cup barbecue sauce

1/3 cup mayonnaise

1/3 cup nonfat yogurt

1/3 cup buttermilk

1 tablespoon white wine vinegar

1/4 teaspoon garlic powder

1/4 teaspoon onion powder

1/4 teaspoon paprika

1/4 teaspoon cayenne pepper

2 tablespoons chopped chives

2 tablespoons chopped fresh Italian flat-leaf parsley

SALAD

4 cups torn romaine lettuce leaves (about 5 ounces)

2 medium vine-ripened tomatoes, quartered

1/2 cup thawed frozen corn or fresh cooked corn kernels

2 cups 1-inch pieces of warm grilled, rotisserie, or fried chicken

1. In a small bowl, toss the cucumber slices in the vinegar, salt, and pepper. Allow these to marinate at room temperature while you prepare the salad.

2. To prepare the beans: In a medium bowl, combine the black beans, peppers, onion, and parsley. In a small bowl, combine the lime juice, olive oil, oregano, honey, and cumin. Toss the dressing with the bean mixture. Set aside.

3. For the barbecue ranch dressing: In a blender or food processor, blend the barbecue sauce, mayonnaise, nonfat yogurt, buttermilk, vinegar, garlic powder, onion powder, paprika, and cayenne pepper. Pour the dressing into a bowl and fold in the chives and the parsley. *

4. To serve the salad: Arrange the romaine lettuce on each plate. Place the tomato quarters on the side of each plate and sprinkle the greens with corn. To the side of the greens place some of the marinated cucumber. Place a spoonful of the black beans on the center of the greens. Top with the warm chicken. Pass the barbecue ranch dressing or drizzle some over the chicken and the greens.

✱ TIP: Doctor your favorite good-quality ranch **dressing** if you don't have time to make the dressing from scratch. Just stir in the spices and the barbecue sauce and your special dressing is ready to serve!

Broiled New York Strip Steaks with Baby Greens

MAKES 4 TO 6 SERVINGS

✓ *SOMETHING SPECIAL*   ✓ *EASY PREPARATION*

I have always enjoyed the combination of blue cheese and beef. In this salad, we begin with a simple way to cook the meat . . . in the broiler. The steaks are ready in minutes, ready to serve on a bed of greens. This salad is the perfect easy-to-fix meal, and it is hearty enough to satisfy just about everyone's appetite, especially when the family clamors for the simple, satisfying flavor of steak.

★ TIP: Grill the steaks **ahead of time** for a quick-prep dinner. Wrap them well and chill in the refrigerator. Remove them about 15 minutes before serving, slice, and put together the salad.

STEAK

2 tablespoons freshly ground pepper

1 tablespoon fresh thyme leaves

1 tablespoon olive oil

3 boneless New York Strip steaks (1½ inches thick)

1 tablespoon salt

SALAD

¼ cup olive oil

2 tablespoons red wine vinegar

1 tablespoon grainy mustard

6 cups mixed baby greens (about 9 ounces)

½ cup stemmed, seeded, deveined, and sliced red bell pepper

1 medium vine-ripened tomato, quartered

½ cup crumbled blue cheese (2 ounces)

1. In a small bowl or dish, combine the pepper, thyme, and olive oil and rub equal amounts of the mixture into both sides of each steak. Season with salt and set aside.

2. Set the oven rack in its highest position and preheat the broiler. Place the steaks on a foil-lined broiler pan. For medium doneness, broil the steaks about 4 minutes per side, until well browned but still pink inside. Remove the steaks from the oven and transfer to a clean serving platter to rest, tented with foil for 3 to 4 minutes. ★

3. In a small bowl, combine the olive oil, vinegar, and mustard.

4. When you are ready to serve, slice the meat on the bias. Toss the salad greens in the dressing.

5. Arrange some dressed greens on each plate with the red bell pepper, tomato, and steak slices. Crumble blue cheese over the top and serve.

Grilled Lamb Chops with Mandarin Orange Salad

✓ *SOMETHING SPECIAL*   ✓ *EASY PREPARATION*

Lamb chops have great flavor, are easy to prepare, and the leftovers make excellent encore dinners. When you're serving them to your family one night, plan to make a few extra and use the leftover meat to make a quick salad or a main dish incorporating your favorite grain later in the week.

12 single baby rib lamb chops

1 garlic clove, cut in half, lengthwise

3 tablespoons plus ¼ cup olive oil

1 teaspoon crumbled dried thyme ✱

⅓ cup white wine vinegar

¼ cup sugar

½ cup chopped fresh mint

½ teaspoon salt

½ teaspoon freshly ground pepper

6 cups torn green leaf lettuce (from about 2 small heads)

One 15-ounce can mandarin oranges, drained

½ cup chopped green onions (from about 8 whole green onions)

¼ cup sliced celery

1 cup toasted slivered almonds

1. Pat the rib chops dry with a paper towel and rub them with the cut side of the garlic clove. Brush the chops with the 3 tablespoons olive oil and sprinkle them with the dried thyme.

2. Preheat an outdoor grill or grill pan for 5 to 10 minutes over medium-high heat. Grill the chops over medium-high heat for about 2 to 3 minutes per side. The chops should be golden on the outside and still pink in the center. ✱

3. Meanwhile, in a small saucepan, bring the white wine vinegar and sugar to a simmer. Cook until the sugar is dissolved. Remove the pan from the heat and stir in the fresh mint, salt, and pepper. Whisk the ¼ cup olive oil into the dressing and set aside.

4. In a large bowl, combine the lettuce greens, oranges, green onions, celery, and almonds. Toss with a small amount of the dressing, just enough to coat the greens—more can be added later, if needed.

5. To serve, arrange the salad on individual salad plates and top each with 2 of the rib chops. Pass the remaining dressing as a dipping sauce for the lamb.

✱ **TIP:** Rub the **dried herb** between your palms before adding to any recipe to release the fragrance.

✱ **TIP:** To **retain the juices** in the grilled meat, place it on a plate and tent it with foil as it comes off of the grill. It will continue to cook a little, but the juices will remain in the meat and it will stay perfectly tender until you are ready to serve it.

Asian Broiled Salmon Salad

✓ *SOMETHING SPECIAL*

The trick to this dish is to broil the salmon under high heat for just a minute or two after cooking it most of the way on the grill pan, so that the spicy coating becomes browned and crusty. The combination of the warm spicy salmon with the crispy cabbage and sweet mango is amazingly delicious.

MARINADE

1 tablespoon freshly grated ginger

1/2 teaspoon ground coriander

Pinch cayenne pepper

1/4 cup panko bread crumbs

1 tablespoon fresh lime juice

1 teaspoon peanut oil

1/2 teaspoon sesame oil

Salt and freshly ground pepper, to taste

1 1/2 pounds salmon fillets in 4 pieces

DRESSING

1 1/2 teaspoons grated fresh ginger

1 1/2 tablespoons low-sodium soy sauce, or more to taste

2 tablespoons rice or white wine vinegar

1 teaspoon finely chopped garlic

Freshly ground pepper, to taste

1 tablespoon fresh lime juice

1/4 cup peanut oil, depending on your taste

1/2 teaspoon sesame oil

SALAD

1 cup halved and very thinly sliced red onion

3 cups finely shredded napa cabbage

1/3 cup shredded carrot

1 cup fresh cilantro leaves, all stems removed

1 small fresh poblano chile, stemmed, seeded, very thinly sliced

1 hard ripe mango, halved and sliced *

1. In a small bowl, combine the grated ginger, coriander, cayenne, panko, lime juice, peanut oil, sesame oil, salt, and pepper. Pat the coating onto the fleshy side of the salmon fillets, pressing to make it adhere.

2. In a small bowl, combine the ginger, soy sauce, vinegar, garlic, pepper, and lime juice. Beat in the oils in a steady stream until the dressing thickens slightly.

3. In a large bowl, combine the onion, napa cabbage, carrot, cilantro, chile, and mango. Toss with about half of the dressing.

4. Heat a grill pan over medium-high heat for 5 minutes. Preheat the broiler. Sear the salmon fillets, skin side down, for 4 minutes. Transfer the grill pan to the broiler and broil 1 to 2 minutes, until the top is crusty and golden—do not turn the fillets.

5. Arrange the dressed salad on chilled plates and top each serving with a hot fillet of salmon. Pass the remaining dressing to drizzle on top. *

★TIP: To prepare mangoes, cut two large cheeks off the flat sides, cutting as close to the stone as possible. Peel the skin from the fruit with a sharp knife, then slice very thinly across.

★TIP: To create a skinless fillet of cooked salmon, perfect for topping a salad, run a very thin spatula between the flesh and the skin before transferring to the serving plate.

Mediterranean Seared Tuna Salad

✓ SOMETHING SPECIAL   ✓ EASY PREPARATION

The flavors of this easy salad evoke the warm, sunny days of a Mediterranean summer. Try to find the smallest cherry tomatoes available—the ones shaped like small grapes are especially sweet. If you cannot find fresh haricot verts or thin green beans, it is fine to use the frozen kind. Serve crisp flat bread and several good cheeses such as feta, manchego, or even Gorgonzola alongside. I like to set the table on the deck with glasses of ice-cold cider for the children, and a well-chilled crisp white wine for the grownups.

∗ TIP: Retain crispness and color in steamed or boiled green vegetables by quickly chilling them in a colander under very cold running water. Drain the chilled vegetables well and dry on a cloth towel.

MARINADE

2 tablespoons dry red wine

2 tablespoons red wine vinegar

1/3 cup olive oil

4 cloves garlic, crushed

1/4 teaspoon salt

Freshly ground pepper, to taste

2 tablespoons chopped fresh rosemary

2 tablespoons chopped fresh parsley

3/4 pound (12 ounces) tuna steaks in 1 or 2 pieces

SALAD

6 ounces very thin green beans (haricots verts if available)

1 English cucumber, thinly sliced

1 cup stemmed, seeded, and very thinly sliced red bell pepper

1 cup marinated artichoke hearts, very well drained

1 cup small cherry tomatoes

4 hard-cooked eggs, peeled and quartered

1 1/2 cups very thinly sliced red onion

Salt and freshly ground pepper, to taste

Extra-virgin olive oil

1 cup Niçoise or Kalamata olives, drained

1/4 cup freshly sliced basil, for garnish

1. In a small bowl, combine the red wine, red wine vinegar, olive oil, garlic, salt, pepper, rosemary, and parsley. Place the tuna steaks in a large resealable plastic bag. Pour in the marinade. Seal and marinate 30 to 40 minutes.

2. Put the green beans in a steamer basket over boiling water. Cover and steam 3 minutes. Remove from the heat and cool under cold, running water. Drain well and set aside. ∗

3. On a large, deep platter arrange the beans, cucumber, bell pepper, artichoke hearts, cherry tomatoes, and egg quarters in an attractive pattern. Spread the onion rings on top. Season well with salt and pepper.

4. Drizzle lightly with olive oil. Sprinkle the olives over the salad.

5. Preheat the grill pan or outdoor grill on high for 5 minutes. Remove the tuna from the marinade and pat dry with a paper towel. Grill for 3 minutes per side, until crusty on the outside and pink on the interior.

6. Break up the tuna into large chunks and arrange over the vegetables. Garnish with the basil and an extra drizzle of olive oil.

Shrimp and Pesto Pasta Salad

✓ SOMETHING SPECIAL   ✓ EASY PREPARATION   ✓ MAKE-AHEAD

This make-ahead salad is perfect for potluck dinners or suppers that have to wait for the last family member to come in. Serve it at room temperature, though it can be refrigerated for several hours and brought out about 30 minutes before serving. Refrigerated varieties of prepared pesto have clearly marked dates and are quite satisfactory, but I do not recommend the jarred variety from the supermarket shelves.

12 ounces penne pasta

¼ cup pine nuts, toasted *

8 ounces shelled, deveined, and poached medium (31–35 per pound) shrimp, tails removed *

1 cup fresh basil pesto from the dairy case of your supermarket

¼ cup freshly grated Parmigiano-Reggiano cheese

Salt and freshly ground pepper, to taste

1. Cook the penne pasta in 6 quarts of boiling salted water for 9 minutes. Drain well.

2. In a large bowl, combine the pine nuts and cooled shrimp with the penne. Toss in the pesto, and finish with the cheese. Season with salt and pepper and serve at room temperature.

＊TIP: Toast pine nuts in the oven for an even brown color. Since they have more oil than other nuts, they will brown faster. Instead of toasting them in a pan, which can cause them to burn in spots, try toasting them in a 350°F oven on a cookie sheet. They will brown evenly within 5 to 7 minutes, but be sure to watch them carefully—they will burn the minute you turn your back.

＊TIP: Gently poach the shrimp so that so they don't become chewy. Bring a large pot of salted water to a boil. Add the shrimp a few at a time, to avoid lowering the temperature of the water. Watch them carefully and remove them as soon as they are pink and firm, no longer than 2 to 3 minutes. Drain them and set them aside until ready to put in the salad. You can use frozen cooked shrimp to save money, but better to buy it raw and poach it yourself.

Butter Leaf Salad with Glazed Scallops

✓ SOMETHING SPECIAL

The mild, sweet flavor of scallops makes them a family favorite, but one we rarely think to make at home. This is unfortunate, because they cook quickly, and take on any great flavor that we might add to them. In this dish, the combination of ginger along with the nuttiness of sesame oil creates a sheen of flavor on the scallops. Just be careful not to overcook, and your family will find a new home treat.

✱ TIP: Rinse **scallops** in cold water and pat them dry before marinating or cooking. Use a small sharp knife to remove the tough muscles on the side of the scallop, if necessary.

1 teaspoon cumin seeds

1 tablespoon sesame oil

1 tablespoon grated fresh ginger

Salt and freshly ground pepper, to taste

18 large sea scallops ✱

¼ cup chopped pitted Kalamata olives

2 tablespoons chopped roasted red bell pepper

2 teaspoons rinsed capers

2 tablespoons red wine vinegar

1 teaspoon Dijon mustard

¼ cup extra-virgin olive oil

6 cups torn butter leaf lettuce (about 9 ounces)

2 medium vine-ripened tomatoes, quartered

1. Stir or toss the cumin seeds in a small skillet over medium-high heat until fragrant and light brown. Transfer the seeds to a spice grinder, mortar and pestle, or into a heavy plastic bag and grind them coarsely.

2. Combine the sesame oil and the ginger in a medium bowl. Season with salt and pepper and add the scallops. Toss gently to coat. Refrigerate for up to 1 hour.

3. In a blender or food processor, combine the olives, ground cumin, roasted bell pepper, capers, red wine vinegar, and mustard. Pulse just to combine. With the machine running, add the olive oil in a thin stream to thicken the mixture.

4. Heat an outdoor grill or grill pan to medium-high heat. Grill the scallops until they are cooked through, about 2 to 3 minutes per side, turning only once.

5. Toss the lettuce with half of the vinaigrette. Divide the lettuce and the tomato quarters among 6 plates. Top each plate with 3 scallops and serve with the remaining vinaigrette on the side.

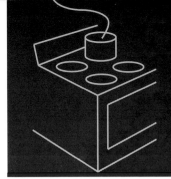

Incredible Eggs

Eggs are not just for breakfast. They are wholesome and filling, usually quick to prepare, and welcome as a change of pace for dinner. I have often taken leftover vegetables, added them to fresh eggs, and created a fantastic frittata when I felt that there was nothing else good for dinner in the refrigerator.

Eggs are something the entire family can enjoy because they can be prepared in so many different ways. Eggs can be baked, fried, poached, boiled, scrambled, or turned into omelets, frittatas, quiches, puddings, or even savory custards—the possibilities are almost endless. Plus, these egg dishes are so easy to prepare, the whole family can gather together to help in the kitchen, whether it's dinnertime or weekend brunch.

Here are some egg tips:

- Trying to eat healthier? Health advisors have given the go-ahead to enjoy eggs regularly. For less fat, though, use only one egg yolk for every three whites when scrambling them, if you like, or use refrigerated egg substitutes in quiches and frittatas. With the blend of the whites and a small amount of yolk they will seem richer than they actually are. Egg whites alone can be fabulous in omelets, too, because you can add so many things to them. Toss in some sharp cheddar or fresh vegetables, and the result is a dish fit for lunch, dinner, or even a late after-the-movies supper.

- Large eggs are used in most recipes and should be 65°F to 75°F or room temperature before using—about 20 minutes out of the refrigerator. If a recipe calls for beating and/or folding egg whites, start with room-temperature eggs and separate them carefully, keeping egg whites free of any yolk. (The whites will not increase to maximum volume if there is any trace of fat in them. Even the bowl and beaters must be scrupulously clean and dry.) After beating egg whites, carefully fold them with a wide wooden spoon or spatula into dry ingredients, trying not to break them down.

- Eggs combine well with all kinds of ingredients you probably already have on hand: onions, tomatoes, potatoes, herbs, leftover ham, or sliced turkey. Most of these dishes can be prepped ahead of time, combined, and cooked at the last minute with little time or fuss, making them perfect for busy night suppers, or as first-time meals for young cooks. On these occasions, eggs can easily and satisfyingly be what's for dinner.

Salmon and Chive Scrambled Eggs

✓ *EASY PREPARATION*

This is a fabulously simple, yet elegant and luscious breakfast dish. It is a new take on an old favorite. The slightly smoky flavor of the salmon goes very well with the creamy texture of the eggs, and the green onions add just the right tang. For a very special experience, top the soft eggs with a dollop each of sour cream and caviar!

¼ cup olive oil

8 large eggs

2 tablespoons chopped fresh chives

¼ teaspoon salt

⅛ teaspoon freshly ground pepper

1 cup chopped smoked salmon from the deli

¼ cup sour cream

1 tablespoon chopped fresh dill, for garnish

1. In a medium bowl, whisk together 2 tablespoons of the olive oil, the eggs, chives, salt, and freshly ground pepper.

2. Heat the remaining 2 tablespoons of olive oil in a medium skillet over low heat. Pour in the egg mixture and stir, using a flat wooden or plastic spatula, until the eggs just begin to set but are still creamy and slightly liquid, about 4 to 6 minutes. ✳

3. Gently stir in the smoked salmon and continue to cook only until the eggs are just barely set, about 1 minute longer. Remove the pan from the heat and stir in the sour cream.

4. Spoon the eggs onto warm plates, sprinkle with fresh dill, and serve immediately.

✳**TIP:** For light, fluffy, delicate scrambled eggs, cook them very slowly over low heat, stirring constantly and very gently as they cook.

Tomato and Ham Quiche

✓ *EASY PREPARATION*   ✓ *MAKE-AHEAD*   ✓ *TAKE-ALONG*

A quiche is a timeless dish to serve for breakfast, lunch, or even dinner—and if it is hearty enough, even "real men" will eat it. For an impromptu meal, the kinds of vegetables, meat, and cheese used can all be varied according to what you have in your refrigerator when you decide to cook—so, as long as you have eggs, milk, and cream on hand, the sky is the limit for you and your quiche possibilities!

Two 9-inch frozen pie crusts, defrosted overnight in refrigerator, or 20 minutes on the kitchen counter

1 tablespoon butter

1/2 cup finely chopped red onion

3/4 cup chopped ham (from about 4 ounces)

1/2 cup seeded and diced tomato

1 cup grated Gruyère cheese (from 4 ounces)

1/2 cup Parmigiano-Reggiano cheese (from 2 ounces)

Salt and freshly ground pepper, to taste

6 large eggs

1 cup whole milk

1 cup heavy cream

1. Preheat the oven to 425°F. Line two 9-inch glass pie plates with the pie crusts and make an attractive edge, then gently line each crust with foil or parchment paper. Fill the lined pans with pie weights or dried beans. Place the weighted shells on a cookie sheet in the preheated oven and bake 18 to 20 minutes, until the shells are barely colored. Remove the weights or beans, and the parchment or foil. Continue to bake the shells blind (unfilled) about 3 minutes more, until light golden brown. Remove the shells from the oven and cool completely. *

2. While the crust is baking, heat the butter in a small skillet over medium-low heat. Add the red onion and season with a pinch of salt. Cook, stirring often, until the onion is tender and sweet, about 6 minutes. Do not brown.

3. Spoon the cooked onion into a medium bowl and add the ham and tomato. Stir gently to combine. Stir in the cheeses, season to taste with salt and pepper, and reserve to cool.

★ TIP: Baking blind means to prebake a tart or pie shell before adding the filling. This step insures a crisp crust because it keeps the liquids from soaking into the pastry when the filling is added. The pastry should be lined, then filled with a weight to keep the surface from blistering and to hold up the sides. The crust is partially baked this way, then the weight and foil are removed, the filling is added, and they are baked together. Pie weights are commercially available, but dried beans or rice work fine.

4. In a medium bowl, beat the eggs, milk, and cream until very well combined and light yellow in color. Season well with salt and freshly ground pepper.

5. Lower the oven temperature to 350°F.

6. Arrange half of the cooled vegetable and cheese mixture in the bottom of each cooled pie shell. Pour half the egg mixture into each of the filled shells, and bake for 40 to 45 minutes, until the filling just sets in the center and is lightly colored on top. *

7. Remove the quiches from the oven and allow them to cool for 5 to 10 minutes—the filling will fall slightly in the middle as it cools. Cut into wedges to serve.

＊TIP: The **quiche filling will be done** when it puffs up, turns golden brown, and does not jiggle in the middle if you gently shake the pie plate.

Vegetable Strata

✓ *EASY PREPARATION*   ✓ *MAKE-AHEAD*   ✓ *TAKE-ALONG*

This vegetable strata is much like a savory bread pudding and is a wonderful way to provide breakfast, brunch, or any light meal for friends and family. If you want to serve it as part of a meal, add a crisp green salad or a small cup of soup (such as the Creamy Roasted Tomato Soup, page 34) to the menu. This dish is especially suitable for serving on hectic mornings, because it can be assembled the night before and baked fresh in the morning.

8 cups cubed French bread, crusts removed before measuring

2 tablespoons butter, plus extra for buttering the dish

1¾ cups whole milk

5 large eggs

Salt and freshly ground pepper, to taste

½ cup chopped onion

1½ cups stemmed, seeded, ½-inch diced red bell pepper

2 teaspoons finely chopped fresh oregano

2 small zucchini, sliced into rounds ⅛ inch thick

1 tablespoon chopped fresh mint

2 cups crumbled feta cheese (from 8 ounces), plus ¼ cup reserved to sprinkle on top

1. Preheat the oven to 250°F.

2. Place the cubed French bread on a cookie sheet in an even layer and bake in the preheated oven for 10 to 15 minutes to slightly dry out but not brown the bread. Cool and reserve.

3. Increase the oven temperature to 350°F. Generously butter a glass 9- × 11-inch baking dish.

4. In a large bowl, whisk together the milk and eggs; season with salt and freshly ground pepper. Add the bread cubes, toss to coat, and allow them to soak for 15 minutes, turning often.

5. Meanwhile, melt 1 tablespoon of the butter in a medium heavy skillet over medium heat. Add the onion and season with salt. Cook, stirring often, until the onion is translucent, about 5 minutes. Add the red pepper and continue to cook until the vegetables are tender, about 6 minutes more. Add half the oregano and cook, 1 minute more, until fragrant. Remove to a bowl and reserve.

6. In the same skillet, melt the remaining 1 tablespoon of butter over medium heat. Add the zucchini slices, season with salt to

taste, and cook about 8 minutes, stirring frequently, until the zucchini just begins to caramelize, turning golden brown. Stir in the remaining oregano and cook, 1 minute more, until fragrant. Add to the bowl with the onion and pepper, and season well with

salt and freshly ground pepper. Add the fresh mint and 2 cups crumbled feta cheese. Stir to combine.

7. Add the vegetable mixture to the soaking bread and gently stir to combine. Pour all into the

prepared pan, sprinkle with the reserved feta cheese, and bake 35 to 40 minutes, until puffy and lightly browned. ⋆

8. Remove from the oven, cool slightly, and serve warm, cut in squares.

⋆**TIP:** You can **make the strata** to this point up to 24 hours in advance and bake when you are ready to serve it. This makes it a perfect busy weekend brunch dish.

Cream Cheese and Egg Frittata

MAKES ONE 10-INCH FRITTATA

✓ *EASY PREPARATION*　　✓ *MAKE-AHEAD*　　✓ *TAKE-ALONG*

Frittatas are great for breakfast or brunch picnics because they can be easily transported and are just as delicious whether served hot or cold. This creamy frittata is redolent of summer with the fresh herbs, but the possible choices for fillings are almost endless.

* TIP: If the skillet handle is **not ovenproof**, keep it from burning by covering it with several layers of aluminum foil.

1 tablespoon butter

1/2 cup finely chopped white onion

Salt, to taste

5 large eggs, at room temperature

1/2 cup half and half

1/2 cup grated Parmigiano-Reggiano cheese (from 2 ounces)

1/4 cup each chopped fresh basil, chive, and parsley; reserve 1 tablespoon of the mixed herbs for garnish

1/8 teaspoon cayenne pepper

1 cup seeded and diced tomato, at room temperature

Freshly ground pepper, to taste

1 tablespoon unsalted butter

8 ounces cream cheese, cut into 1/2-inch cubes

1. Preheat the oven to 325°F. Melt the butter in a 10-inch skillet over medium heat. Add the onion, season with salt and cook, stirring from time to time, until soft and tender but not browned, about 10 minutes. Remove the onion to a small bowl, wipe the skillet clean and set aside.

2. While the onion is cooking, in a large bowl, whisk together the eggs, half and half, Parmigiano-Reggiano cheese, herbs, pinch of salt, and cayenne.

3. In a small bowl, combine the diced tomato and reserved chopped herbs. Season with salt and freshly ground pepper to taste.

4. Heat the 1 tablespoon of unsalted butter over medium heat in the same 10-inch skillet. Add the cooked onion and pour the egg mixture into the skillet. Stir the eggs with a heat-resistant spatula, in a circular motion, until they just begin to set, about 3 minutes.

5. Sprinkle the cubed cream cheese over the top of the eggs and stir once or twice to barely combine.

6. Place the pan in the preheated oven and bake for about 7 minutes, until the cheese melts and the frittata is puffed, lightly golden, and the center is just set. *

7. Remove from the oven and cool slightly. Garnish with reserved mixed herbs.

8. Slide the frittata onto a warmed serving plate, cut into wedges, and serve warm or at room temperature, with the tomato salad spooned over the top.

Mediterranean Egg Cups

✓ SOMETHING SPECIAL   ✓ MAKE-AHEAD   ✓ TAKE-ALONG

This distinctive method of preparing eggs is easy to do, yet very impressive. Eggs baked in a nest of fresh vegetables are colorful and delicious—children love not only helping put them together, but they dive right in to the finished dish. The individual servings are perfect for buffet brunches, lunch outside, or times when everyone deserts the dinner table for special activities, eating at different times. The fennel, thyme, and olives evoke the flavors of the Mediterranean.

★TIP: For a more elegant look, **this dish can be made and served in individual ramekins** and brought straight from the oven on cloth napkin–lined plates.

2 tablespoons olive oil, plus more for greasing muffin cups

¼ cup finely sliced shallot (from about 6 to 8 cloves)

1 cup halved and thinly sliced fennel, with the root and stalk trimmed away

Salt, to taste

½ teaspoon finely chopped fresh thyme

1½ teaspoons chopped garlic (from about 2 small cloves)

1 cup seeded and diced tomato

1½ cups cleaned and dried baby spinach (from 4 ounces baby spinach)

½ teaspoon salt

⅓ cup low-sodium chicken broth

18 Kalamata olives, pitted, sliced in thirds

6 large eggs

Freshly ground pepper, to taste

¼ cup extra-virgin olive oil, for garnish

1. Preheat the oven to 300°F.

2. Heat the 2 tablespoons olive oil in a large skillet over medium heat. Add the shallot and fennel, season with salt and cook until soft and tender without browning, about 6 minutes. Add the thyme and garlic, and cook 1 minute more.

3. Add the tomato and stir to combine. Arrange the spinach on top of the mixture and sprinkle with ½ teaspoon salt. Using tongs, gently toss the spinach so that it wilts evenly. When the spinach is just wilted add the stock to moisten the ingredients. Remove from the heat and stir in the olives. Reserve.

4. With a pastry brush, liberally grease six 3¼-inch-diameter muffin cups with olive oil. Divide the cooked fennel and spinach mixture among the prepared muffin cups. Drizzle a tablespoon of the cooking liquid from the skillet into each cup. Using the back of a spoon, make a small well in the center of the vegetables in each cup, creating a nest for the egg.

5. Crack 1 egg into each nest. Season with salt and freshly ground pepper, cover loosely with foil, and place in the preheated oven. Bake for about 10 to 12 minutes, until the egg whites are set but the yolks remains soft. Remove the muffin tins from the oven, run a small knife around the inside of each muffin tin, and gently lift the egg and vegetable cups to warm plates. Garnish with a drizzle of extra-virgin olive oil and serve immediately. ★

Santa Fe Mini Tortes

✓ *EASY PREPARATION*

This dish is a unique southwestern take on quiche, using corn tortillas as a "crust." The resulting individual tortes are excellent when served with sour cream, fresh salsa, and cilantro—or top them with the tomato salad from the Cream Cheese and Egg Frittata recipe (page 58).

2 tablespoons butter

½ cup sliced green onions (from about 7 onions, or 1½ bunches)

1 medium red bell pepper seeded, deveined, and finely chopped (about 1 cup)

Salt, to taste

1 teaspoon minced garlic

1 tablespoon chopped fresh cilantro

¾ teaspoon ground cumin

⅛ teaspoon cayenne pepper

Olive oil to grease muffin cups

Six 6-inch fresh corn tortillas, cut into quarters

4 large eggs

2 tablespoons whole milk

¼ teaspoon salt

½ cup grated Monterey Jack cheese (from 2 ounces)

2 ounces green chiles, chopped (about half of a 4-ounce can)

1 cup seeded and diced tomato

3 cups mixed baby greens (4½ ounces)

Extra-virgin olive oil, for tossing

Sour cream, salsa, and fresh cilantro sprigs, for garnish

1. Preheat the oven to 325°F.

2. Melt the butter in a large skillet over medium heat. Add the green onions, red bell pepper, and a pinch of salt, and cook until tender, about 5 minutes, stirring frequently. Add the garlic, cilantro, cumin, and cayenne, cooking until fragrant, 1 minute more. Remove the skillet from the heat and reserve.

3. Use a pastry brush to liberally grease six 3-inch muffin cups with the olive oil. In each muffin tin, place 4 tortilla triangles, curved side down. Gently push the tortilla cup down so that the tips extend ¼ inch over the top of the muffin cup. Be gentle so that the tortillas do not tear. ∗

4. In a medium bowl, whisk together the eggs, milk, and ¼ teaspoon salt.

5. Place 1 teaspoon of the grated cheese in the bottom of each tortilla-lined muffin cup, and top it with one-sixth of the cooked

∗**TIP:** Using fresh, pliable corn **tortillas is a must here.** Arrange the 4 quarters, rounded edges overlapping in the bottom of the muffin cup, points sticking up over the edge. Press gently so the entire inside of the cup is covered, working the tortillas the same way you would pastry.

vegetables. Divide the egg mixture among the cups, filling to within ½ inch of the top edge of the shell. Sprinkle each with green chiles, tomato, and top with the remaining cheese.

6. Bake the tortes in the preheated oven for 15 to 20 minutes, until just set in the center.

7. In a large bowl, toss the greens with a little extra-virgin olive oil—just enough to barely moisten the leaves.

8. Remove the pans from the oven, cool slightly, and remove the individual tortes from the muffin cups.

9. Divide the greens among 6 salad plates and set 1 torte on each. Serve the tortes warm, topped with a dollop of sour cream and some fresh salsa. Garnish with cilantro sprigs. Pass more extra-virgin olive oil on the side.

Potato and Onion Omelets

✓ *EASY PREPARATION*

Omelets are a fun way to involve your family in making breakfast or brunch; just show them the way and then let everyone make their own. Once your children are comfortable using the stovetop, omelets can become their "specialty" dish, and weekend brunches can occasionally be their responsibility. Potato and eggs form a perfect partnership in an omelet and are made even tastier by the addition of leeks, shallot, and cheese.

1 cup diced red-skinned potatoes, unpeeled *

Salt, to taste

2 tablespoons white wine vinegar

Freshly ground pepper, to taste

1 tablespoon butter, plus 2 tablespoons cut into 4 equal pieces of 1½ teaspoons

½ cup sliced leek, white part only, washed well

½ cup thinly sliced shallot (from about 8 to 10 large cloves)

1 teaspoon minced garlic

1 teaspoon chopped fresh oregano

12 large eggs

1 cup grated cheddar cheese (from 4 ounces)

1. After dicing the potatoes, quickly plunge them in a bowl filled with enough water to cover all the potato pieces so they will remain white until ready to be used. Drain the diced potatoes and place them in a medium pot. Cover with cold water by 2 inches, season with salt, and bring to a simmer over high heat. Reduce the heat to medium-high and simmer about 10 minutes until the potatoes are tender but not falling apart. Drain the potatoes well and spread out on a cookie sheet. Sprinkle with white wine vinegar and freshly ground pepper. Cool.

2. Melt the 1 tablespoon butter in a small skillet over medium-low heat. Add the leek and shallot, season with salt, and cook until tender, 4 to 6 minutes. Do not let them brown. Add the garlic and oregano and cook 1 minute more. Remove from the heat and spoon the mixture into a medium bowl. Add the cooled potatoes, mix well, and season to taste with salt and freshly ground pepper. Reserve.

3. Break 3 large eggs into a small bowl and whisk well. Season the eggs with salt and freshly ground pepper.

✱ TIP: Soaking the potatoes is an important step for this omelet. If you leave them uncovered, the air will turn them an unappetizing reddish-brown color. Drain the potatoes well just before cooking them, and dry them on a towel if you are going to fry them so they will not spit and sputter in the oil.

4. Melt one 1½ teaspoon piece of the butter in a 6-inch nonstick skillet over medium heat. When the butter is melted and the foam has subsided, pour in the whisked eggs and let sit for 15 seconds. Using a wooden spoon or heat-resistant spatula, pull the cooked eggs from the edges toward the center and allow the liquid to spill back out onto the hot pan. Continue this process until much of the liquid egg is set. Let the omelet cook for 10 seconds and then spread one-quarter of the potato/onion filling in a line down the center of the open omelet. Tilt the pan, and using a spatula, roll one-third of the omelet over the filling. Hold the pan over the serving plate so the unfolded side begins to slide out. Using the spatula, slide the omelet onto the plate so the unfolded side slides under the folded side and the seam is on the bottom.

5. Repeat steps 3 and 4 three more times, to make the remaining omelets. As your skill increases, you can make 2 omelets simultaneously in 2 separate pans, or put your spouse or children to work alongside you.

6. Omelets may be kept warm in a 200°F oven for 5 to 10 minutes, but are best when served right away.

Croissant French Toast

✓ *EASY PREPARATION*   ✓ *MAKE-AHEAD*   ✓ *FREEZER READY*

This luscious, richly decadent version of French toast will surely satisfy any crowd. The sliced almonds offer a crunchy texture to contrast with the tender croissant. This is a great way to use any slightly stale croissants that might be leftover from yesterday's breakfast.

4 large eggs

1¼ cups whole milk

1 tablespoon flour

1 tablespoon plus 2 teaspoons sugar

½ teaspoon baking powder

Salt, to taste

1 teaspoon vanilla extract

¼ teaspoon almond extract

⅛ teaspoon ground nutmeg

6 croissants, halved lengthwise

2 tablespoons unsalted butter, cut into 4 equal pieces of 1½ teaspoons each

2 tablespoons vegetable oil

1 cup sliced almonds, toasted (4 ounces)

Butter, room temperature, for garnish

1 cup maple syrup, warmed, for garnish

Fresh seasonal fruit, preferably berries, for garnish

1. Preheat the oven to 250°F.

2. In a medium bowl, using a fork or whisk, beat together the eggs, milk, flour, sugar, baking powder, salt, vanilla extract, almond extract, and ground nutmeg. Dip both halves of each croissant in the egg mixture and place in a shallow pan or on a rimmed cookie sheet, cut side up. Pour the remaining mixture over the croissant halves and let them soak for 15 minutes.

3. In a large skillet, over medium heat, heat 1½ teaspoons each of the butter and oil. When the mixture sizzles, sprinkle one-third of the almonds into the skillet, and place 4 croissant halves cut side down on top of the almonds. Press the croissants onto the almonds and fry until golden brown, about 3 minutes. Turn and brown the other side. Keep the cooked croissants—almond coated side up—warm on a baking sheet in the oven and repeat with the remaining croissant halves.

4. Serve each person 2 croissant halves, passing more butter, warm maple syrup, and fresh fruit on the side. Sprinkle with powdered sugar and serve with fresh sliced strawberries if you like.

Fish and Shellfish

Fish and shellfish have become an essential part of the American diet. Due in part to the demands of a more health-conscious public and, because of improved preservation and transportation techniques, good seafood is now widely available. Flash-frozen shrimp, prawns, and scallops, as well as salmon steaks and fillets, tuna, trout, halibut, and other fish are as close as your nearest quality supermarket. Many fish and shellfish types are expensive, and all are highly perishable so they must be treated with care—keep it refrigerated constantly until you are ready to prepare it, plan to eat it within a day or two of purchase, and cook it attentively because fish cooks fast and can overcook in the blink of an eye.

One reason to serve your family fish is all of its health benefits. Fish and shellfish are low in calories, fat, and sodium, and are high in vitamins A, B, and D, as well as protein. Fish and shellfish are also high in phosphorus, potassium, and iron, and some are high in a group of fatty acids called omega-3, which has been proven to help lower high cholesterol levels. Shellfish are not as high in cholesterol as once thought, and both crustaceans and shellfish have less fat and cholesterol than red meat or eggs. However, the way you choose to prepare the fish will determine how healthy it will be for you and your family.

While fresh from the sea, lake, or river is obviously better, fish that is flash frozen as soon as it is caught is far superior to any that has languished in transit and then in the fish case for days. Look for these signs to ensure freshness:

- Whole fish should look glossy, the eyes should be clear, and the gills should be a bright red.

- Smell is by far the best way to determine freshness. Fresh fish should have a slight sea smell or no odor at all. Any off odors or ammonia smell are a sure sign of age, or poor handling.

- Most fish are sold in fillets and should appear to be moist and glistening. Any sign of dryness around the cut surface is a sure sign of age. The fillets should be firm to the touch, not the least bit spongy when poked.

- When you buy fish, the fishmonger will enclose the fish and shellfish in plastic bags and then wrap it in paper. Once at home, place the bag on ice in a colander. Put the colander over a bowl to catch the water and set it in the refrigerator. Change the ice every 24 hours and use the fish within 48 hours.

If you have skittish fish eaters in the family, delicately flavored fish such as flounder or tilapia, when braised in a broth or placed on the grill, are perfect to introduce to the family. The light texture and great flavor will prove there's nothing "fishy" about it. Fish soups and stews are great for cold nights when a steaming bowl of fragrant seafood is a welcome remedy for cold bones and spirits. Shrimp and fish take to the grill easily. Just remember they need little cooking, and should only be turned once. Because their cooking times are generally short and their flavors are delicate, special attention must be given to how they are cooked. Be sure to wait until everyone is seated to begin cooking the fish. Unless the dish is to be served at room temperature, it is the diner who should wait, not the fish.

Grilled Salmon Fillets with Lime Butter Baste

✓ *EASY PREPARATION*　　✓ *SOMETHING SPECIAL*

Salmon is a fish that pleases almost everyone in the family, and this method of preparing it is simple and delicious. Salmon has high amounts of omega-3 fatty acids, which makes it an excellent choice for cholesterol-conscious families. Serve with a salad of mixed greens, crunchy jicama, sweet red peppers, sliced oranges, and toasted pine nuts to perpetuate the subtle Southwestern flavors of the fish.

* TIP: A good quality **stove-top grill pan** is perfect for preparing this dish, especially if weather or space prohibit outdoor grilling.

1 teaspoon whole coriander seeds

1 teaspoon whole fennel seeds

1 teaspoon paprika

1 tablespoon kosher salt

1/8 teaspoon cayenne pepper

Four 6-ounce pieces of salmon fillet

1/4 cup (4 tablespoons) butter

1 teaspoon chopped or grated lime zest

1 tablespoon fresh lime juice

2 teaspoons chopped fresh cilantro

Salt and freshly ground pepper, to taste

2 tablespoons olive oil

1. Preheat the grill for 10 minutes to medium-high heat. Clean and season the grill. *

2. Cook the whole coriander and fennel seeds in a small skillet over medium heat just until fragrant, for 1 to 2 minutes. Spoon the seeds from the skillet into a spice grinder and grind to a coarse powder. Place in a small bowl and stir in the paprika, kosher salt, and cayenne pepper.

3. Lightly sprinkle the dry rub evenly over the salmon fillets and let stand for 15 minutes at room temperature. Reserve any remaining rub for another use.

4. Melt the butter in a small saucepan. Remove from the heat and add the lime zest, lime juice, and cilantro. Season to taste with salt and freshly ground pepper.

5. Gently brush the seasoned salmon fillets with olive oil. Place on the preheated grill or grill pan, skin side down, and grill, without moving, for 4 minutes.

6. Using a fish or grill spatula, gently turn the fillets over and baste with the lime/cilantro butter. Continue grilling 4 minutes more. The fillets will be a beautiful medium rare. Cook a minute or two longer on both sides if you like your salmon well done. Remove the fillets from the grill, baste again with the flavored butter, and serve warm.

Ratatouille-Stuffed Tilapia Fillets

✓ *SOMETHING SPECIAL*   ✓ *MAKE-AHEAD*   ✓ *FREEZER READY*

Tilapia is a large-flake, mild-flavored fish, so a simple seasoning of salt and pepper is all you need. The vegetable-rich ratatouille adds color, texture, and a depth of flavor that complements but does not overwhelm the fish.

¹⁄₃ cup olive oil

4 small Japanese eggplant, cut into ¹⁄₄-inch dice

Salt, to taste

2 teaspoons minced garlic (from 2 medium cloves)

1¹⁄₂ cups ¹⁄₄-inch diced onion

1¹⁄₂ cups trimmed, seeded, and ¹⁄₄-inch diced red bell pepper

¹⁄₂ cup diced zucchini

¹⁄₂ cup diced yellow squash

1 cup diced tomato

Freshly ground pepper, to taste

¹⁄₄ cup freshly chopped basil

¹⁄₄ cup chopped fresh parsley

1 tablespoon butter

¹⁄₄ cup finely chopped shallots (from about 6 to 8 cloves)

Eight 5- to 6-ounce tilapia fillets, skinned

¹⁄₂ cup dry white wine

Sweet paprika, for garnish

1. Heat about 1 teaspoon olive oil in a large skillet over medium heat, until hot but not smoking. Add only enough eggplant to make an even layer in the bottom of the pan. Season with salt. Do not move the eggplant until it has caramelized, or begun to brown, on the bottom, about 5 minutes. With a spatula, carefully turn the eggplant over in the pan, trying not to mash the cubes. Continue to cook until the eggplant is completely cooked through, turning it gently from time to time, about 5 minutes more. Add the minced garlic, toss gently, and cook until the garlic is just fragrant, 1 minute. Remove the eggplant and garlic to a bowl. Repeat the process, until all of the eggplant has been cooked.

2. Heat another teaspoon olive oil in the same skillet and add the onion. Season with salt and cook for 2 minutes. Add the bell pepper and season with a little more salt. Continue to cook the onion and pepper together until tender, about 6 minutes. Add the onion and pepper to the eggplant in the bowl.

3. Again, in the same skillet, heat a teaspoon olive oil and add the zucchini and yellow squash. Season with salt and cook until tender, 2 to 3 minutes. Add the tomato and cook just long enough to heat the tomato, 2 minutes. Add to the bowl with the other vegetables. Season all the vegetables with freshly ground pepper and more salt if desired. Add the chopped basil and parsley. Reserve at room temperature.

(continues on page 68)

4. Preheat the oven to 400°F. Use about 1 teaspoon butter to grease a 9- × 11-inch or 9- × 13-inch baking dish, or one just large enough to hold the stuffed fillets in a single layer. Sprinkle the bottom of the baking dish with the chopped shallots.

5. Lay the fillets skin side up on the work surface, season with salt and freshly ground pepper, and place 2 tablespoons of the reserved ratatouille on the head end of each fillet. Roll the fillets starting at the wide end and ending with the tail—secure with a round toothpick if the roll will not stay together. Arrange the rolled fillets, seam side down, in the prepared pan and pour in the white wine. Cover with buttered parchment or waxed paper. ★

6. Bake in the preheated oven for 8 to 10 minutes, just until the fish is cooked through and the ratatouille is warm. Serve immediately, dusted with a little paprika.

VARIATION

For another presentation, lay 4 of the fillets side by side, skin side down, in the prepared baking dish. Spread a layer of ratatouille on each fillet. Top with the 4 other fillets, also skin side down. Continue with the recipe. With this method you can cut servings of any size, just right for each family member.

★ **TIP:** The fish may be prepared up to the point of pouring in the white wine, covered and refrigerated for several hours before cooking.

Spiced Dover Sole Fillets with Creamed Spinach

✓ SOMETHING SPECIAL   ✓ EASY PREPARATION

This preparation is somewhat reminiscent of Indian food because of the spice rub and the coconut milk in the spinach. Do not overdo the spice rub—Dover sole is a very delicately flavored fish, easily overwhelmed by big flavors. Prepare lots of spinach, as this presentation is always a favorite—and it is a wonderful way to introduce spinach to all your family members!

2 teaspoons ground turmeric

2 teaspoons kosher salt

1/4 teaspoon ground cardamom

1/4 teaspoon ground cinnamon

1/8 teaspoon cayenne pepper

1/8 teaspoon ground ginger

1 1/2 pounds Dover sole fillets, cut into 12 long thin strips if the fillets are large ✱

1 tablespoon butter, plus more, melted, for greasing the dish

2 tablespoons finely chopped shallot (from about 4 medium cloves)

Salt, to taste

1 tablespoon finely chopped fresh ginger

2 teaspoons minced garlic (from 2 medium cloves)

8 cups cleaned and dried baby spinach (from 12 ounces baby spinach)

1/3 cup unsweetened coconut milk

1/4 cup heavy cream

Freshly ground pepper, to taste

1. Preheat the oven to 350°F.

2. In a small bowl, combine the turmeric, kosher salt, cardamom, cinnamon, cayenne, and ground ginger, and mix well. Lightly sprinkle the spice mixture over both sides of the fish fillets, pressing down so that it will adhere. Marinate 10 minutes at room temperature. Reserve any excess spice rub for another use.

3. Grease a 12-cup muffin tin with melted butter. Arrange 1 fillet in each muffin tin so that the fillet lines the outside of the tin and leaves the center open for stuffing. Reserve.

4. Melt 1 tablespoon butter in a large pot over medium-low heat. Add the shallot, season with salt, and cook until translucent, about 3 minutes. Add the fresh ginger and garlic and cook until fragrant, 1 minute. Add the spinach and season with more salt. Toss the spinach gently to wilt evenly. When the spinach is just beginning to wilt, add the coconut milk and cream. Stir to combine and cook only until the spinach has wilted. Remove the pot from the heat and season with freshly ground pepper. Reserve. ✱

5. Bake the fish in the preheated oven for 6 to 8 minutes, until the fillets are firm to the touch. Remove the fish from the oven, turn out of the molds, and gently place 3 fillet rolls on each of 4 warmed flat soup plates. Fill the center of each fillet with wilted spinach, spoon some of the hot coconut milk around them, and serve immediately.

✱ **TIP:** Dover sole fillets can be quite large, as the fish can weigh as much as 10 pounds. Ask your fish market for the smallest fillets it has, or cut the large ones into smaller strips.

✱ **TIP:** Don't overcook fresh spinach. To wilt spinach means just that—heating it just until it is no longer crisp, and is tender and hot. Spinach gives off plenty of moisture and usually doesn't require any additional liquid, but it may be added for flavor.

Tuna Steaks with Olive Tapenade

✓ *SOMETHING SPECIAL*

Fresh tuna on the grill is a real treat. The nutty coating on these steaks becomes a crisp crust when they are seared, and the salty olive-based tapenade goes especially well with the richness of the tuna. If there are very young children in your family, you may want to serve their tuna without the tapenade on top. They can always have it on the side to taste. Take care not to overcook the tuna; it should be pink and tender in the middle.

3 teaspoons finely chopped fresh thyme

2 tablespoons finely chopped parsley

1 tablespoon kosher salt

1/2 teaspoon freshly ground pepper, plus more to taste

1/2 cup sliced and finely chopped almonds, toasted (from 2 ounces)

1/4 cup extra-virgin olive oil

Four 6-ounce steaks of sushi-grade tuna, each steak 1 inch thick

1 cup Kalamata olives, pitted

1 teaspoon minced garlic

2 anchovy fillets, minced

1 tablespoon capers, rinsed

1/3 cup extra-virgin olive oil, plus 1 teaspoon

1. In a small bowl, combine 2 teaspoons of the thyme, the parsley, salt, 1/2 teaspoon pepper, and almonds. Stir in 1/4 cup extra-virgin olive oil to form a paste with the consistency of wet sand.

2. Dredge the tuna steaks on both sides in the paste and let them dry at room temperature for 1/2 hour.

3. Meanwhile, prepare the tapenade by combining the olives, garlic, anchovy, capers, and the remaining 1 teaspoon thyme in the bowl of a food processor. Pulse, just until it becomes a very coarse paste. With the machine running add the olive oil through the funnel in a slow, steady stream until the mixture is thick and smooth. The amount of olive oil may vary depending on the consistency desired—add more if you want the tapenade to be more like a sauce, less if you want a thick paste. Season with freshly ground pepper and reserve. ✱

4. Heat 1 teaspoon oil in a heavy nonstick skillet over medium-high heat. When hot, but not smoking, add the tuna steaks and cook just until lightly browned on the bottom, 2 minutes on the first side. Turn the steaks over and cook again to golden brown, 2 minutes more. The fish should be seared on the outside and still pink or rare on the inside. Remove the fish from the pan and serve, either hot or cold with a dollop of tapenade on top. ✱

✱ **TIP:** High-quality commercially made **tapenade** is a fine substitute, especially if time is short. It is better to use the ready-made product than to bypass making this dish.

✱ **TIP:** These **tuna steaks can be grilled on a** preheated, lightly greased **grill pan** if you prefer. Just preheat the grill pan for 5 minutes over medium-high heat. Sear the tuna on one side for 2 minutes; turn and sear on the other side.

Cornmeal-Crusted Trout

✓ *EASY PREPARATION*

Cornmeal-crusted trout is an all-American camping favorite, so why not cook and enjoy it at home, too. It is best cooked and served whole, in all its glory! Everyone in the family can help with dinner, either by catching it, cleaning it, or coating it with cornmeal before cooking. Even young children can easily learn to cook the trout, a real culinary accomplishment. If you have served this on a family trip, making it at home brings back wonderful memories and sparks laughter and conversation at the table. A spinach salad with warm bacon vinaigrette is a perfect accompaniment, whether you are eating at home or sitting around the campfire.

*TIP: Cook all four trout at once in two separate skillets, if the rest of the menu permits (and if a single camp burner is not your only cooking source). Just keep an eye on the fish as they will all be ready at pretty much the same moment.

Four 12-ounce whole trout, gutted, scaled, completely boned

Salt and freshly ground pepper, to taste

4 sprigs fresh dill

1/4 cup flour

1/4 cup fine yellow or white cornmeal

2 tablespoons butter

2 tablespoons safflower oil

2 tablespoons finely chopped fresh parsley

Juice from 1/2 medium lemon

Parsley sprigs, for garnish

4 lemon wedges, for garnish

1. Preheat the oven to 250°F. Rinse and dry the cleaned trout. Season with salt and freshly ground pepper, inside and out. Place a sprig of dill inside the cavity of each trout.

2. In a large bowl, combine the flour and cornmeal. Dredge each fish in the cornmeal mixture, patting off any excess coating.

3. In a large skillet over medium-high heat, heat 1 tablespoon each of the butter and safflower oil. Add 2 of the trout to the pan and cook for about 4 minutes on each side, depending on thickness,

turning once. The trout skin should turn crispy and golden brown. Remove the trout from the skillet and place on a plate lined with paper towels. Keep the fish warm in the oven or covered with foil while the remaining trout are cooked in the same manner. When all the trout are cooked, drain for a minute or two on paper towels and then place each trout on a warm plate. Sprinkle with parsley and a spritz of lemon juice. Serve immediately, garnished with parsley sprigs and a lemon wedge. *

Baked Whole Snapper with Tomato Tartare

✓ *SOMETHING SPECIAL*   ✓ *EASY PREPARATION*

Baking and serving a whole fish not only results in a succulent dish, it makes for a beautiful presentation to your family. While this may seem to be a sophisticated dish, it is actually a simple way to prepare fish, and the end result is perfect for all ages. Serve this fish with your favorite green vegetable, such as green beans or roasted asparagus, along with the classic fish accompaniment of tiny boiled new potatoes seasoned with melted butter and chopped parsley.

2 tablespoons olive oil, plus more to coat baking dish

1 medium leek, dark green part trimmed away, quartered lengthwise, well washed

2 medium carrots, peeled, trimmed, quartered lengthwise

2 medium stalks celery, cleaned, halved lengthwise

2 whole red snapper, about 1½ to 2 pounds each, gutted, gills removed, scaled *

Salt and freshly ground pepper, to taste

1 medium lemon, cut across into 6 thin slices

2 sprigs fresh rosemary

½ cup mayonnaise

1 tablespoon finely chopped cornichons *

1 teaspoon finely chopped shallot

1 teaspoon finely chopped fresh chives

1 teaspoon tomato puree

1. Preheat the oven to 350°F. Brush a baking dish, large enough to hold the 2 fish in an even layer, with olive oil.

2. Arrange the leek, carrots, and celery in the bottom of the prepared pan in an overlapping crisscross pattern to form a cushion for the fish. *

3. Prepare the fish: with a small knife scrape off any scales that might still adhere, rinse in cold water, and dry well—inside and out. Rub the fish with the 2 tablespoons olive oil and season the cavity and the outside with salt and freshly ground pepper. Place 3 slices of lemon and 1 sprig of rosemary in the cavity of each fish.

4. Arrange both fish on the layer of vegetables, make several angled slashes—nearly to the bone— in the flesh of each fish, and bake in the preheated oven for 30 minutes, until the flesh is opaque and pulls away from the bone when a sharp paring knife is inserted along the backbone.

5. In a small bowl, mix together the mayonnaise, chopped cornichons, shallot, chives, and tomato puree. Season to taste with salt and freshly ground pepper. Reserve.

6. Serve the fish whole, arranged on a platter and surrounded by the vegetables. Use a sharp, thin-bladed knife and a spatula to

✱ TIP: Unless you have a friendly fisherman among your circle of friends, the local fishmonger will be happy to **prepare the fish** for you. The fish will be gutted and scaled and the gills will be removed. Sometimes the dorsal and side fins will be clipped off as well. Leave the heads on during cooking, but discard them before serving if you like. I prefer the whole fish on the platter, but some family members might be put off by the sight of the head at the table.

✱ TIP: A **cornichon** is a type of tiny little cucumber that is pickled in vinegar and eaten with gusto all over Europe. They are especially good with fish, cold meats, and pâtés.

✱ TIP: The **vegetable cushion** adds flavor and keeps the fish from sticking to the bottom of the baking pan, making it easier to remove and serve.

remove the fillets from the bones of both fish. Cut along the backbone of the fish with the knife, sliding it about halfway down the fillet. Replace the knife with the spatula and lift the fillet off the carcass and onto a plate. Remove any bones and fins from the fillet and place on a warm plate. Remove and discard the spine from the second fillet, as well as any remaining bones and fins, and arrange on the same plate as the first. Serve with the tomato tartare.

Fish Stew

✓ *SOMETHING SPECIAL*

This fish stew is intended to be a simple version of the wonderful bouillabaisse found in the south of France. The use of shellfish not only adds flavor to the dish, but color and body as well. Any type of firm white fish can be used, so choose your favorite, or whatever is available. Teenagers and adults love this stew and small children might enjoy some of the shrimp and fish in the broth without the rest of the shellfish.

Pinch of saffron, steeped in ¾ cup dry white wine *

2 tablespoons olive oil

1 leek, rinsed well, halved lengthwise, and thinly sliced

Salt, to taste

½ cup carrot, peeled, halved lengthwise, and thinly sliced

1 cup fennel bulb, halved, cored, and thinly sliced

2 teaspoons fennel seed

½ teaspoon crushed red pepper

One 14-ounce can vegetable broth

½ cup canned, chopped, or diced tomatoes

1 fresh bay leaf

1 sprig fresh thyme

3 sprigs fresh parsley, stems included

Extra-virgin olive oil for greasing dish and seasoning fish

8 ounces monkfish, cleaned of outer membrane, cut into four 2-ounce pieces

8 ounces halibut fillet, cut into four 2-ounce pieces

4 large scallops, approximately 1½ inch in diameter

12 large (21–30 per pound) shrimp, deveined, but not peeled

Freshly ground pepper, to taste

Pinch saffron

2 tablespoons Pernod or white vermouth *

12 mussels, cleaned, beards removed *

1. Combine the saffron threads with the wine in a measuring cup 10 minutes before you're ready to use them. Stir from time to time to release the flavor and color from the saffron.

2. Heat 2 tablespoons olive oil in a large soup pot over medium heat. Add the leek, season with salt, and cook, without browning, until soft, about 5 minutes. Add the carrot and fennel and stir to combine. Continue to cook, without browning, until all vegetables are soft and tender, about 8 to 10 minutes. Add the fennel seed and crushed red pepper. Cook until fragrant, 2 minutes.

3. Add the saffron and the white wine in which it was steeped, the broth, and tomatoes. Stir to combine and bring to a simmer, reducing the heat to medium-low to maintain a gentle simmer. Tie the bay leaf, thyme, and parsley together with a string and add

★ TIP: Saffron threads are actually the stigmas of a particular kind of crocus. A small pinch or a few threads add a delicate flavor and lovely orange color to finished dishes. Look for saffron in specialty food stores. Try to avoid powdered saffron, which may actually be turmeric or safflower (both fine spices, just not saffron). A little vial of threads will last a long time.

★ TIP: Pernod is an anise-flavored liqueur widely drunk in Europe. It is clear, pale yellow-green, but turns cloudy when added to water, so don't be alarmed.

★ TIP: Clean the mussels by scrubbing with a stiff brush. Use a pair of needle-nose pliers to grasp the hairy beard that emerges from between the two shells, and pull it out. Discard the beard. Discard any mussels that are broken or do not clamp shut when you debeard them.

the fresh herb bundle, simmering to develop the flavors for 30 minutes. ✱

4. Meanwhile, prepare the fish. Grease a 9- × 11-inch baking dish with extra-virgin olive oil and arrange the monkfish, halibut, scallops, and shrimp in rows in the pan. Sprinkle the fish with salt, freshly ground pepper, saffron, and a little extra-virgin olive oil. Turn the seafood over and repeat the process. Sprinkle with Pernod and marinate the seafood for 30 minutes, at room temperature.

5. Preheat the oven to 350°F.

6. Season the broth with salt and freshly ground pepper to taste. Remove and discard the herb bundle. Gently ladle enough broth into the baking dish to come a quarter of the way up the seafood. Cover with a piece of buttered parchment or foil, and cook in the preheated oven for 10 to 12 minutes. ✱

7. Meanwhile, bring the remaining broth to a simmer, add the mussels, cover, and simmer 6 minutes, until mussels just open. Remove the broth from the heat—discarding any mussels that fail to open.

8. Heat the bowls. Immediately place some of the vegetables from the broth in the center of each bowl and pour a ladleful of broth over them. Arrange 3 mussels in each bowl. Pile 3 shrimp on top of each bowl, and top with 1 piece of monkfish, halibut, and a scallop. Serve immediately, passing extra broth, if desired.

SERVING SUGGESTION

Pass a bottle of very green and fruity extra-virgin olive oil for diners to drizzle into the stew if they like.

✱ **TIP:** Bouquet garni are fresh herbs that are tied together into bundles, cooked in a dish for flavoring, then removed before serving. Traditionally one is made by cutting two 3-inch pieces celery from a large rib. Combine 2 sprigs fresh thyme, 4 or 5 sprigs fresh parsley with stems, and a bay leaf. Enclose them in the 2 pieces of celery and tie them all together with kitchen twine, or tie them in a length of cheesecloth.

✱ **TIP:** Be careful not to **overcook** the seafood. It is better to cook it a little less than the suggested time, since the seafood continues to cook when added to the steaming broth in the bowls.

Shrimp, Sausage, and Vegetable Stew

✓ *EASY PREPARATION*   ✓ *SOMETHING SPECIAL*

This vegetable-filled stew is very similar to the Louisiana dish called gumbo. Without the addition of either okra or filé powder it isn't the real thing, but the concept is the same. If you can find some fresh okra with pods only an inch or so long, cut them into chunks and add them when you add the green pepper and celery. With the okra, the stew will be slightly thicker than this one. Reduce the amount of Creole seasoning by half if your family prefers milder dishes.

1 tablespoon vegetable oil, such as canola or corn oil

¼ cup flour

1 tablespoon olive oil

1 cup finely chopped onion

Salt and freshly ground pepper, to taste

½ cup finely chopped celery

¾ cup finely chopped green bell pepper

3 teaspoons minced garlic (from 3 medium cloves)

1 teaspoon dried thyme

2 teaspoons commercial Creole seasoning

1 bay leaf

½ pound very spicy andouille or other sausage, sliced *

One 28-ounce can chopped tomatoes

1 cup chicken broth

24 large (21–30 per pound) shrimp, peeled and deveined

2 cups hot steamed rice

1. In a small skillet, heat the vegetable oil over medium heat. Sprinkle in the flour and stir so that a smooth paste forms. Continue to cook, stirring continuously, until the flour turns a dark coffee brown and smells rich and nutty. Remove the pan from the heat and set aside. *

2. Heat 1 tablespoon olive oil in a large pot over medium heat. Add the onion and a pinch of salt and cook, stirring, just until translucent, 3 minutes. Add the celery and green pepper and continue to cook, stirring frequently, until the vegetables are tender, about 6 minutes more. Add the garlic, thyme, Creole seasoning, and bay leaf. Cook until fragrant, 1 minute. Nestle the sausage slices into the vegetables and cook, 4 minutes, turning once halfway through. Add the chopped tomatoes and chicken broth. Bring to a simmer and whisk in half of the reserved, warm roux. Cook 5 minutes and add more roux to thicken, if desired. Simmer over low heat for 15 minutes and season with salt and freshly ground pepper. *

3. Just before you are ready to serve, add the shrimp and cook until they just turn pink, 2 to 3 minutes. Remove and discard the bay leaf.

4. Serve the stew in warm bowls over a large spoonful of freshly cooked rice.

*TIP: Gumbo usually features Cajun andouille **sausage,** but hot chorizo is a good substitute, or, in a pinch, cooked, hot Italian sausage can be used.

*TIP: Watch the flour mixture very carefully during this stage. Sometimes, depending on the elements (heat, humidity, etc.), there might be only about a 10-second window between a dark, richly colored *roux*—what this oil and flour mixture is called in Louisiana, a version of the similar French *roux*, which uses butter instead of oil—and a burned mess that cannot be salvaged and must be thrown away. If you're unsure, better to stop early, with a slightly lighter-colored roux, than to burn it.

*TIP: A little **filé powder is stirred into the stew** at this point to **thicken it** a little further if you are in Louisiana. Filé is a powder made from ground sassafras root, and is an excellent though very tricky to use thickener. You will still have a fine stew without it.

Perfect Poultry

What do you order when you go to a new restaurant? I almost always order chicken. The ability to prepare a perfectly cooked chicken, however simple, is a sign of a great cook, and marks the quality of the restaurant or home cook.

Chicken is the essential building block for many great dishes. It can be used as a starting point and whatever is added to it can create a completely new meal. So let's get started. Roasting a chicken on your own is not hard. It does not require any great skill at all, but it does require attention. Just begin with a clean whole roasting chicken, follow a recipe, such as Classic Roasted Chicken (page 78), and you will have the same perfect results as your mom did.

Tips for roasting chicken:

- Choose the highest-quality chicken you can afford—free-range chickens are always very good.

- Whole chickens will have more flavor and natural juiciness, and are cheaper to buy, than the parts.

- Roasters weigh anywhere from four to six pounds, and serve five to eight depending on appetites, though for a small family—three or four—you can always roast a three-pound fryer, or even roast individual Cornish hens as large ones are often big enough to serve two.

- It will take about one hour for the first four pounds and about eight minutes after that for each additional pound.

- You can speed the roasting by splitting the chicken down the backbone, flattening it out, and roasting it butterflied.

When you roast a whole chicken at home and your family does not finish all of the meat, carve the remaining meat off the bone and freeze the carcass for later. The chicken bones will be the basis for great broth for soup on a rainy day, and you can find plenty of recipes in the next chapter, Poultry Encores, for the leftover meat.

Bring home a chicken tonight and you cannot go wrong.

For a change of pace, turkey is easy to find and adds great flavor to chili, braised dishes, salads, soups, and more. Once you've mastered working with chicken and turkey, consider other options, like cornish hens or duck, in some of these recipes. Ask the poultry manager for guidance on time and temperature changes.

Classic Roasted Chicken

✓ EASY PREPARATION   ✓ MAKE-AHEAD   ✓ TAKE-ALONG   ✓ FREEZER READY

Chicken is one of the most important meats to master for family cooking—it is often quick to fix, low in fat if you remove the skin, and exceptionally versatile. Most of us use pieces of chicken, especially the breast, in everyday cooking. But the succulent, juicy, whole roasted chicken has so much better flavor than the parts alone. Once you have tried this recipe, you can look to the next chapter, Poultry Encores, for more uses for the extra meat. Why not roast two chickens at the same time, one for eating immediately, one to use as the basis for a meal or two later in the week? Twice as much is leftover for very little extra work.

★ TIP: For crisp skin all around, set the chicken on a low rack in the roasting pan—this keeps the chicken off the bottom of the pan and lets air and heat circulate all around.

★ TIP: When roasting two chickens at once, use a large 10- × 14-inch or 10- × 15-inch roasting pan with a rack. Place the chickens side by side, with plenty of space between them so the heat will circulate freely, and follow the recipe as you would for 1 chicken. You may need to increase the cooking time by 10 or 15 minutes, but be sure to check the interior temperature with an instant-read thermometer before leaving the birds in for the added time.

One 6- to 7-pound roasting chicken

3 tablespoons fresh thyme

1/4 cup extra-virgin olive oil

2 tablespoons chopped garlic (from about 6 medium cloves)

2 teaspoons lemon zest, lemon reserved and cut into 4 pieces

Salt and freshly ground pepper, to taste

1/4 cup Marsala wine or white Vermouth

1/2 cup low-salt chicken broth

1 tablespoon flour

1. Preheat the oven to 425°F. Rinse the chicken and pat it dry, inside and out. Place it in a roasting pan. ★ Rub the chicken with thyme, olive oil, garlic, and lemon zest. Season with salt and pepper. Place the lemons in the cavity of the chicken. Tie the legs together with kitchen twine.

2. Roast the chicken for 20 minutes. Reduce the heat to 350°F and roast for another hour, or until a thermometer inserted in the thickest part of the breast registers 160°F. ★

3. Remove the chicken from the oven. Carefully tilt the chicken to drain the juices from the cavity. Remove the chicken from the roasting pan and place it on a platter. Tent it with aluminum foil.

4. Pour the pan juices into a fat skimmer or a measuring cup and remove the fat by skimming it off of the top. Heat the roasting pan on the stove over medium-high heat and add the wine. Scrape the roasting pan until all the browned bits are loosened. Add the chicken broth to the measuring cup with the pan juices and pour all of it into the roasting pan. Whisk in the flour and cook over 2 burners until the mixture is thickened. Season the mixture with salt and pepper, to taste.

5. Carve the chicken and serve with the sauce on the side.

Carving Poultry

Carving poultry is an art that can be learned. Here are some tips on how to become an adept carver. The directions that follow are for a chicken but may be used for a turkey or any other poultry.

Begin carving the chicken by removing each leg. Arrange the chicken, breast side up, on a cutting board. Steady the chicken with a carving fork. Cut the skin between the thigh and breast.

Using a large knife as an aid, press the thigh outward to find the hip joint. Slice down through the joint and remove the leg. (Alternatively, you can grasp the leg, twist it at the joint, and remove.)

Cut between the thigh and drumstick at the joint to divide the leg into 1 thigh piece and 1 drumstick.

To carve the drumstick, steady it with a carving fork and cut a thick slice of meat from one side of the drumstick, along the bone.

Next, turn the drumstick over so that the cut side faces down. Cut off another thick slice of meat. Repeat, turning the drumstick onto a flat side and cutting off meat, carving a total of 4 thick slices.

To slice the thigh, place it flat side down on a cutting board. Steady the thigh with a carving fork. Using the knife, cut parallel to the bone and slice off the meat.

The wing must be removed before carving the breast. Slice diagonally down through the bottom edge of the breast toward the wing. Using the knife as an aid, press the wing out to find the shoulder joint, cut through the joint, and remove the wing.

To carve the breast meat, hold the back of the carving fork against the breastbone. Starting parallel to the breastbone, slice diagonally through the meat. Lift off each slice, holding it between the knife and fork.

Continue until you have carved all the meat on one side of the breast. Turn the chicken around and repeat carving on the other side of the breast.

Chicken and Rice—with Variations

✓ *MAKE-AHEAD*   ✓ *TAKE-ALONG*   ✓ *FREEZER READY*   ✓ *READY AND WAITING*

There are so many versions of this basic dish that everyone can develop their own favorite. Just use this classic version to cut your teeth on and then try one or more of our suggested variations. This is an excellent family dish, simple enough for young appetites, interesting enough to tempt even picky adults.

2 tablespoons olive oil

1 cup chopped yellow onion (about 1 medium onion)

1 green bell pepper, stemmed seeded and thinly sliced

2 teaspoons finely chopped garlic (from 2 medium cloves)

3/4 cup chopped ham (from 4 ounces)

8 chicken thighs, skinned if you prefer, or not

Salt and freshly ground pepper, to taste

1/4 teaspoon saffron (optional)

1/4 cup chopped fresh cilantro, plus more for garnish

One 14-ounce can diced tomatoes with green chiles

2 cups chicken broth, boiling

1 cup raw long-grain rice

1. Preheat the oven to 200°F. Heat the oil in a deep casserole over medium heat. Add the onion and pepper. Cook, stirring, until the onion is golden brown, about 8 minutes. Add the garlic and ham. Cook 1 minute more. Add the chicken thighs and season with salt, pepper, saffron, and cilantro.

2. Cook for 10 minutes, turning the chicken pieces once. Stir in the tomatoes and boiling broth. Cover and simmer for 30 minutes, until the chicken is very tender.

3. Remove the chicken from the broth and keep warm, covered with foil, in the preheated oven.

4. Stir in the rice, cover, and simmer for 20 to 25 minutes until the rice is cooked. Fluff with a fork to incorporate the vegetables and mound on a serving platter. Arrange the warm chicken on top and garnish with a little more chopped cilantro. Serve very hot in flat soup bowls.

VARIATIONS

- Substitute 1 cut-up 3-pound chicken and 3 ounces of sliced kielbasa for the chicken thighs. Instead of the tomatoes, stir in ¼ cup fresh lemon juice, 4 ounces sliced mushrooms, and 4 cooked artichoke hearts, sliced. Continue with the master recipe.

- Substitute 1⅓ cups cider for 1 cup of the broth. Eliminate the tomatoes and saffron. Peel, seed, and thinly slice 1 Golden Delicious apple and cook it in 1 tablespoon butter over medium heat until tender, about 10 minutes. Add to the rice. Continue with the master recipe.

- Replace the tomatoes with 4 ounces sliced mushrooms. Replace ½ cup of the broth with ¾ cup dry white wine and stir in 1 tablespoon Dijon mustard. Use chopped flat-leaf parsley rather than the cilantro. Continue with the master recipe.

- Use butter rather than oil to cook the onions. Replace the green pepper and tomatoes with 1 cup mixed dried fruit that has been cut up, soaked in boiling broth, and drained before adding. Eliminate the ham. Continue with the master recipe.

Chicken with Feta Cheese and Tomatoes

MAKES 6 SERVINGS

By using chicken breasts with the skin on, you end up with a moist, tender piece of chicken, here garnished with olives and feta cheese. These two ingredients can be kept on hand and used whenever you are in the mood to bring the flavors of the Mediterranean to your family. You may always remove the skin before serving. Serve it with couscous or rice.

★TIP: Pitted olives are available in many specialty food stores. If you cannot find them, a cherry pitter will do the job, or use a sharp knife to cut the olive in half and pick out the seed with the knife tip.

8 boneless skin-on chicken breast halves

Salt and freshly ground pepper, to taste

¼ cup olive oil

1 cup finely chopped onion

2 teaspoons garlic (from about 2 medium cloves)

4 cups diced vine-ripened tomatoes (from about 4 large tomatoes)

4 cups chicken broth (1 quart)

2 tablespoons fresh oregano

2 cups crumbled feta cheese (from about 8 ounces)

⅔ cup Kalamata olives, pitted and chopped, for garnish ★

1. Rinse the chicken breasts and pat dry. Season with salt and pepper. Heat the olive oil in a large deep skillet at medium-high heat. Place 4 of the chicken breasts in the pan, skin side down, and cook the chicken until the skin browns, about 5 minutes. Turn the chicken and brown it on the other side, about 4 minutes more. Remove the chicken to a plate and repeat with the remaining chicken.

2. Add the onion and the garlic to the pan and cook until tender, about 5 minutes. Add the tomatoes and broth and bring to a boil. Return the chicken to the pan. Cover the pan. Reduce the heat to medium-low. Simmer until the chicken is just cooked through, 10 to 15 minutes more.

3. Transfer the chicken to the plates. Boil the pan juices over high heat until reduced by half and thickened, about 5 minutes. Stir in the oregano and cheese, and simmer until heated through, about 5 minutes. Garnish with the olives and serve.

Spicy Chicken Curry with Side Dishes

✓ *SOMETHING SPECIAL* ✓ *MAKE-AHEAD*

In many parts of southern Asia, especially in India, Malaysia, and Indonesia, curries are often served with an array of relishes or spicy side dishes called sambals. When you prepare this curry dinner at home, serve any or all of my relish suggestions and let each diner add his or her favorites to season the spicy stew and rice. These relishes can be as simple as raisins, and as complex as homemade chutneys. Children love the idea of picking and choosing their accompaniments, especially if you give them the job of setting them out in small dishes before dinner.

3 tablespoons peanut oil

2½ pounds chicken breasts, skinned, boned, and cut into large cubes

½ cup finely chopped yellow onion

4 teaspoons finely chopped garlic (from 4 medium cloves)

1 teaspoon hot curry paste, or more or less to taste *

1 tablespoon ground cumin

1 teaspoon finely chopped fresh ginger

2 tablespoons tomato paste

½ cup chicken broth

1 cup unsweetened coconut milk

3 tablespoons chopped fresh cilantro, plus more for garnish

4 cups freshly steamed rice

1. In a deep, heavy straight-sided skillet, heat 2 tablespoons peanut oil over medium heat. Brown the chicken in batches, for about 2 minutes per batch. Set aside.

2. In the same skillet, add the remaining oil and cook the onion and garlic, stirring, for 5 minutes. Stir in the curry paste, cumin, and ginger. Cook, stirring, 1 minute more. Stir in the tomato paste. Remove from the heat. *

3. Combine the chicken broth and coconut milk in a 2-cup measure. Pour into the skillet. Add the chicken. Stir to mix well. Reduce the heat to low and simmer gently, uncovered, 40 to 45 minutes, stirring from time to time—do not let it boil or the chicken will toughen. The chicken should be very tender and the sauce thickened. *

4. Add 3 tablespoons cilantro and cook until heated through, 5 minutes more.

5. Serve the curry, garnished with more cilantro, in a deep bowl with plenty of steaming rice on the side. Pass your choice of side dishes.

(continues on page 84)

★ TIP: This amount of **curry paste makes the dish very hot.** If your family is sensitive to spice, start with less than 1 teaspoon curry paste and add more a little at a time—or use a milder curry paste.

★ TIP: Cooking the **curry paste and spices** before adding the liquid brings out their fragrance and flavor.

★ TIP: To prepare a quick **dinner** another night, freeze the chicken at this point. Pour the cooled mixture into a heavy resealable plastic bag and freeze flat. Thaw completely before reheating and continuing with the recipe.

Possible side dishes:

Chopped hard-cooked egg;

Raisins;

Thinly sliced green onions;

Chutney—especially mango or pineapple;

Chopped roasted peanuts;

Toasted coconut;

A mixture of 1 cup plain yogurt, 1/2 cup thinly sliced halved and seeded English cucumber, 1/4 cup thinly sliced green onions, 1/4 cup freshly chopped mint, well seasoned with salt and pepper;

2 large ripe tomatoes, peeled, seeded, chopped, and mixed with 2 tablespoons minced onion, 1 teaspoon Asian chili/garlic sauce, and 2 tablespoons chopped fresh cilantro;

Sliced hard ripe bananas or mango;

Deep fried onion rings—even the canned variety is good here.

Apricot-Glazed Chicken with Sweet Apricot Stuffing

✓ *EASY PREPARATION*   ✓ *MAKE-AHEAD*

I have used this glaze on chicken, turkey, and Cornish game hens. I have always believed that a jar of marmalade, jam, or jelly, goes a long way toward pleasing the family at dinnertime. I often melt it to glaze carrots or green beans, but in this case we are going to make a delicious glaze for the chicken.

1 cup apricot jam

¼ cup very finely chopped dried apricots

¼ cup balsamic vinegar

1 tablespoon dried English mustard

1 teaspoon crushed red pepper *

1 whole chicken, split in half

3 tablespoons butter

½ cup finely chopped onion

½ cup finely chopped celery

1 teaspoon dried thyme

½ cup chopped dried apricots

6 cups chopped bread cubes

¼ cup shelled pistachio nuts

2 large eggs, lightly beaten

Salt and freshly ground pepper, to taste

1. In a small saucepan over medium heat, simmer the apricot jam, ¼ cup dried apricots, balsamic vinegar, dried mustard, and red pepper.

2. Preheat the oven to 350°F. Rinse the chicken and pat it dry. Place the 2 halves in a buttered baking dish, or in a small roasting pan lined with aluminum foil. Brush with the glaze and bake for 25 minutes. Remove from the oven.

3. In a small skillet, melt the butter over medium-high heat. Add the onion, celery, thyme, and ½ cup apricots. Cook until the vegetables are soft, about 5 minutes.

4. Transfer the mixture to a large bowl. Add the chopped bread cubes, pistachios, and eggs. Stir to combine the ingredients, then mound into 2 separate portions in the baking dish. Top each mound with a chicken half, skin side up. Season with salt and pepper.

5. Bake for ½ hour, brushing the chicken with the glaze at least twice. Remove from the oven. Serve, sliced or cut into pieces, with the stuffing alongside.

SERVING SUGGESTION

Steamed carrots go very well with this truly excellent dish.

＊TIP: Crushed red pepper is the same thing you find in shakers on the tables of pizza parlors: small flakes of dried hot pepper that add some zip when sprinkled over food.

Turkey-Chipotle Chili

✓ *SOMETHING SPECIAL*

This quick-recipe stew is thickened by the masa, a finely ground cornmeal used in Mexican cuisine to make tortillas, that is added to the broth. The spiciness comes from the smoked and dried jalapeño, also known as chipotle. When you have any leftover turkey meat, this is a great recipe to try, or just roast a turkey breast and go from there.

Two 15-ounce cans small white beans, like navy beans, drained and rinsed

6 cups low-salt chicken broth (1½ quarts)

2 teaspoons minced garlic (from 2 medium cloves)

2 cups finely chopped white onions (from 2 medium onions)

½ cup masa flour ✱

One 15-ounce can diced tomatoes

2 teaspoons Mexican oregano ✱

2 tablespoons canned chipotle chiles, minced

2 tablespoons olive oil

Two 4-ounce cans chopped green chiles

2 teaspoons ground cumin

1½ teaspoons dried oregano

⅛ teaspoon ground cloves

¼ teaspoon cayenne pepper

4 cups diced cooked turkey breast

Garnishes: Monterey Jack cheese, chopped tomatoes, cilantro, green onions, and sour cream

1. In a 4-quart kettle, combine the beans, broth, garlic, and ½ cup of the onions, and bring to a boil.

2. Whisk the masa into the broth then add the tomatoes, Mexican oregano, and chipotle chiles to taste. Bring the mixture back to the boil and stir often.

3. Heat the oil in a medium-sized heavy skillet over medium-high heat. Add the remaining onions and cook for 3 minutes. Add the green chiles, cumin, oregano, cloves, and cayenne. Cook for 2 minutes and add to the bean mixture. Stir in the turkey and continue to simmer for 15 minutes.

4. Serve the chili in deep bowls and let each diner garnish his or her serving with Monterey Jack cheese, chopped tomatoes, cilantro, green onions, and sour cream.

✱ **TIP:** Masa flour is available in the Spanish section of your local supermarket.

✱ **TIP:** Mexican oregano is a bit stronger than the Greek oregano we normally use. Add more or less depending on your preference for the flavor.

Braised Turkey Breast with Olives

✓ *MAKE-AHEAD*   ✓ *TAKE-ALONG*   ✓ *FREEZER READY*

Not only is this turkey breast succulently moist, but it is extremely easy to slice and serve. It is quite simple to buy a whole turkey breast, remove the breastbone, and roll and tie it yourself, or buy one that has been prepared by your supermarket meat cutter.

One 3-pound turkey breast, boned and tied ∗

Salt and freshly ground pepper, to taste

¼ cup olive oil

3 cups sliced onions (from 2 large onions)

2 cups seeded and sliced green peppers (from 2 medium green peppers)

4 teaspoons finely chopped garlic (from 4 medium cloves)

One 28-ounce can Italian tomatoes, coarsely chopped

1 teaspoon lemon zest

⅓ cup chopped flat-leaf parsley

½ cup chicken broth, plus more if needed

½ cup dry white wine

1½ cups pitted green olives (without pimiento), rinsed well in cold water

1. Season the turkey breast with salt and pepper.

2. Heat 2 tablespoons olive oil over medium heat in a heavy covered casserole large enough to hold the turkey breast in one piece. ∗

Brown the breast on all sides, about 10 minutes all together. Remove the breast and set aside.

3. Add the remaining oil and cook the onions and peppers over medium heat until soft, about 6 minutes. Add the garlic and cook 1 minute more. Stir in the tomatoes, zest, and parsley. Stir in the broth and wine and return the turkey breast to the casserole. Simmer, covered, over very low heat for 1 hour, adding broth a little at a time if it begins to look

dry. Remove the cover, add the olives, and simmer gently for 30 minutes more, until the turkey breast reads at least 160°F on an instant-read thermometer inserted in the center, and the sauce is reduced and thick.

4. Remove the turkey breast to a heated serving platter. Cover with foil and let rest for 10 to 15 minutes. Slice and serve with the vegetables and sauce spooned over the top.

SERVING SUGGESTION

Pile steaming hot, freshly cooked pasta (angel hair, linguine, egg noodles, etc.) in a deep platter and then arrange the turkey slices on top with the vegetables and sauce spooned over all—dinner in a dish!

∗ **TIP:** If you cannot find a fresh turkey breast, there is a boned, rolled, and frozen turkey breast available in most supermarkets that will be an excellent substitute. Just thaw in the refrigerator or in cold water and proceed with the recipe.

∗ **TIP:** Casseroles made of enamel over cast iron are especially good for long-cooking as they distribute heat evenly and retain heat once removed from the heat source. Le Creuset and Staub are two popular brands. Old-fashioned plain cast iron is also a good choice and available in many stores. Or, use any other heavy, covered casserole, such as one made of stainless steel or anodized aluminum.

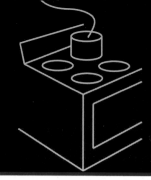

Poultry Encores

In your many grocery shopping trips, you have probably bought large packages of chicken on sale or have even cooked a large amount only to have your family eat just a small portion—leaving too much left over to use quickly, and possibly making you think you need to throw it out.

But this chapter looks at that situation in another light. Having too much is actually a good thing, here. It's a great opportunity for a quick family dinner tomorrow or the next busy night that comes around. If you have leftover chicken, or you have bought a rotisserie chicken, you can not only prepare dinner for tonight but you're halfway to making a new family meal for another time.

How will you know when the occasion arises for a quick chicken fix? Ask yourself:

- Is everyone going to be at the table tonight?

- Does everything need to be made all at once or is it an evening when schedules will keep you apart?

- Does your refrigerator turn into a drive-through so you have to have food ready to grab by whomever's hungry?

The answers to these questions always determine whether I'll prepare extra chicken and what I will be making with it.

Chicken in the refrigerator or freezer is just begging to be turned into something delicious. If chicken is seemingly dry, adding a sauce will make it more moist and flavorful. For instance, a chicken breast that is cubed and tossed in yogurt, as in the Chicken and Yogurt Pitas (page 89), will develop a fuller flavor. The cooked chicken is the beginning; the rest can be up to whatever sparks your imagination on any given night.

For more varied options, canned enchilada sauce, jarred pasta sauce, or commercial pesto can make a terrific meal when paired with your leftover chicken. (Remember to heat the chicken in the sauce over a low heat for just enough time to have the sauce infuse the chicken with flavor. Be careful not to cook it too long or the meat will still be dry inside, even if covered with a sauce.)

So stock your pantry with these instant helpers, along with any others your family may enjoy. There are many great sauces on supermarket shelves that are nutritious and can be kept on hand for any occasion. Also keep a stock of your favorite cheese for a quick chicken parmesan, frozen pie crusts for a pot pie, or your favorite pasta shapes for a chicken-filled pasta entrée. There will be no need for a recipe once you realize everyone will rave at your own encore presentations. In this chapter, we give you just a few good recipes to get you started. After that, you can branch out on your own. Leftover cooked chicken is not a boring, last-ditch choice, but a perfect building block for a meal.

Chicken and Yogurt Pitas

✓ *EASY PREPARATION*   ✓ *NO COOKING NEEDED*

This is a great quick meal when there is no time to cook. With some leftover cooked chicken in the refrigerator, you will be able to make the pita sandwiches in 15 minutes. Call everyone into the kitchen and set the children to work filling the pitas while you prepare the rest of the meal. A simple dinner is on the table in no time, and so satisfying. Serve with fresh steamed vegetables and a tossed green salad.

4 cups shredded cooked chicken
(from 2 breast halves)

1 cup plain nonfat yogurt (8 ounces)

1 cup mayonnaise

1 cup finely chopped celery

½ cup chopped green onion
(from 8 whole green onions)

3 tablespoons coarse-grained
mustard

1 teaspoon chopped fresh dill

Salt and freshly ground pepper,
to taste

6 pita rounds, sliced in half across

1 head of green leaf lettuce

4 tomatoes, sliced

1. In a medium bowl, combine the chicken, yogurt, mayonnaise, celery, onion, mustard, and dill. Season this with salt and pepper.

2. Line the pita pockets with lettuce and tomato and then fill with the chicken mixture. Serve.

Herbed Chicken Patties

MAKES 4 TO 6 SERVINGS

✓ *EASY PREPARATION*   ✓ *MAKE-AHEAD*   ✓ *FREEZER READY*

This is a very tasty way to use cooked chicken. Kids love them served on a bun, but they are equally delicious as a plated main course along with mashed potatoes and grilled asparagus. They are easily frozen before pan frying, for quick out-of-the-freezer busy night meals.

2 cups chopped cooked chicken
or turkey

2 tablespoons butter

2 tablespoons flour

Salt and freshly ground pepper,
to taste

1/2 cup milk or half and half

1 teaspoon Dijon mustard

2 tablespoons chopped fresh oregano

1 teaspoon chopped fresh thyme

2 tablespoons chopped fresh
curly-leaf parsley

2 tablespoons finely chopped
green onions (from 2 whole onions)

1/3 cup panko bread crumbs

2 tablespoons olive oil

1. Grind the chicken by pulsing in a food processor—but not to a paste. The chicken should still have some texture.

2. Melt the butter in a 2-quart saucepan over medium heat. Add the flour and season with salt and pepper. Cook, stirring, for 3 minutes. Stir in the milk or half and half all at once. Cook, stirring, until very thick, about 3 minutes more. Remove from the heat and stir in the mustard.

3. In a medium bowl, mix the chicken, oregano, thyme, parsley, and green onions. Add the panko. Stir in the cooled cream sauce and season the mixture very well with salt and pepper.

4. Refrigerate 1 hour, then shape into 4 to 6 patties. ✱

5. Heat the olive oil in a heavy skillet over medium-high heat. Fry the patties until golden brown, about 3 minutes per side.

VARIATION

Grill the patties on a fish screen on a well-heated grill. The smoky flavor will be a nice enhancement.

✱ **TIP:** Freeze the patties at this point, if you like, by arranging them in a single layer on a baking sheet and placing it in the freezer. Once fully frozen, transfer the patties to a resealable freezer bag. Take out as many as you need for a quick busy night dinner. Fry straight from the freezer, just add a few minutes to the cooking time.

90 KITCHEN COACH: FAMILY MEALS

Old-Fashioned Chicken and Dumplings

✓ *SOMETHING SPECIAL*

Dumplings can be almost any flavor, shape, size, and texture—the unifying element being that dumplings are made with flour, water, and some sort of fat. They can be thick and floury; crusty on the top like biscuits; big, softly steamed balls; or thin and pastalike, as in this recipe. This is a wonderful dish to serve when something comforting is called for—a homey dish, not overly spiced or fussy—sort of chicken noodle stew. This is a good opportunity for the kids to help fix dinner. They can roll out and cut the dumplings, and they love to drop them (carefully) into the simmering broth.

2 tablespoons butter

1 medium yellow onion, thickly sliced

4 medium carrots, cut into 1/2-inch slices (about 2 cups)

3 ribs celery, cut into 1/2-inch slices (about 2 cups)

Salt and freshly ground pepper, to taste

3 cups cut-up cooked chicken

Bouquet garni

4 cups chicken broth (1 quart)

Dumplings (next page)

1 tablespoon butter, softened

1 tablespoon flour

3 tablespoons chopped fresh curly-leaf parsley, for garnish

1. Heat the butter over medium heat in a heavy covered casserole such as Le Creuset (see ★ **TIP** on page 87). Add the onion, carrots, and celery, and cook, stirring, just until soft, but not browned, about 6 to 8 minutes. Season with salt and freshly ground pepper, and add the cooked chicken. Drop in the bouquet garni. Pour in the chicken broth, reduce the heat to low, cover, and simmer 30 minutes.

2. While the broth is cooking, make the dumplings.

3. Lower the heat until the broth is just barely simmering and add the dumplings, a few at a time, until all are in the pot. Simmer, covered, over very low heat until the dumplings are cooked through, about 12 to 15 minutes. The dumplings will swell while cooking.

4. With a fork, combine the butter and flour into a smooth paste. Stir in the butter paste a little at a time, just until the broth thickens to the consistency of heavy cream; this takes about 3 to 4 minutes and you probably won't need to use all the paste. Garnish with chopped parsley and serve in pasta bowls.

(continues on page 92)

Dumplings

1 cup all-purpose flour

½ **teaspoon baking powder**

½ **teaspoon salt**

2 **tablespoons butter**

¼ **cup milk**

1. In a medium bowl, use a fork to stir together the flour, baking powder, and salt. Cut in the butter with a pastry cutter until the lumps look like coarse crumbs. Stir in the milk and gather the dough into a ball. The dough will be stiff.

2. On a floured board, knead the dough twice to just mix well.

3. Roll out the dough very thinly—about ⅛ inch. Cut into 1- × 2-inch strips. Lay the dumplings on a plate or board to dry for 20 minutes.

Creamed Chicken and Mushrooms on Toast

✓ EASY PREPARATION   ✓ MAKE-AHEAD   ✓ FREEZER READY

This quick, but satisfying dish can be on the table in a matter of minutes. If you like a lighter dish, try using broth instead of milk in the mushroom sauce. Or, for a more elegant dish, substitute half a cup of dry white wine for half a cup of the milk or broth. The same basic recipe can be used with cooked cubed ham, tuna, salmon, even crumbled cooked ground beef. Let the kids decide which one they want tonight.

3 tablespoons butter

½ cup sliced green onions (from 8 whole onions)

2 teaspoons finely chopped garlic (from 2 medium cloves, optional but recommended)

2 cups fresh button mushrooms (from 4 ounces), stems removed, halved or quartered if larger around than a nickel

2 tablespoons flour

Salt and freshly ground pepper, to taste

2 cups whole milk, chicken broth, or half and half

2 cups cubed cooked chicken or turkey

3 tablespoons chopped fresh curly-leaf parsley, plus more for garnish

4 slices sour dough bread, toasted and lightly buttered, cut in quarters

1. Heat 1 tablespoon of the butter in a heavy skillet over medium-high heat. Add the green onions and cook, stirring, until soft and transparent, about 6 minutes. Stir in the garlic and mushrooms. Cook, stirring, until the mushrooms are soft, about 3 minutes. Drain the vegetables and set aside.

2. Melt the remaining 2 tablespoons butter in a 2-quart saucepan over medium-high heat. Stir in the flour and season well with salt and pepper. Cook, stirring, for 3 minutes—but do not let the flour brown. Whisk in the milk or broth all at one time.

Cook, whisking, until thickened, about 3 to 4 minutes. Stir in the mushroom mixture, chicken, and parsley. Season again with salt and pepper, if necessary. Cook over low heat until the chicken is hot, for 5 minutes.

3. To serve: Arrange 4 toast quarters on each plate. Spoon chicken over the top. Garnish with a little more chopped parsley. Serve hot.

VARIATION

Serve over split biscuits, English muffins, or in puff pastry cups for a special party luncheon main dish. Add a mixed vegetable salad to finish off the meal.

Quick and Easy Chicken Pot Pie

✓ SOMETHING SPECIAL   ✓ FREEZER READY

We all need a hearty dinner recipe that can be made easily. This quick pot pie is a dinner in one dish, it can be made any time of the week, and it is a great recipe for leftovers. Put it together in the morning, refrigerate, then pop it in the oven the minute you get home. By the time the table is set and you have made a big salad, the pot pie is ready and everyone can sit down to eat together. The pot pie can also be frozen, unbaked, until you are ready to use it. Take it out of the freezer and bake while still frozen, for one hour or until hot and bubbly.

1½ tablespoons olive oil

1 cup finely chopped white onion

2 medium carrots, thinly sliced (about 1 cup)

2 large ribs celery, sliced (about ½ cup)

4 cups cooked shredded chicken

3 tablespoons butter

⅓ cup all-purpose flour

1 cup chicken broth

1½ cups whole milk

Salt and freshly ground pepper, to taste

3 tablespoons dry Sherry

1 cup frozen green peas

3 tablespoons minced flat-leaf Italian parsley

Pastry for a 1-crust pie, frozen or homemade, at room temperature

1. Preheat the oven to 375°F. Add the oil to a large skillet and heat over medium-high heat. Add the onion, carrots, and celery. Cook until the vegetables are tender, about 5 minutes. Combine them in a medium bowl with the chicken.

2. Heat the butter in the same skillet over medium-high heat. Add the flour and cook for 2 minutes. Beat in the stock and milk all at once. Bring to a simmer and cook until slightly thickened, about 3 minutes. Season to taste with salt and pepper and then add the Sherry.

3. Pour the sauce over the chicken and vegetable mixture. Stir in the peas and the parsley. Pour the mixture into a 3-quart casserole dish. Roll out the pastry, top the casserole with the pie crust, and form a decorative rim. Cut steam vents in the surface.

4. Bake for 40 minutes until the crust is golden and the filling is bubbling. Serve immediately.

Chicken Fried Rice

✓ *EASY PREPARATION*

Rice is a wonderful grain for any meal. It is easy to fix, adaptable, filling, and best of all, it tastes great. Children seem to love this dish anytime, as a snack after school, for a quick dinner on sports nights, or even in front of late-night television. Once they are stove savvy, they can make this dish whenever they need a wholesome snack. You can cook the rice the night before, keep it on hand in the refrigerator, and have this encore dish ready in no time.

3 tablespoons peanut oil

3 large eggs, lightly beaten with a fork

¼ cup sliced green onions (from 4 whole onions)

½ cup frozen green peas, thawed

¼ cup chopped carrot

1½ cups diced cooked chicken

3 cups cooked rice

2 tablespoons light soy sauce

2 tablespoons finely chopped fresh cilantro or Italian flat-leaf parsley

1. Heat 1 tablespoon of the oil in a large, deep, heavy skillet or wok over medium-high heat. Pour in the eggs and cook, stirring from time to time, until just set, about 2 minutes. Remove the eggs to a plate and break them up with a fork.

2. Return the skillet or wok to the heat. Add the remaining oil. Add the green onions, peas, and carrot. ✱ Cook, stirring, for 2 minutes. Add the chicken and rice. Cook, tossing lightly, until the rice is hot and beginning to brown a little, about 5 minutes.

3. Stir in the soy sauce, cilantro, and cooked egg. Stir over the heat for 1 minute, until well mixed. Serve very hot with more soy sauce on the side.

> ✱**TIP:** Literally **any variety of cooked vegetable** that might be on hand in the refrigerator will work in this stir-fry. Try asparagus tips, roasted peppers, corn cut from the cob, cut-up green beans, lima beans, or diced zucchini.

Chicken, Cheese, and Portobello Quesadillas

✓ EASY PREPARATION   ✓ MAKE-AHEAD

Every day when my 12-year-old son, Matthew, comes home from school he asks me to make him a quesadilla. After more than a year, I thought he would have tired of the same snack, but he never does. His steadfast preference for them does not stop at home—even when we go out to dinner, he will often order a quesadilla. The creativity of restaurant chefs often inspires me to try new filling combinations. I bet your family will love these as much as mine does.

4 portobello mushrooms, brushed clean, and the beard removed *

2 tablespoons olive oil

1/2 teaspoon salt

1/2 teaspoon freshly ground pepper

Six 12-inch flour tortillas

2 cups shredded cooked chicken

2 cups grated cheddar cheese (from 8 ounces)

2 cups grated Monterey Jack cheese (from 8 ounces)

2 tablespoons pickled jalapeño pepper slices

3 tablespoons butter

1. Preheat the grill or grill pan over medium-high heat.

2. Brush the mushrooms with olive oil and season them with salt and pepper. Place the mushrooms, cap side down, on the grill pan and grill until the caps are lightly browned and the mushrooms are tender, about 3 to 4 minutes. Remove the mushrooms from the grill and let them rest for 5 minutes. Slice thinly.

3. Lay 3 of the tortillas on a work surface. Divide the chicken, cheese, mushroom slices, and jalapeños among 3 tortillas. Top each with a second tortilla.

4. Melt 1 tablespoon of the butter in a medium skillet over medium heat. When the butter is hot and bubbly, carefully add 1 quesadilla to the skillet. Brown lightly on both sides, turning once. Repeat with the other 2 quesadillas. *

5. Cut into quarters while still very hot and serve with a green salad or vegetable soup, or pass your favorite fresh salsa alongside.

★ TIP: The portobello "beard" or gills can be removed easily before cooking. You may want to do this as they are very dark in color, and can dye the final dish almost black. Pop out the stem, then, using the tip of a teaspoon, carefully scrape out the gills leaving only the cap.

★ TIP: If you are in a hurry or trying to cut down on fat, **try steaming the quesadilla** for 2 minutes in the microwave. You will end up with a soft quesadilla in a flash. If your grill is still hot from cooking the mushrooms, then try grilling the quesadilla for a real authentic flavor.

Chicken Enchiladas with Tomatillo Sauce

✓ MAKE-AHEAD   ✓ FREEZER READY

This is an inviting new variation on the old reliable family enchilada recipe with the addition of a green tomatillo sauce. The enchiladas can be made with any type of filling, such as grilled or cooked vegetables, fish, chicken, or meat. Try taking leftover meats and vegetables from the refrigerator to make your own interesting combinations. Once the ingredients are all at hand, even young children can help assemble the dish. Be sure to make an extra pan to freeze for another time!

SAUCE

6 husked, stemmed, cleaned, and roasted tomatillos *

1 cup chopped white onion

1 small stemmed, seeded, and minced serrano chile

2 teaspoons chopped garlic (from 2 medium cloves)

2 cups low-salt chicken broth

1/2 cup toasted pumpkin seeds

6 roasted, peeled, and seeded poblano chiles *

1/2 cup chopped cilantro, stems included

1 leaf of romaine lettuce

1 1/2 teaspoons salt

1 tablespoon peanut oil

FILLING

1/4 cup half and half

8 ounces cream cheese, at room temperature

2 cups cooked shredded chicken

3/4 cup finely chopped white onion

1/2 teaspoon salt

1 tablespoon unsalted butter for greasing the microwave dish

Twelve 8-inch corn tortillas

3/4 cup grated cheddar cheese (from 3 ounces)

3/4 cup grated Monterey Jack cheese (from 3 ounces)

Shredded iceberg lettuce, tomatoes, sour cream, olives, and salsa

1. Make the tomatillo sauce: In a small saucepan, place the roasted tomatillos, onion, serrano chile, garlic, and broth. Bring to a boil, cover the pan, and simmer for 10 minutes.

2. Combine the pumpkin seeds and 4 tablespoons of the cooking liquid in a food processor and pulse until finely chopped. Add the tomatillo mixture, poblano chiles, cilantro, lettuce, and salt to the food processor. Puree until the mixture is smooth. *

3. Heat the oil in a large skillet over medium-high heat. Add the pureed mixture and stir over medium heat until some of the moisture evaporates and the sauce is thickened, about 5 minutes. This can be made up to 2 days ahead and refrigerated or frozen for up to 3 months.

4. Make the enchilada filling: In the bowl of a mixer fitted with the paddle, on medium speed, beat together the half and half and cream cheese until smooth and fluffy. Fold the chicken, onion, and salt into the cream cheese mixture.

(continues on page 98)

*TIP: It is easy to roast the tomatillos and the poblano chiles under the broiler. Just place the tomatillos on a jellyroll pan or rimmed cookie sheet, and broil close to the heat for about 2 to 3 minutes, turning several times until the skin is lightly browned and beginning to blister. To roast the poblano, or any other pepper, place them close to the heat and broil for about 4 to 5 minutes, turning several times, until blackened on all sides. Place a damp paper towel over the chile for 5 minutes and then gently peel away the skin. Remove the vein and seeds. These roasted peppers can be kept in the refrigerator for several days.

*TIP: Make this sauce a day in advance to save time and refrigerate until you want to make the enchiladas.

5. Butter a small dish and stack the tortillas in it. Cover the dish with plastic wrap and heat the tortillas in the microwave at half power for 1 minute, until they are lightly steamed.

6. Preheat the oven to 350°F. Spoon a thin layer of the sauce into the bottom of a 9- × 13-inch glass baking dish.

7. Assemble the enchiladas: Spread a thin layer of the tomatillo sauce on 1 tortilla. Arrange ¼ cup of the chicken mixture down the center of the tortilla. Roll the tortilla and place it, seam side down, in the baking dish. Repeat with all of the tortillas. Spoon the remaining sauce over the rolled tortillas. Cover the dish with foil and bake for 20 minutes or until hot. Remove the foil and sprinkle the enchiladas with the cheddar and Monterey Jack cheese. Bake, uncovered, until the cheese melts, about 10 minutes more.

8. Serve with shredded iceberg lettuce, chopped tomatoes, sour cream, olives, and salsa on the side.

Curried Turkey with Herbed Couscous

MAKES 6 SERVINGS

Serving turkey throughout the year jazzes up dinner and provides some variation from eating yet another chicken. This healthy dish brings the flavors of Morocco right to your own dinner table. In this recipe, begin by poaching the turkey in broth until fully cooked. Allow the meat to cool, then cut it into pieces.

★**TIP:** Although optional, the **yogurt is highly recommended** in this dish to provide a creamy texture with no added fat.

4 tablespoons olive oil

1 cup finely chopped white onion

1 teaspoon chopped garlic

1 teaspoon turmeric

1/2 teaspoon crushed red pepper

1 tablespoon tomato paste

3 cups low-salt chicken broth

1 1/2 cups water

2 medium carrots, sliced (about 1 cup)

1 teaspoon ground cinnamon

2 cups cooked turkey

1 cup canned chickpeas, rinsed well and drained

2 cups couscous

2 tablespoons chopped Italian flat-leaf parsley

1/4 cup nonfat plain yogurt (optional) ★

1. Heat 3 tablespoons of the olive oil in a medium skillet over medium-high heat. Add the onion and garlic to the pan and cook over medium heat, stirring, until softened, about 5 minutes. Add the turmeric and crushed red pepper, and cook the mixture, stirring, for 1 minute.

2. Stir in the tomato paste, broth, water, carrots, and cinnamon, and simmer, covered, until the vegetables are tender, about 20 minutes. Add the turkey slices and the chickpeas and simmer the mixture for 5 minutes.

3. Pour 2 cups of the cooking liquid into a small saucepan, add the remaining 1 tablespoon olive oil; stir in the couscous. Remove the pan from the heat and let the mixture stand, covered, for 5 minutes. Fluff the couscous with a fork and add the parsley. Divide the couscous between 6 shallow bowls. Spoon the meat and vegetables over the couscous. Drizzle with the yogurt if you like, and serve very hot.

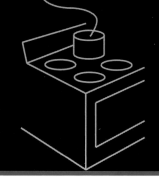

Beef, Pork, Veal, and Lamb

It's no secret that one of the easiest and most family-pleasing dinners is a richly flavored pot roast and for many of us, cutting into a perfectly cooked, tender, juicy steak, with some roasted potatoes on the side, is one of the most satisfying of all meals, period. For ease and particularly for taste, family meals are often based around a meat entrée but finding balance and variety is challenging.

No longer a dietary no-no, due to methods of breeding and feeding, beef has changed over the years. It has become notably leaner—in fact, according to the National Cattleman's Association, much of the beef we eat today is 27 percent leaner than it was 20 years ago. The "new" pork is even leaner. Cuts of meat are trimmed more closely before being sold than they used to be, which also contributes to the leanness of the meats we eat. With this leanness, though, you need to be more careful about handling and cooking meat properly in order to get the best flavor from it. Here are some guidelines.

- Always begin by bringing meat to room temperature before you cook it. This only takes about 20 to 30 minutes out of the refrigerator depending on the size of the cut. Starting with the meat at room temperature gives you a better gauge for cooking time and results in a crustier exterior.

- The flavor of the leaner cuts is generally good, but you have to be careful not to dry them out when you cook them. The solution is to monitor the cooking very carefully, to add liquid to the pan as necessary, and to check it with an instant-read meat thermometer to determine doneness, so you can stop the cooking as soon as, or shortly before, it is done.

- You can enhance the flavor of meat with a rub or marinade. These work really well for many cuts. Remember that you can keep red meat in a marinade in the refrigerator for up to 48 hours. Take a look at the Wine and Rosemary Marinated Leg of Lamb (page 105). You can use this marinade for almost any type of meat. It would be delicious with New York strip steaks. A dry rub can also be great because you can put it on just before you are ready to cook. Rubs are real time savers and can be made ahead in bulk, as in the Herb-Crusted Lamb Chops (page 107), to use any time you want.

- Another great way to add flavor to meat is to make small cuts in the surface and stuff them with assertively strong flavors like slivers of garlic, fresh herbs, bits of onion, or mixed oils and spices. Once the meat begins to cook, the flavor mixtures may brown quickly, but that only adds to the flavor.

- Slow cooking is an excellent method for cooking leaner modern cuts, such as in Cumin-Crusted Chuck Roast (page 101). If you are cooking a roast and want to slow simmer it, a slow cooker is a great help. You can throw all the ingredients together in the morning and come home after work to a beautiful dinner already cooked and waiting.

Cumin-Crusted Chuck Roast

✓ *MAKE-AHEAD*   ✓ *FREEZER READY*   ✓ *READY AND WAITING*

This is a great "rainy days and Sundays" slow-cooking dish you can put in the oven and forget for a few hours. Buy a roast larger than you will need for dinner (adjust cooking time accordingly) and save any leftovers for a quick "encore" dish later in the week, such as Hearty Salad with Asian Dressing (page 116) or Irish Stew (page 114).

1 teaspoon finely chopped garlic

1/2 teaspoon ground coriander

2 tablespoons ground cumin

2 tablespoons panko bread crumbs

2 tablespoons finely chopped green onion (from 2 to 3 whole onions)

Salt and freshly ground pepper, to taste

Pinch cayenne pepper

1 tablespoon olive oil

One 3-pound chuck roast (or larger if you wish)

1. Preheat the oven to 300°F.

2. Mix all the ingredients except the roast in a small bowl. Rub the mixture generously over one surface of the roast, pressing so it will adhere.

3. Place the roast, rub side up, in a heavy covered casserole, such as Le Creuset (see ★ TIP on page 87). Cover and cook in the oven for 4 hours, or up to 5 hours if your schedule changes.

4. Remove the cover and cook 30 minutes more. Remove the roast

to a cutting board, tent with foil, and let it rest for 10 minutes. Pour off as much fat as you can from the pan juices.

5. To serve: Slice the roast into thick slices, drizzling a little of the pan juices over each serving. Pass any remaining juices in a separate bowl and serve.

SERVING SUGGESTION

Serve with baked potatoes, mashed potatoes, noodles, or rice.

Classic Beef Stroganoff on Buttered Noodles

✓ *SOMETHING SPECIAL*

This elegant dish was originally made with beef tenderloin, but if that cut strains the budget, substitute New York strip steak or even chuck steak for a delicious family dinner that is also perfect for entertaining friends.

2 pounds beef tenderloin, strip steak, or chuck steak, frozen for 2 hours ✳

3 tablespoons butter

¾ cup thinly sliced onion

1½ cups sliced fresh mushrooms (from about 4 ounces)

1 teaspoon finely chopped garlic

Salt and freshly ground pepper, to taste

1 cup beef broth

1 tablespoon tomato paste

1 teaspoon softened butter

1 teaspoon flour

1 cup sour cream

2 tablespoons chopped fresh curly parsley

8 ounces thick egg noodles, cooked, drained, and kept hot

Pinch paprika, for garnish

1. With a very sharp knife, slice the beef into ⅛- to ¼-inch-thick slices.

2. Heat 2 tablespoons of the butter in a large, deep straight-sided skillet over medium-high heat. Brown the beef, a few slices at a time, about 2 minutes per batch. Remove the browned meat to a dish and set aside.

3. Reduce the heat to medium and add the onion, mushrooms, and garlic to the same skillet. Cook, stirring, until soft, about 5 to 6 minutes. Add more butter if necessary—if the mixture begins to dry out—a little at a time. Season well with salt and pepper. Return the beef to the skillet. Stir together the broth and tomato paste and add to the skillet. Cover and simmer over low heat for about 30 minutes. ✳

4. With a fork, combine the softened butter and flour to form a thick paste. Stir into the sauce and cook until slightly thickened, about 3 to 4 minutes.

5. Stir in the sour cream and parsley. Heat through but do not boil, about 2 minutes. ✳

6. Toss the hot noodles with the last 1 tablespoon of butter.

7. Serve the stroganoff very hot over the buttered noodles and garnish with a sprinkling of paprika.

✳**TIP:** To easily cut the meat into even slices, freeze the meat just until firm, but not frozen. By the time all the meat is cut, the slices will have thawed and be ready to cook.

✳**TIP: If using chuck,** which is not as tender as either tenderloin or New York strip, simmer a little longer, about 45 minutes.

✳**TIP: Do not let sour cream** boil as it will curdle and the resulting dish will look very unappetizing.

Jerked Roast Filet of Beef with Coconut Rice

✓ *SOMETHING SPECIAL*   ✓ *EASY PREPARATION*

Like many other cooking terms, the origin of "jerk" is murky at best. Today, however, it is generally associated with Jamaican jerk cooking. It can be fiery hot, but generally results in succulently juicy beef, pork, chicken, and seafood. This extravagant but delicious dish could well be the star of your next family celebration or dinner party. Our version is not too hot, but if your family does not like spicy foods, cut the cayenne and crushed pepper in half.

✶TIP: Letting roasted meats and poultry rest before carving permits the meat to firm up and reabsorb the juices, making slicing easier.

Coconut Rice (next page)

RUB

2 tablespoons ground allspice

1 teaspoon cayenne pepper, or more or less to taste

1 teaspoon crushed red pepper, or more or less to taste

1 teaspoon sweet paprika

2 teaspoons dried thyme

2 teaspoons salt

1/2 teaspoon ground pepper

1 tablespoon dried minced onion

1 teaspoon garlic powder

1/8 teaspoon ground cinnamon

ROAST

One 2½-pound piece filet of beef

Olive oil

1. Make the coconut rice. Preheat the oven to 450°F.

2. Prepare the rub: Stir all the ingredients together in a small bowl.

3. Rub the surface of the filet with oil. Generously coat all surfaces of the meat with the rub, pressing hard so it will adhere. Place the meat on a rack set in a roasting pan.

4. Roast in the preheated oven for 15 minutes. Lower the heat to 375°F and roast 10 to 15 minutes more, or just until an instant-read thermometer reads 125°F when inserted in the middle of the thickest part of the roast. If you like your meat less rare, cook several minutes longer until the thermometer reads 135°F.

5. Remove the roast from the oven and let it stand, tented with foil, for 10 minutes before serving. ✶

6. Serve the filet sliced, accompanied by coconut rice and lots of crusty bread.

(continues on page 104)

Coconut Rice

✓ EASY PREPARATION   ✓ SOMETHING SPECIAL

The coconut milk in this rice tends to calm down the spiciness of the jerk seasonings, and the flavor is unusually delicious.

1 tablespoon butter

½ cup very finely chopped onion

Salt, to taste

1 cup uncooked long-grain white rice

1 cup water

1 cup unsweetened coconut milk

2 tablespoons finely chopped fresh curly-leaf parsley

1. Melt the butter in a 2-quart saucepan over medium heat. Stir in the onion and cook, stirring, until soft, 4 to 5 minutes. Season well with salt. Stir in the rice and cook 1 minute.

2. Combine the water and coconut milk in a 2-cup measure. Add to the rice and stir to combine. Lower the heat slightly and cook, uncovered, until the liquid is evaporated and deep holes appear in the surface. Remove from the heat, place a thick kitchen towel over the saucepan, and top with the cover. Let stand for 15 minutes.

3. Stir in the parsley and fluff the rice well with a fork. Serve very hot.

Wine and Rosemary Marinated Leg of Lamb

MAKES 8 SERVINGS

✓ *SOMETHING SPECIAL*   ✓ *MAKE-AHEAD*

This leg of lamb fits into any busy family schedule because it can be marinated, stored in the refrigerator, forgotten, and grilled at your own convenience. You can substitute other types of meat for the lamb, as the flavors in the marinade go well with many other cuts of red meat. Most cuts of lamb, beef, and pork can be marinated for up to 48 hours. Remember when it comes to wine, cook with what you would be willing to drink. You don't need to use an expensive wine, but make sure that the flavor is good.

4 cups Honey Kiwi Salsa (next page)

One 5-pound leg of lamb, boned, butterflied *

½ cup finely chopped fresh rosemary

½ cup finely chopped fresh mint *

2 cups Cabernet or other hearty red wine *

¼ cup olive oil

¾ cup red wine vinegar

4 teaspoons chopped garlic (from 4 medium cloves)

2 teaspoons freshly ground pepper

1. Make the honey kiwi salsa.

2. Cut the lamb into 3 pieces. You will notice that since the lamb is butterflied, it unfolds naturally into 3 long strips. It can be cut into 2 thick pieces and 1 thin piece. The thick pieces are on the outside and the middle piece is thinner.

3. In a 2-cup measure, blend the rosemary, mint, wine, olive oil, vinegar, garlic, and pepper. Place the lamb in a resealable plastic bag. Pour the marinade over the lamb. Seal and place in the refrigerator. Marinate for at least 4 hours, turning several times.

4. Prepare the grill to medium-high heat. Grill the lamb pieces to desired doneness, about 10 to 12 minutes per side for medium-rare. I generally grill all 3 pieces the same length of time so 1 piece will be pretty much well done, as there are always some folks who do not like rare or even pink lamb. *

5. Remove the lamb to a cookie sheet, board, or platter, tent with foil, and allow to rest 10 minutes. (The lamb can be prepared up to 2 hours ahead. Cover and let stand at room temperature.)

6. Serve the lamb sliced, with the honey kiwi salsa alongside.

✱ TIP: Ask your butcher to butterfly and trim the lamb for you. The butcher will remove the bone and open the meat out like a large steak.

✱ TIP: To preserve the life of your fresh herbs, trim the stems and place them in a small cup of water. Loosely cover the cup and the herbs with plastic wrap. Place the herbs in the refrigerator. Leave them towards the front so that every time you make a salad or serve some fruit, you will use them—and they will be gone before you know it.

✱ TIP: For an alcohol-free dish, try using nonalcoholic red "wine" or an equal amount of nonalcoholic beer in the marinade.

✱ TIP: This dish can also be roasted in a preheated 425°F oven for 20 to 30 minutes.

(continues on page 106)

Honey Kiwi Salsa

✓ *SOMETHING SPECIAL*   ✓ *MAKE-AHEAD*

With grilled lamb on the menu, an Australian specialty, this salsa with a Down Under accent of kiwis is just the right accompaniment. The delicate fruit flavor of this colorful side dish appeals to almost everyone, and provides just the right sweet complement for the lamb.

4 cups peeled and chopped kiwi (from about 10 kiwi fruit)

¼ cup finely chopped fresh mint leaves

¼ cup honey

1½ teaspoons chopped fresh rosemary

Up to 4 hours before serving, mix all ingredients together in a small bowl. Cover and chill up to 24 hours. Bring to room temperature before serving.

Herb-Crusted Lamb Chops

✓ *SOMETHING SPECIAL*   ✓ *EASY PREPARATION*

Dry rubs are not just great flavor enhancers for meat, but they can be made in larger quantities than you will need right away and kept in an airtight container for several months. I brush the meat with oil and then gently press on the rub. It is a great way to add flavor at the last minute without having to work too hard or too far in advance.

2 teaspoons dried dill

2 teaspoons dried basil

1 teaspoon dried thyme

2 teaspoons sweet paprika

1 teaspoon dry mustard

2 teaspoons onion powder

1/2 teaspoon garlic powder

1 teaspoon freshly ground pepper

1/4 teaspoon cayenne pepper

1 teaspoon salt

1 teaspoon lemon zest

12 loin lamb chops, each 1¼ to 1½ inches thick

1/4 cup olive oil

1. In a small bowl, combine the dill, basil, thyme, paprika, mustard, onion powder, garlic powder, pepper, cayenne, and salt. This mixture can be saved in an airtight container at room temperature. When you are ready to rub it on the lamb chops, fold in the lemon zest. ✱

2. Heat a large cast-iron skillet, grill pan, or outdoor grill over high heat.

3. Brush each lamb chop with olive oil. Press the rub mixture firmly into both sides of each chop, patting them so the spices will adhere.

4. Grill the chops uncovered over high heat, turning once, for 2 to 3 minutes on each side. The chops should be charred on the outside and rare inside. Serve hot or warm.

✱ **TIP:** Keep the **herb and spice combination** on hand for spur-of-the-moment special meals. Use on strip steaks, pork chops or tenderloins, whole leg of lamb for roasting, even chicken breasts. You might even sprinkle a little on cooked green beans or roast potatoes.

Bollito Misto with Green Sauce

✓ SOMETHING SPECIAL   ✓ READY AND WAITING   ✓ MAKE-AHEAD   ✓ FREEZER READY

Here is a modern version of a very old Italian home-cooking favorite. Nothing could be simpler to make than this "mixed boil" of meats, cooked until tender. Simple as it is, it requires the best-quality ingredients. The combination of several kinds of meat makes this a substantial dish, and guarantees there will be some left for freezing or making into a quick work-night dinner later in the week. I like to have this when it is cold or raining outside, or after a long day raking leaves, or challenging the ski slopes. It is definitely a dish for healthy appetites.

＊TIP: Substitute a large **Cornish game hen** for the chicken if you're feeding fewer than four people.

3 large ribs celery, cut into 1-inch pieces (about 2 cups)

3 medium carrots, cut into 1-inch pieces (about 4 cups)

2 small onions halved through the root end

2 pounds chuck roast in 1 piece, most of the fat trimmed

Water

Green Sauce (next page)

3 pounds veal shoulder or breast in 1 piece

One whole 3-pound or smaller chicken (depending on the size of your family) ＊

Salt and freshly ground pepper, to taste

1½ pounds fennel-flavored chicken sausages or Italian sweet sausages

3 tablespoons chopped fresh Italian flat-leaf parsley

1. In a soup pot large enough to hold all the ingredients except the sausages, over medium heat, combine the celery, carrots, and onions. Add the chuck roast and enough water (2 to 4 quarts) to cover completely. Simmer over low heat for 1 hour. Meanwhile, make the green sauce.

2. Add the veal and chicken, and season well with salt and pepper. Simmer until the veal and the chicken are very tender, 45 minutes to 1 hour more.

3. While the chicken and veal are simmering, pierce the sausages with a fork and place them in a 2-quart saucepan. Add water to cover and simmer over low heat until the sausages are cooked. Turn off the heat and let the sausages stand in the water, covered, until ready to eat.

4. Just before serving, remove the meats and sausages from their broths and slice as much as you will need for dinner. Arrange the meats on a deep platter and ladle the vegetables over the top, along with just enough broth to moisten the meat. Garnish with chopped parsley. Serve the strained meat broth on the side in mugs. Discard the sausage broth.

5. Pass the green sauce to eat with the meats.

Green Sauce

1/3 cup finely chopped fresh Italian flat-leaf parsley

2 tablespoons minced red onion

1 teaspoon fresh lemon juice

1 teaspoon finely chopped garlic

1 teaspoon rinsed capers

2 tablespoons broth from the cooking pot

1 teaspoon Dijon mustard

Salt and freshly ground pepper, to taste

1/4 cup olive oil

In the jar of a blender, combine all the ingredients except the olive oil. Pulse to combine. With the blender running, add the olive oil in a thin steady stream until the sauce in thickened. It will not be as thick as mayonnaise. Serve in a bowl on the side.

Veal Scallops with Onions and Mushrooms

✓ *FREEZER READY*   ✓ *MAKE-AHEAD*

The next time you invite family or friends for a special dinner, try this simple but elegant dish of thinly sliced veal. Serve some steamed broccoli or asparagus on the side to make a colorful and delicious meal. If you want an alternative to rice, creamy mashed potatoes also make a great accompaniment.

¼ cup flour

Salt and freshly ground pepper, to taste

1 pound veal scallops ✳ ✳

¼ cup (4 tablespoons) butter

1 white onion, halved and thinly sliced (about 1½ cups)

1½ cups sliced mushrooms (from about 4 ounces)

2 teaspoons finely chopped garlic (from 2 medium cloves)

1 cup canned petite diced tomatoes, drained

½ cup beef broth

¼ cup dry white wine

½ cup heavy cream

2 tablespoons finely chopped fresh parsley

3 cups hot cooked rice

1. In a deep plate, mix the flour, salt, and pepper. Dust the veal with the seasoned salt and set aside.

2. Melt 2 tablespoons of the butter in a large, heavy skillet over medium-high heat. Cook the veal in the hot butter, 2 or 3 pieces at a time, until golden, about 1 minute per side. Remove to a large plate and set aside.

3. Melt the remaining butter in the same skillet over medium-high heat. Add the onion, mushrooms, and garlic. Cook, stirring, for 5 minutes. Stir in the tomatoes, broth, and wine. Season well with salt and pepper. Bring to a boil and cook until the sauce is reduced by nearly half, about 3 minutes.

4. Stir in the cream and parsley. Reduce the heat to medium-low and barely simmer for about 3 minutes. Return the veal to the pan and heat through, about 4 minutes more.

5. Serve very hot with rice on the side.

★**TIP:** If veal scallops or scaloppini are not available in your supermarket, cut veal cutlets into 3-inch pieces and use a wooden mallet to pound them very thin between two pieces of plastic wrap.

★**TIP:** Substitute very thin scallops of chicken breast if your family does not care for veal.

Mustard-Crusted Pork Roast

✓ *EASY PREPARATION*   ✓ *FREEZER READY*

This recipe is so simple, and the mustard crust is a tasty complement to the pork. Serve it to your family one night and have enough left over for hot pork sandwiches the next. The delicious mustard coating can be used when roasting, as is done here, or for grilling. I have often used this same coating for chicken, beef, and lamb, too. Mustard is a great complement to vegetables and meats. I always keep at least four or five different types of mustards in my refrigerator. They will keep up to one year.

6 tablespoons coarse-grained Dijon mustard

¼ cup horseradish Dijon mustard

2 tablespoons yellow mustard

2 tablespoons Dijon mustard

4 teaspoons chopped garlic (from 4 medium cloves)

2 teaspoons dried thyme

1 teaspoon cayenne pepper

2 tablespoons olive oil

2 tablespoons white wine vinegar

1 tablespoon chopped fresh rosemary

One 3-pound boneless center-cut pork loin roast *

Salt and freshly ground pepper, to taste

1. Preheat the oven to 375°F. In a small bowl, combine the mustards, garlic, thyme, cayenne, olive oil, vinegar, and rosemary. Beat well to blend.

2. Dry the pork with paper towels. Sprinkle with salt and pepper. Spread the mustard mixture on the pork. Set the pork on a rack in a roasting pan. Roast about 1 hour, until an instant-read thermometer inserted into the center registers 150°F. Let stand, tented in aluminum foil, for 15 minutes. Transfer the roast to a serving platter. Slice and serve. *

*TIP: Pork tenderloin is a quicker-cooking and leaner **alternative** to pork loin. This premium cut is almost fat-free and very moist, and is a much smaller roast in diameter so it requires less roasting time.

*TIP: If using 2 **pork tenderloins** for this recipe, roast them side by side for about 30 to 35 minutes. Let stand, covered, for 10 minutes before slicing.

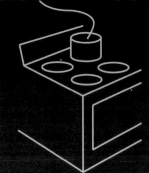

Beef, Pork, Veal, and Lamb Encores

Do you hesitate to cook a large roast because it seems complicated or time-consuming to prepare? Do you think you will be facing a week's worth of sandwiches and reheated meat and potatoes? Instead, think of it as an efficient way of cooking satisfying food that can be used again in a variety of dishes—you cook once to serve twice or more.

Another key benefit of having the main course thought out in advance also allows you to be a little more creative with appetizers or side dishes—if you have the time and interest.

Tips and Ideas for Meat Encore Meals:

- In the summer (or if you can grill year-round), add a tri-tip of beef to the grill while it is still hot from a cookout of steaks or chops. You will have meat on hand to make great tacos and the preparation requires very little effort.

- Most meats will roast in the oven or simmer in a slow cooker without a lot of fuss, such as Mustard-Crusted Pork Roast (page 111) or Cumin-Crusted Chuck Roast (page 101) from the previous chapter.

- Whenever you cook a roast, slice only what you think you will need for that meal. Leave the rest in one whole cooked piece. Refrigerate the leftover roast, tightly wrapped in plastic wrap. Once it has chilled completely, cut the meat into cubes or slices, or shred it by hand. It is easiest to handle when it is fully cooled. Freeze the meat in airtight resealable plastic bags for up to two months, or refrigerate for five days.

- Once you have your leftover meat on hand, using it will be easy. Stews can be created in minutes when cooked meat is folded into the vegetables and sauce.

- Shredded meat is fantastic in burritos and enchiladas, or added to a pasta dish. After all, ragus are classically rich dark meat sauces.

- Shredded or cubed meats can be turned into chili, or even added to a salad for lighter fare. Cold sliced meat can be the basis for a great cold platter, along with hard-cooked eggs, cucumbers, tomatoes, a wedge of great cheese, mixed greens—and of course, some excellent mustard.

We're all familiar with the tradition of enjoying special occasion leftovers for days to come. When I was young, my grandmother would roast the largest brisket she could find for a Friday night dinner. Saturday was warm brisket sandwiches on egg bread, and Sunday was a wonderful sautéed brisket with potatoes. It was served with ketchup and was always relished after a cherished family weekend.

Next time you are setting up your menus for the week, think about the added benefits you can reap by creating encores from a large piece of meat.

Spicy Pork Casserole

✓ *EASY PREPARATION*   ✓ *MAKE-AHEAD*   ✓ *TAKE-ALONG*   ✓ *FREEZER READY*

I like to make this nourishing dish using leftover pork for a special spicy cold-weather brunch main course. It is reminiscent of chiles rellenos, in a casserole. Serve it along with hot flour tortillas and a refreshing salad of fresh slices of oranges and red onions tossed with a tangy vinaigrette. It is equally good for lunch or as a simple Sunday supper before a busy week of school and work. See the **TIP** on page 97 for roasting poblano chiles.

★ TIP: A glass baking dish works well here because the glass will not react with eggs and change the color of the final dish. Glass also provides easy cleanup.

2 tablespoons olive oil

1 cup finely sliced onion (from 1 small onion)

2 cloves garlic, thinly sliced

1 cup finely chopped cooked pork

Salt and freshly ground pepper, to taste

8 ounces fresh poblano chiles, roasted, peeled, seeded, and cut in strips

2 cups shredded Monterey Jack cheese (from 8 ounces)

1½ cups half and half

1 tablespoon chili powder

5 large eggs

½ cup panko bread crumbs

1. Preheat the oven to 350°F.

2. Heat the olive oil in a medium skillet over medium heat, and cook the onion and garlic until soft, about 4 minutes. Stir in the pork. Remove from the heat and set aside. Season well with salt and pepper.

3. Spread half the onion and meat mixture in a well-greased 8-inch square baking dish. Arrange half the chiles over the vegetables.

Spread half the cheese on top. Season well with salt and pepper. Repeat the layers once more. ★

4. In a small bowl, beat together the half and half, chili powder, eggs, and panko bread crumbs. Pour over the casserole. Let stand 15 minutes. Bake 40 to 45 minutes, until puffed and golden. Remove from the oven and cool 10 minutes. Serve warm.

Irish Stew

✓ *EASY PREPARATION*   ✓ *MAKE-AHEAD*   ✓ *TAKE-ALONG*   ✓ *FREEZER READY*

I love to serve my family stew, but most stews take so long to cook that I would only make one on the weekend. This quick stew, in a light broth full of freshly cooked vegetables, eliminates that concern. Since it starts with cooked meat, it is ready in a fraction of the time, which makes it perfect for a busy family Saturday supper, or as weeknight reprise of a delicious Sunday roast.

1 tablespoon butter

1 tablespoon olive oil

2 medium carrots, thinly sliced (about 2 cups)

2 medium onions, peeled and chopped (about 2 cups)

1 teaspoon finely chopped garlic

1/4 teaspoon cayenne pepper

1 teaspoon ground cumin

1 teaspoon salt

1/2 teaspoon freshly ground pepper

2 cups beef broth or water

1 cup stout, such as Guinness

1/2 cup tomato paste

4 cups cooked cubed beef or lamb, at room temperature

1 tablespoon chopped fresh curly-leaf parsley

1 tablespoon chopped fresh chives

1. In a large stew pot, heat the butter and oil over medium high heat. Add the carrots and onions, and cook until soft, about 5 minutes. Add the garlic and cook, stirring, for 1 minute more.

2. Add the cayenne, cumin, salt, and pepper. Stir in the broth, stout, and tomato paste. Simmer until the vegetables are tender and the broth begins to thicken, 20 minutes.

3. Add the cubed meat, parsley, and chives. Heat through and serve. ✱

✱ TIP: Adding the cubed **meat** just before you are ready to serve keeps it tender. The longer you cook the meat in this fashion, the tougher it will get.

Roasted Beef or Lamb with Gnocchi and Sherry Cream Sauce

✓ *EASY PREPARATION*

This recipe takes advantage of the gnocchi (Italian potato dumplings) that are readily available in supermarkets and specialty stores. I love the cream sauce with the added richness of the Sherry. Children seem to love this Italian-style dish, a change from familiar pasta dishes, and one that comes together in less than 30 minutes. So next time there is leftover meat from a roast, save some for this recipe and you can have a delicious meal with little effort.

1 cup finely chopped shallots
(from about 12 medium cloves)

1 cup dry Sherry

1½ cups nonfat sour cream
or plain yogurt

1 cup low-salt beef broth

1 pound fresh gnocchi, cooked
according to package instructions *

2 cups cooked shredded beef or lamb

⅓ cup finely chopped curly-leaf
parsley

Freshly ground nutmeg, to taste,
for garnish

Sea salt and freshly ground pepper,
to taste, for garnish

1. In a large stockpot over high heat, combine the shallots and Sherry, and cook until the shallots are soft, about 6 minutes. *

2. Add the sour cream, broth, gnocchi, beef or lamb, and parsley. Stir until the gnocchi is hot, about 5 minutes, but do not boil the sauce as the sour cream has a tendency to curdle when boiled.

3. Spoon into bowls and serve garnished with the nutmeg, salt, and pepper.

✳ TIP: You will **find fresh gnocchi under vacuum-pack** in the deli or pasta section of the supermarket. You can store them at room temperature for several weeks, so add them to your pantry list. Generally gnocchi only requires boiling for 2 to 3 minutes to cook.

✳ TIP: Boiling the Sherry allows most of the alcohol to evaporate but **if you want an alcohol-free dish,** use non-alcoholic white wine or beer in this recipe.

Hearty Salad with Asian Dressing

✓ *EASY PREPARATION*   ✓ *TAKE-ALONG*

Cold salads incorporating meat are especially good in warm weather, or when family members are going to eat at staggered times. If everyone isn't eating together, arrange the salad on individual plates, cover with plastic wrap, and refrigerate until needed. The dressing isn't added until the last minute, so the salads will remain fresh and crisp.

SALAD

2 tablespoons olive oil

2½ cups sliced fresh mushrooms (from 8 ounces mushrooms) *

1 teaspoon finely chopped garlic

3 cups mixed salad greens (from 4½ ounces)

2 cups sliced cooked meat—beef, pork, or lamb *

1½ cups seeded and thinly sliced red bell pepper

1 cup very thinly sliced red onion

1 cup crumbled feta cheese with herbs (4 ounces)

2 small tomatoes, cut into wedges

DRESSING

¼ cup lime juice (from 2 medium limes)

1 shallot, very finely chopped (1½ teaspoons)

2 tablespoons light soy sauce

2 tablespoons chopped fresh cilantro

1 tablespoon hot sesame oil

¼ cup canola, peanut, or extra-virgin olive oil

Freshly ground pepper, to taste

1. For the salad: Heat the olive oil over medium heat in a medium, heavy skillet. Cook the mushrooms for 3 to 4 minutes, stirring from time to time. Add the garlic and cook 1 minute more. Drain and cool.

2. Arrange the greens on a serving platter. Distribute the meat over the greens in an attractive pattern. Spoon mushrooms into the middle of the platter. Mound the pepper and onion slices on top.

3. Sprinkle the salad with the cheese and garnish with tomato wedges.

4. For the dressing: Beat together the lime juice, shallot, and soy sauce. Beat in the cilantro, sesame oil, and salad oil. Season well with pepper.

5. Serve the dressing in a bowl alongside the salad so diners can drizzle at will.

∗TIP: Serve a mixture of **mushrooms** such as portobello, cremini, white, shiitake, or oyster for maximum flavor. Use whatever is on hand or available in your local supermarket.

∗TIP: The potential for **flexibility is one of** the best features of this salad. Use any type of leftover meat you have on hand, and let your family suggest the type of cheese and vegetables you add.

Pork or Beef Enchilada Pie

✓ TAKE-ALONG   ✓ MAKE-AHEAD   ✓ FREEZER READY

Make these enchiladas with leftover pork or steak, or just fill them with cheese for an easy main course. Children can easily help put these together, so set them up at the kitchen counter and let them help get dinner ready. Serve the enchiladas with refried beans and packaged Mexican style rice.

Twelve 6- or 8-inch fresh corn tortillas

1 tablespoon butter

1 large can red enchilada sauce

Salt and freshly ground pepper, to taste

3 cups shredded pork or beef

One 4-ounce can chopped green chiles

2 cups grated Monterey Jack cheese (from 8 ounces)

2 cups grated cheddar cheese (from 8 ounces)

3 cups shredded iceberg lettuce, for garnish

1/2 cup chopped cilantro leaves

Fresh salsa, for garnish

Sour cream, for garnish

Black olives, for garnish

1. Place the corn tortillas in a buttered pie plate. Cover the plate with plastic wrap and steam them on high in the microwave for 2 minutes.

2. Preheat the oven to 375°F. Butter a 9- × 13-inch glass dish. Pour the enchilada sauce into a shallow bowl and season with salt and freshly ground pepper. Spread a thin layer of the sauce on the bottom of the glass dish. Dip a tortilla in the sauce and place it on the right half of the glass dish. Place 2 or 3 pieces of pork on the tortilla, some of the chopped green chiles, and some of each of the cheeses. Top with

another tortilla that has been dipped in the sauce. Repeat the layering process until you reach the sixth tortilla. Finish with a layer of sauce and cheese. Make another enchilada pie on the left-hand side of the dish with the remaining ingredients.

3. Bake for 20 minutes or until heated through. Meanwhile, combine the lettuce with the cilantro in a medium bowl. Remove the enchilada pies from the oven and cut them into wedges to serve. Garnish with the lettuce, salsa, sour cream, and olives.

Stuffed Eggplant Mediterranean

✓ *MAKE-AHEAD* ✓ *TAKE-ALONG* ✓ *FREEZER READY* ✓ *SOMETHING SPECIAL*

Eggplant is an important part of nearly every Mediterranean cuisine. The combination of onion, garlic, and tomatoes goes wonderfully well with eggplant. Add some goat cheese, along with any leftover meat you may have in your refrigerator, and you have a main course redolent with the flavors of Greece. This is a wonderful way to introduce a new vegetable to the family. These can be prepared ahead of time, refrigerated, and baked just before serving.

2 medium eggplants, halved lengthwise

2 tablespoons olive oil, plus more for brushing the eggplant

1 cup finely chopped yellow onion

3 teaspoons finely chopped garlic (from 3 medium cloves)

1/2 cup chopped curly parsley

2 tablespoons chopped fresh oregano

3 fresh Roma tomatoes, halved lengthwise, seeded, and chopped

Salt and freshly ground pepper, to taste

1 cup finely chopped cooked lamb, beef, or pork

1 cup crumbled feta cheese (from 4 ounces) ✳

Extra-virgin olive oil

1. Preheat the broiler. Cut deep slashes in the flesh of the eggplant, being careful not to cut through to the skin.

2. Brush the cut side with olive oil, and broil the eggplant, cut side up, just until the flesh is softened, for 5 to 6 minutes. Cool the eggplant for 5 minutes, then scoop the flesh into a medium bowl and chop it finely. Reserve the shells.

3. Lower the heat to 375°F.

4. Heat 2 tablespoons of the olive oil in a heavy skillet. Cook the onion, stirring, until soft. Add the garlic, parsley, oregano, and tomatoes. Cook 3 minutes more. Season well with salt and pepper. Add the meat to the onion mixture. Toss. Stir into the chopped eggplant.

5. Stuff the mixture evenly into the eggplant shells. Divide the cheese among the eggplants and sprinkle on top. Drizzle with a little extra-virgin olive oil. ✳

6. Place the filled shells on a rimmed baking sheet. Bake for 45 minutes.

7. Serve hot, warm, or at room temperature, along with a tossed green salad and hot crusty bread.

✳ TIP: For a more Italian-flavored dish, substitute shredded mozzarella for the feta, and pass a bowl of grated Parmigiano-Reggiano to sprinkle on individual servings.

✳ TIP: If you want to **cook the eggplant later** in the day or at another time, it can be well wrapped in plastic wrap, sealed in a freezer bag, and frozen at this point. Bring to room temperature before baking.

Lamb and Brown Rice Salad

✓ *EASY PREPARATION*

How often do you accompany meals with rice? If your family is like mine, rice is a staple side dish, ready to soak up whatever flavors are on the dinner plate. The next time brown rice is on the menu, make extra for a delicious main dish salad in a day or two—meat is not the only staple that can be prepared in excess and used later. While you're in prep mode, make sure you store any unused herbs properly (see the **TIP** on page 105) and you will have all of the makings of a perfect quick encore meat dish. Serve it warm or cold garnished with tomatoes, or not, depending on your preference.

★TIP: Prepare this salad up to 1 day ahead. Cover and refrigerate and let the flavors mature.

1 cup canned garbanzo beans, drained and well rinsed

2 cups chopped tomatoes (from 2 medium tomatoes)

1½ cups chopped fresh Italian flat-leaf parsley

1 cup chopped green onions (from about 16 green onions)

1 cup fresh lemon juice (from about 8 medium lemons)

⅓ cup chopped fresh mint

⅓ cup extra-virgin olive oil

3 cups cooked brown rice, white rice, or other grain

Salt and freshly ground pepper, to taste

3 cups cooked cubed lamb or beef

1 large head butter leaf lettuce, well-washed, dried, leaves separated

1. In a large bowl, combine the garbanzo beans, tomatoes, parsley, green onions, lemon juice, mint, and the olive oil along with the rice. Season to taste with salt and pepper. Toss the lamb into the salad. ★

2. Serve the salad in a large salad bowl lined with the butter leaf lettuce.

Lentils with Shredded Beef and Feta Cheese

✓ *SOMETHING SPECIAL*   ✓ *EASY PREPARATION*

The combination of the meat, lentils, and vegetables make this the perfect all around family meal. If the kids won't go for the lentils, try cubed potatoes, or even rice in their place. Serve on a bed of greens.

1 cup Puy, or green, lentils ∗

¼ cup red wine vinegar

1 tablespoon chopped fresh garlic (from 3 medium cloves)

1 teaspoon cumin

½ teaspoon salt

1 teaspoon freshly ground pepper

¼ cup olive oil

1 cup finely chopped red onion

½ cup finely chopped red bell pepper

3 cups shredded beef, pork, or lamb

¼ cup chopped fresh mint leaves, for garnish

½ cup crumbled feta cheese (from 2 ounces), for garnish

3 cups well washed and dried baby greens (from 4½ ounces)

1. Pick over the lentils, rinse, and drain them. Add the lentils to a saucepan and cover them with water 2 inches over the lentils. Bring them to a boil over high heat. Reduce the heat and cook them uncovered, over medium-low heat until tender, about 45 minutes to 1 hour. Drain them immediately and place them in a bowl. ∗

2. In a small bowl, whisk together the vinegar, garlic, cumin, salt, and pepper. Whisk in the olive oil in a slow stream until the dressing thickens. Pour this over the warm lentils and toss to coat evenly. Add the onion, bell pepper, and shredded beef, pork, or lamb.

3. Season to taste with salt and pepper. Garnish with the mint and feta cheese. Season with more vinegar if necessary.

4. Serve the salad at room temperature, on a bed of crisp greens.

∗**TIP:** Green lentils have a more robust flavor than most of the other varieties. While they take a little longer to cook, they do not tend to fall apart when added to salads or other dishes.

∗**TIP:** Lentil cooking time may vary, depending on their size, type, and how fresh they are. If you are not using Puy lentils, be sure to check them from time to time to be sure not to cook them into a mush.

Gooey Cinnamon Rolls (page 169) and Santa Fe Mini Tortes (page 60)

Technique tip: For quick tomato prep, cut off the sides, discard core with seeds and juice

Technique tip: To keep mushrooms dry and fresh, store them in a paper bag in the refrigerator

Technique tip: Until needed, store cut carrots in cool water to keep them crisp

Carving chicken: Pull chicken leg away to cut through the bone (page 79)

Cut away whole chicken breast then slice it (page 79)

Handling dough for pastry spirals: Roll dough under plastic wrap (page 24)

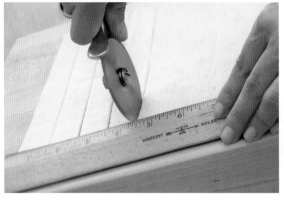
Measure dough before cutting (page 24)

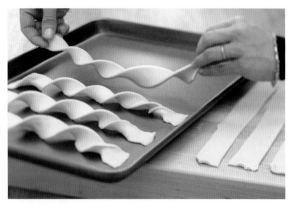
Space spirals evenly on baking sheet (page 24)

Creamy Roasted Tomato Soup (page 34)
with Herbed Cheddar Cheese Spirals (page 24)

Classic Roasted Chicken (page 78)

Chicken and Yogurt Pitas (page 89)

Classic Roasted Chicken (page 78)
and Orzo with Vegetables and Herbs (page 123)

Asian Broiled Salmon Salad (page 48)

Wine and Rosemary Marinated Leg of Lamb
with Kiwi Honey Salsa (page 105)

Lamb and Brown Rice Salad (page 119)

Cheesy Quesadillas (page 193)

Chocolate Chip Bread Pudding (page 177)
and Frothy Marshmallow Hot Chocolate (page 187)

Vegetables for Everyone

With constant media attention on the health benefits of vegetables, you may often feel pressured to make them a part of your everyday cooking, simply because they are "good" for you and your family. The key to getting your family to eat their vegetables—and to enjoy cooking them—is to come up with creative and interesting ways to cook them. And this chapter is a good place to start.

For best flavor and texture, serve vegetables in their proper season. Modern shipping and storage make it easy to obtain just about any vegetable any time of year, but no vegetable is fresh and sweet all year long. Those in their prime change from month to month so your menus should change, too. Look for the freshest seasonal vegetables wherever you do your vegetable shopping, whether at the farmers market, supermarket, or natural food store. If you see interesting produce that you don't recognize, ask the purveyors, store clerks, or even nearby shoppers for details—people often love to share their enthusiasm (and even recipes) for unheralded vegetables such as parsnips or beets in winter and special salad greens in summer.

When you bring produce home, clean and trim the vegetables. If you have time, steam the carrots, broccoli, or green beans and then place them in ice water to stop the cooking. Make sure you dry them well and they will keep for up to three days in the refrigerator, ready to stir-fry, to pop on the grill, or even to slide under the broiler for dinner.

Preparing vegetables the whole family will eat is an ongoing challenge. No matter whose turn it is to put dinner on the table, choosing a main course can be just the beginning of the project. The star dish needs a supporting cast and vegetable sides are a very important part of the show. Don't get stuck in a rut with the usual choices: Mashed potatoes, steamed broccoli, boiled carrots—all certainly have their place in your meals, just not every day.

Sometimes vegetable dishes can be the most important element of the meal, especially if you have a vegetarian in your family. The dishes in this chapter are hearty and filling enough to be stand-alones when someone doesn't want to indulge in the meat or fish course. Fresh vegetables combined with pasta or grains make excellent companions for grilled foods, and best of all, kids love them.

Family cooking and overall family health can benefit tremendously from well-prepared vegetables. Cooking methods are almost as important to the quality of vegetable dishes as freshness. I have long thought raw vegetables are somewhat overrated—for unless they are super-fresh, right out of the farm or garden, their flavor often needs to be coaxed gently forward. Steaming brings out more of their flavor, but roasting them in the oven or cooking them on the grill caramelizes them, rendering them sweet and succulent.

The vegetable dishes in this chapter can be made and enjoyed around your schedule. Tuck our Baked Onions (page 126) or Pumpkin and Onion Casserole (page 128) into the oven alongside a roasting chicken and dinner nearly cooks itself. Most of the recipes in this chapter can be prepared ahead and cooked when you're ready for dinner. These slower-cook dishes are great for comfortable family meals when there is time to linger over both cooking and eating. These dishes are excellent when just cooked, but are also delicious if the leftovers are frozen and reheated in the microwave for another meal when time is short. They can be brought out of the freezer and reheated really quickly.

Even if the first attempts with certain vegetables don't meet with much success, try serving them again, prepared slightly differently or with different dishes. New combinations or just repeat taste testing might bring the family around. Of course, also keep offering your family new vegetable choices. There will eventually be something on the menu that pleases your crowd.

Mixed Vegetables and Quinoa

✓ *MAKE-AHEAD*   ✓ *TAKE-ALONG*

Although similar in flavor and texture to a grain, quinoa is actually a distant relative of spinach. Sometimes called the super grain, quinoa supplies almost as much protein as milk. When cooked, the grains have the fluffy texture of cooked wheat, though they have just a hint of crunch as well.

1½ cups quinoa *

2 tablespoons olive oil

1 cup chopped white onion

1 teaspoon chopped garlic

½ cup chopped red bell pepper

1 cup chopped tomato

2 cups Italian parsley, leaves only, chopped

½ cup extra-virgin olive oil

¼ cup Cabernet wine vinegar, or other red wine vinegar

2 tablespoons fresh lemon juice

2 teaspoons salt

½ teaspoon freshly ground pepper

1. Bring 3 quarts of salted water to a boil in a 6-quart stockpot. Meanwhile, rinse the quinoa well to remove the natural resin. Add the quinoa to the boiling water. Return to a boil and cook, uncovered, for about 10 minutes. Drain the quinoa well in a colander, rinsing with cold water, then shake to dry it as much as possible.

2. While the quinoa is cooking, heat the olive oil in a medium skillet at medium-high heat. Add the onion and garlic to the pan. Cook, stirring, for 3 minutes and add the red bell pepper. Cook, stirring, 3 minutes more and add the tomato. Remove the mixture from the heat and set aside.

3. Spoon the grain into a large bowl and add the cooked vegetables, parsley, extra-virgin olive oil, vinegar, lemon juice, salt, and pepper. Toss well and serve. *

✳ TIP: Quinoa is pronounced "keen-wa." It is important to be sure to rinse quinoa well before you cook it. The soapy resin on the outside of the grain needs to be rinsed off before cooking or it leaves a bitter aftertaste.

✳ TIP: Serve the quinoa hot out of the pan or serve it cold, straight out of the refrigerator, like a chilled salad. It is great to take to a party, because you can also serve it at room temperature and it will still be as good as it was when you made it.

Orzo with Vegetables and Herbs

✓ MAKE-AHEAD　　✓ EASY PREPARATION　　✓ SOMETHING SPECIAL

Orzo, a small pasta shape that looks like grains of rice, is available in most supermarkets. While I like the texture of the pasta for this salad, you can also make this recipe with couscous or even cooked grains such as bulgur or brown rice. This dish goes very well with grilled fish or roasted chicken.

✻ TIP: Make the salad to this point **up to 12 hours ahead.** Cover and chill. Bring to room temperature before continuing.

2 cups broccoli florets

2 cups uncooked orzo (about 16 ounces)

1/4 cup finely chopped shallots (from 8 medium cloves)

1/2 cup chopped red bell pepper

11/4 cups chopped tomatoes (from 2 large tomatoes)

5 green onions, sliced, including 1-inch of the dark green

1/2 cup chopped fresh Italian parsley

4 teaspoons lemon zest (from 4 medium lemons)

11/2 teaspoons salt

1/2 teaspoon freshly ground pepper

1/4 cup plus 2 tablespoons fresh lemon juice (from 3 medium lemons)

1 teaspoon garlic, smashed to a paste with the back of a knife

3/4 cup olive oil

1. Bring salted water to a boil in a 4-quart saucepan. Add the broccoli and cook 3 minutes. Using a slotted spoon, transfer the broccoli to a strainer. Rinse with cold water and drain. Add the orzo to the same pot. Boil until tender, 8 to 10 minutes, drain and cool.

2. In a large bowl, mix together the orzo, broccoli, shallots, red bell pepper, tomatoes, green onions, parsley, and 2 teaspoons of the lemon zest. Season well with salt and pepper.

3. In a medium bowl, combine the lemon juice, the remaining 2 teaspoons lemon zest, and the garlic. Gradually whisk in the olive oil. Season to taste with salt and pepper.

4. Pour half of the dressing over the salad; toss to coat. ✻

5. Just before serving, toss the salad with enough remaining dressing to coat generously.

Cheese and Vegetable Enchiladas

✓ *MAKE-AHEAD*   ✓ *TAKE-ALONG*

Serve these delicious enchiladas with your favorite salsa, some shredded iceberg lettuce, and a bowl of packaged Mexican rice for a great family dinner. I have found that children love this south-of-the-border dish, and it is a quick and easy alternative to fast food.

1/4 cup olive oil

2 cups grated carrots
(from 2 medium carrots)

2 large ribs celery, thinly sliced
(about 1 cup)

1 cup sliced white onion *

3/4 cup stemmed, seeded, deveined, and sliced red bell pepper

2 cups canned tomatoes

2 tablespoons ground cumin

1 tablespoon chili powder

2 teaspoons chopped garlic
(from 2 medium cloves)

One 10 3/4-ounce can tomato puree

1 tablespoon lemon juice

Eight 10-inch flour tortillas

2 cups shredded smoked Gouda
(from about 8 ounces)

2 peeled, stoned, and thinly sliced avocados, for garnish

1 cup plain yogurt, for garnish

1 cup fresh salsa, for garnish

1. Preheat the broiler and line a broiler pan with aluminum foil. Heat the olive oil in a large skillet over medium heat. Add the carrots, celery, and onion and cook, stirring, for 2 minutes. Add the bell pepper to the pan and cook 3 minutes more.

2. Roughly chop the tomatoes and add them to the vegetable mixture along with the cumin, chili powder, garlic, tomato puree, and lemon juice. Simmer for 5 minutes more over high heat.

3. Puree one-third of the vegetable mixture in the jar of a blender with the lid on and covered with a dish towel to prevent spilling. Pour the resulting sauce into a flat dish. Dip each tortilla into the sauce, coating both sides. Place some of the reserved vegetables in the center of each tortilla and roll up. Place the rolled tortilla, seam side down, in the pan. Repeat with the remaining tortillas. Sprinkle the enchiladas generously with the cheese and broil for 2 to 4 minutes, until the cheese melts and begins to brown. *

4. Serve hot, with the sliced avocado, yogurt, and salsa to garnish.

*TIP: The easiest way to **slice a peeled onion** is to cut it in half from root to tip and lay each half cut side down on the cutting board. Slice across as thinly or thickly as you need.

*TIP: Bring the children into the kitchen to put the enchiladas together while you set the table.

Roasted Onions and Potatoes

✓ *EASY PREPARATION*   ✓ *MAKE-AHEAD*   ✓ *SOMETHING SPECIAL*

Roasting vegetables takes only a little preliminary preparation, after which they pretty much cook themselves. This is a perfect dish if you are looking for recipes the kids can get started before you return from work. They can peel or wash all the vegetables, dry them, toss them in the seasoned oil, and set them out in the roasting pan ready to pop in the oven when you get home. Serve them along- side almost any main course such as our Classic Roasted Chicken (page 78) or Jerked Roast Filet of Beef (page 103) for a hassle-free dinner that's ready when you need it.

1 pint red boiling onions, peeled (or white if red are not available) *

1 pound smallest new potatoes, washed

6 whole garlic cloves, still in the skins, or more (up to a whole head if you really love garlic; just remember to separate the cloves)

3 tablespoons olive oil

1½ teaspoons ground cumin

Salt and freshly ground pepper, to taste

2 tablespoons fresh rosemary leaves, chopped

1. Preheat the oven to 450°F.

2. In a large bowl, toss together the onions, potatoes, and garlic. Toss with the olive oil, ground cumin, salt and pepper, and chopped rosemary.

3. Spread the vegetables in the bottom of a roasting pan. Roast 35 to 40 minutes, tossing from time to time, until well browned and tender when pierced with a fork. *

4. Serve very hot.

★ **TIP:** The easiest way to **peel** these tasty **little onions** is to plunge them into a saucepan of boiling water, boil 1 minute, drain, cool slightly, and slip off the skins. You can always peel them right from the bag, but it will take you much longer.

★ **TIP:** Roast these vegeta- **bles ahead of time**, refrigerate, and then reheat them slowly in a 275°F oven for 15 to 20 min- utes.

Baked Onions

✓ *EASY PREPARATION*   ✓ *MAKE-AHEAD*

This ultra-simple, make-ahead vegetable dish goes very well with many main courses, especially Wine and Rosemary Marinated Leg of Lamb (page 105) or Mustard-Crusted Pork Roast (page 111). The sweetness of the onions combined with the herbs and cheese creates a succulent richly flavored dish. You can prepare these delicious onions whenever the mood strikes, as most of the ingredients come directly from your pantry and the shelves of your refrigerator. I think it will become a family favorite.

3 tablespoons butter, softened

Salt and freshly ground pepper, to taste

2 tablespoons chopped fresh oregano

1/4 cup panko bread crumbs

1/4 cup grated Parmigiano-Reggiano cheese

Pinch of cayenne pepper

4 large sweet onions (Vidalia are nice), peeled and halved across

1/3 cup beef or chicken broth, or dry white wine

1. Preheat the oven to 375°F.

2. In a small bowl, beat together the butter, salt, pepper, oregano, panko, cheese, and cayenne.

3. Slash the cut surface of each onion half in a crosshatch pattern. Spread the butter mixture thickly over the slashed surface, pressing it into the cuts. Arrange the onions, cut side up, in one layer in a glass or china baking dish. Pour the broth or wine around the onions. Cover with foil. *

4. Bake 1 hour. Uncover and bake 30 minutes more until lightly browned on top.

5. Let these onions stand for 10 minutes before serving as they are extremely hot. Serve hot or warm.

* TIP: Prepare these onions **ahead** to this point and refrigerate up to 8 hours. Bring to room temperature for about 20 minutes before continuing with the recipe. They are excellent take-alongs for your next multi-family potluck supper.

Oven Ratatouille

✓ *EASY PREPARATION*   ✓ *MAKE-AHEAD*   ✓ *FREEZER READY*

This dish contains all the wonderful fresh flavors of a southern French summer meal. I love to serve it at room temperature as a relish with cold meats, or warm with grilled chicken. It's also excellent hot, sandwiched between two thick fish fillets and baked for 20 minutes. This dish will bring more vegetables to your family table and is a great recipe to have in your repertoire because it is flexible, depending on your preferences and what's available.

3 tablespoons olive oil

2 large green bell peppers, seeded and cut into chunks

1 large sweet onion, cut into chunks

3 cloves garlic, sliced

1 cup pearl onions (frozen ones are fine)

3 large tomatoes, halved, seeded, and cut into chunks

1 large globe eggplant, well washed and cut into chunks

2 medium zucchini, cut into chunks

2 teaspoons finely chopped fresh thyme

1 tablespoon finely chopped fresh oregano

Salt and freshly ground pepper, to taste

1/2 cup dry white wine or vegetable broth

2 tablespoons chopped fresh parsley

1. Preheat the oven to 350°F.

2. Heat the oil in a deep oven-proof casserole with a tight-fitting cover (such as Le Creuset) over medium heat. Add the green peppers, chopped onion, and garlic. Cook, stirring, for 5 minutes.

3. Add the small onions, tomatoes, eggplant, zucchini, thyme, and oregano. Season well with salt and pepper. Pour in the wine or broth.

4. Bake 45 minutes, stirring several times. ✱ Uncover, reduce the heat to 325°F, add the parsley, and bake 20 minutes more. Serve hot, warm, or cold. ✱

✱ **TIP:** Shorten the first baking time by 20 to 25 minutes if you like your vegetables on the crunchy side.

✱ **TIP:** Make this dish ahead of time if you know you will be pressed for time later in the week. It refrigerates very well for up to 2 days and is easily reheated. Store it in a refrigerator-to-oven dish and pop it into a 350°F oven for 25 minutes. Serve right away. Or serve it cold as a relish with cold roast meat or poultry for a hot-weather meal.

Pumpkin and Onion Casserole

✓ *EASY PREPARATION*   ✓ *MAKE-AHEAD*   ✓ *FREEZER READY*

Bring the kids into the kitchen when Halloween is coming up (or anytime flavorful squashes and pumpkins are in season) and let them help prepare this delicious fall dish. The blending of the sweet and savory flavors of fruit, onions, and pumpkin make this a good accompaniment to roasted meats or poultry, especially pork or lamb. Although the pumpkin is familiar as a decoration, this is a wonderful opportunity to get the family to try it as a vegetable.

★ TIP: Substitute any hard squash, such as butternut, turban, or hubbard, for the pumpkin in this recipe. If it is late in the season, the outside of the squash may be quite hard; use a heavy knife or cleaver to make the first cuts.

1/3 cup (5 tablespoons) butter, plus more for buttering the dish

2 medium onions, chopped (about 3 cups)

1 teaspoon minced garlic

2 Granny Smith apples, peeled, cored, and cut into 1/2-inch cubes

3 pounds pumpkin, peeled, cut into 1-inch cubes ★

Salt and freshly ground pepper, to taste

1 1/2 teaspoons herbes de Provence

3/4 cup heavy cream

3/4 cup panko bread crumbs

1. Preheat the oven to 375°F. Generously butter a 1 1/2-quart ovenproof casserole.

2. Melt 3 tablespoons of the butter in a heavy skillet. Add the onions, garlic, apples, and pumpkin. Cook, tossing, for 5 minutes.

3. Toss with the salt, pepper, and herbes de Provence. Spoon the mixture into the casserole. Pour in the cream.

4. Bake, covered, 1 hour.

5. Combine the panko crumbs and the remaining 2 tablespoons butter. Remove the casserole from the oven and uncover. Spread the buttered crumbs over the top. Bake, uncovered, 20 minutes more, until lightly browned.

6. Let stand for 10 minutes before serving.

Roasted Tomatoes and Bulgur

✓ *MAKE-AHEAD*　　✓ *TAKE-ALONG*　　✓ *FREEZER READY*　　✓ *SOMETHING SPECIAL*

Bulgur wheat is a great alternative to rice or pasta. The rich flavor of the roast tomatoes adds a new dimension to this risotto-like dish and makes it the perfect accompaniment to your next grilled steak dinner. I find that children love the toasty flavor of bulgur—it reminds them of popcorn.

½ pound (about 5 medium) Roma tomatoes, halved lengthwise

3 cloves garlic, very thinly sliced

Salt and freshly ground pepper, to taste

3 tablespoons olive oil, plus more for drizzling

1½ cups chopped onion

¼ teaspoon ground cinnamon

¼ teaspoon ground ginger

½ teaspoon paprika

1 teaspoon salt

1 cup bulgur wheat

1½ cups chicken or vegetable broth

⅓ cup chopped fresh curly-leaf parsley

1. Preheat the oven to 475°F.

2. Arrange the tomatoes in one layer, cut side up, in a small roasting pan. Sprinkle with the garlic slices. Season with salt and pepper. Drizzle with olive oil. Roast 30 minutes, turning once about halfway through. ✻

3. Remove from the heat.

4. Heat the 3 tablespoons olive oil in a 3-quart covered saucepan. Add the onion and spices. Season with the 1 teaspoon salt and pepper. Stir until the onion is transparent and well browned around the edges. Sprinkle in the bulgur and stir to coat the grains with oil.

5. Stir in the broth, cover, and simmer for 20 minutes.

6. Stir in the parsley. Remove the pot from the heat, cover with a kitchen towel and then the pot lid. Let stand for 10 minutes.

7. Slice the tomato halves across into thick strips. Toss with the bulgur, along with any juices from the roasting pan.

8. Serve very hot, or at room temperature.

SERVING SUGGESTION

Split 2 Cornish game hens in half. Make 4 mounds of the tomato bulgur mixture on a baking sheet. Place 1 game hen half on each mound, skin side up. Brush with melted butter; season with salt and pepper. Bake for 1 hour at 375°F. Serve the remaining bulgur mixture hot, on the side.

✻ TIP: The **roasted tomato skins** will blister a bit as they cook, but don't worry, this adds to the **smoky flavor**. If the outdoor grill is already hot, this step can be done on the grill, adding another flavor layer to the dish.

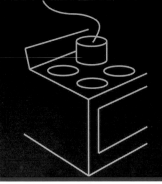

Ready and Waiting:
Slow Food

Slow food has finally come back into its own after years of emphasis on dishes that seem to be quick fixes but often require great amounts of last-minute preparation and cooking.

Although some of these recipes call for the slow cooker, slow cooking doesn't have to require a special appliance. In fact, some of the most flavorful, beloved dishes I have ever served are slow-cooked dishes made in regular pots cooked in regular ovens or in heavy stove-top casseroles. These require closer attention, but are unbelievably satisfying. They are often the dishes my family asks for again and again.

Slow cookers definitely do have a place in the busy cook's kitchen. Some of the slow cookers on the market today have removable parts so that they can be used not only as an appliance but as a pot on the stove or in a standard oven. If your old model has seen better days you may want to investigate these multipurpose cookers.

I have to confess that, as a cook and food-lover, I used to dread the idea of "dump and wait" recipes—I thought that somehow slow cooker recipes wouldn't result in tasty, satisfying food and all my contribution as a cook would be taken away. I thought that whatever foods went into them automatically came out bland and overcooked. But having my son in the house and my parents next door, I have come to see the need for a meal that is ready and waiting when the family is. Now, I put all kinds of interesting foods into the slow cooker just to see what the results will be—and they can be quite delicious.

Slow cooking can benefit from some minor preparation, if you have the time. Here are some preparation tips to make the most of your slow cooker:

- If you know that you are going to use the slow cooker tomorrow, begin by washing, trimming, and chopping the vegetables today.

- Before putting vegetables in the pot, cook them in a heavy skillet over low heat in a small amount of olive oil to bring out the sugars and flavors. Remember, you are not cooking them in the skillet, just starting the process.

- Brown meats in the skillet, too, for flavor. I read an article a few years back in a major food magazine that said, "Don't bother browning; it doesn't make much difference in the flavor." Well, it does. If you don't believe me, try it once with vegetables and meat unbrowned, then try them browned the next time. You will notice a big difference in the flavor and texture of the finished foods.

- Once you have put everything into the slow cooker, don't open it until the cooking time is up. Opening the lid will reduce the interior temperature and increase the cooking time.

Long cooking, whether on the stove, in the oven, or in a slow cooker, makes meat so tender it will melt in your mouth. Any leftovers can be used for hot sandwiches using crusty French bread or home-baked frozen biscuits. You can also spread leftovers in a baking dish, top with cheesy mashed potatoes, and serve a quick version of shepherd's pie. Or add to vegetable soup for a hearty winter dinner dish.

Once you try slow cooking it will become something you do routinely, because it is easier—and the results are delicious!

Corned Beef Dinner

✓ MAKE-AHEAD   ✓ READY AND WAITING

This New England favorite is a perfect cold-weather, one-pot meal. Peel and chop the vegetables ahead of time and they will be ready to add just before dinner. Put them in the pot, set the table, make a salad, and by the time everyone sits down, dinner is ready to serve.

1 piece corned beef, approximately 3½ pounds, rinsed, dried

Cold water

1 tablespoon plus 1 teaspoon pickling spice *

3 large garlic cloves, peeled, smashed to a paste with the back of a knife

2 sprigs fresh rosemary

4 carrots, peeled, cut into thirds

8 small red potatoes, peeled, halved

1 small head green cabbage, halved, each half cut into 4 wedges

Whole-grain mustard, for serving

Prepared horseradish, for serving

1. Place the corned beef in a 4-quart kettle and add enough cold water to cover the meat by 3 inches. Bring to a simmer over medium heat. Skim off any foam or scum that floats to the surface.

2. Add the pickling spice, garlic, and rosemary. Reduce the heat to low, cover, and continue to cook at a simmer for approximately 3 hours, until the meat is fork tender. If needed, add more hot water during the cooking process to keep the corned beef covered. Remove the corned beef from the cooking liquid and tent to keep warm. *

3. Add the carrots, potatoes, and cabbage to the cooking liquid and bring to a simmer over medium heat. With the lid slightly askew, cook the vegetables until tender, approximately 15 minutes.

4. As the vegetables are cooking, slice the corned beef across the grain into ⅛-inch slices. Arrange the slices on a heated platter and keep warm, tented, in a 200°F oven.

5. When all the vegetables are cooked, remove them from the kettle with a slotted spoon and arrange on the platter with the beef. Ladle a little hot cooking liquid over the top of the beef. Serve immediately with bowls of whole-grain mustard and prepared horseradish on the side. Pass a small pitcher of cooking liquid in case someone wants to remoisten their serving of beef.

* TIP: Pickling spices and herbs come inside some packages of corned beef. I prefer my own pickling spices, but this packet is easy to use and the taste of the final dish will still be good. There are several good commercial blends, but all contain some combination of coriander seed, cumin seed, mustard seed, fennel seed, peppercorns, and whole cloves, many with dried hot red pepper or crushed red pepper. Use one of these commercial mixtures, or experiment and come up with your own.

* TIP: The cooking water should barely simmer throughout cooking. Boiling the meat at too high heat will make it tough rather than tender.

New England Baked Beans

✓ *MAKE-AHEAD*   ✓ *TAKE-ALONG*   ✓ *FREEZER READY*

Originally a Native American dish, cooked in maple syrup rather than molasses, this economical, nutritious, and filling food became a staple dish for the first settlers when they arrived in rocky New England. Sometimes cooked overnight in stone-lined bean holes, or in cooling ovens (in which bread had been baked), this was the essence of real slow cooking. Our recipe, which takes advantage of already cooked canned beans, is ready in a fraction of the time without sacrificing flavor. Add a big salad, full of greens and chopped or sliced vegetables, along with some crusty whole-grain bread, and you will have a meal the whole family will enjoy.

★**TIP:** If you would rather a totally **hands-off dish**, pour all the ingredients into a slow cooker and cook on low for 4 hours.

¼ cup molasses

½ cup canned chopped tomatoes, with juices

3 tablespoons cider vinegar

2 tablespoons packed dark brown sugar

1½ teaspoons dry mustard

½ teaspoon salt

⅛ teaspoon cayenne pepper

½ pound smoky bacon, chopped, or more if you like

½ cup diced onion

3½ cups canned navy beans, rinsed and drained (from two 15-ounce cans)

1. In a small bowl, combine the molasses, chopped tomatoes, vinegar, brown sugar, dry mustard, salt, and cayenne pepper. Whisk to combine and reserve.

2. Cook the chopped bacon in a large skillet over medium heat until fat is rendered and the bacon is just beginning to crisp. Remove the bacon from the skillet with a slotted spoon and drain on paper towels.

3. Discard all but approximately 1 tablespoon of bacon fat. Returning the pan to the heat, add the onion to the fat and cook, stirring, until tender, 3 to 4 minutes.

4. Return the bacon to the skillet, add the beans and the reserved tomato mixture. Stir gently to combine the ingredients and bring to a simmer. Reduce the heat to low, cover and cook 30 minutes to allow the beans to absorb liquid, stirring from time to time. The beans should be thick, not soupy. Serve hot. ★

Ropa Vieja

✓ *MAKE-AHEAD*   ✓ *TAKE-ALONG*   ✓ *READY AND WAITING*   ✓ *FREEZER READY*

"Old Clothes" or "rags" may not sound very appetizing, but that's the literal name of this traditional and tantalizing Cuban dish of long-cooked shredded beef with a spicy tomato sauce and vegetables. The beef absorbs lots of flavor. As with many traditional dishes, the core ingredients—flank steak, onions, peppers, and garlic, along with tomatoes and herbs—remain the same, though additions—such as our jalapeño and olives—can vary greatly. Even though the ingredient list is long, it isn't expensive, and this recipe is actually very easy to prepare and requires little hands-on time. The result is a meltingly tender, flavorful dish that will impress and delight. Children love it served in soft sandwich rolls—sort of like a Sloppy Joe; adults prefer it with rice. Obviously, this isn't a weeknight dish, unless most of the prep is done the night before, but it makes a wonderful winter weekend family dinner.

✷ TIP: If you don't have a **slow cooker**, slowly braise the meat in a heavy covered casserole, such as Le Creuset, in a 325°F oven for 2½ to 3 hours. If you have an older slow cooker with only a low heat setting, cook the flank steak for 8 or more hours, until it is nearly falling apart.

✷ TIP: **Prepare the ropa vieja to this point** up to 2 days before it will be served. Simply store the beef in the braising liquid in the refrigerator.

2½ pounds flank steak, trimmed of any excess fat, cut in half across the grain

4 cups water

1 medium onion, peeled, chopped (about 1 cup)

2 medium carrots, peeled and chopped (¾ to 1 cup)

2 celery ribs, chopped (about 1 cup)

1 bay leaf

3 garlic cloves, peeled and lightly crushed

2 teaspoons chopped fresh oregano

3 teaspoons ground cumin

2½ teaspoons salt

¼ teaspoon whole black peppercorns

2 tablespoons olive oil

1 small red onion, peeled and sliced (about ¾ cup)

½ large green bell pepper, seeded and cut into ¼-inch strips

1 small red bell pepper, halved, seeded, and cut into ¼-inch strips

1 jalapeño, seeded and finely chopped

1 tablespoon chopped garlic (from 3 cloves)

2 cups beef braising liquid or beef broth, plus additional if desired

1½ cups chopped tomatoes, with juice (from about 2 medium tomatoes)

¼ cup tomato paste

⅓ cup sliced pimento-stuffed Spanish olives

¼ teaspoon ground pepper

Juice of ½ lime

8 lime wedges, for garnish

½ cup sour cream mixed with ½ teaspoon lime zest and a pinch of salt, for garnish

4 cups hot freshly cooked rice

1. In a large slow cooker, place the beef, water, onion, carrots, celery, bay leaf, 3 crushed garlic cloves, 1 teaspoon of the oregano, 1½ teaspoons of the cumin, 1 teaspoon of the salt, and the peppercorns. Cover and cook on high for 4 to 5 hours, until the meat is completely tender. ✷

2. Remove the meat from the liquid and set it aside. Strain the cooking liquid through a mesh strainer and reserve, discarding the cooked vegetables, bay leaf, and peppercorns. Skim any fat from the cooking liquid. ✷

3. Shred the beef using two forks or your fingers. Warm the

(continues on page 134)

olive oil in a large skillet over medium heat. When the oil is hot, add the red onion, peppers, and the remaining 1½ teaspoons salt, stirring to combine. Cook until the vegetables are barely tender, about 6 minutes. Add the 1 tablespoon chopped garlic, the remaining 1 teaspoon oregano, and the remaining 1½ teaspoons cumin and cook 1 minute more.

4. Add the shredded beef to the skillet, along with the 2 cups reserved cooking liquid, the chopped tomatoes, and the tomato paste, stirring well to combine. Bring to a simmer and cook for 30 minutes. Stir in the olives, ground pepper, and lime juice. Add more cooking liquid if the mixture is too thick. Adjust the seasoning, adding salt and pepper if desired, and serve hot, garnished with lime wedges and sour cream, and lots of freshly cooked white rice.

Grillades and Grits

✓ *READY AND WAITING*   ✓ *SOMETHING SPECIAL*

Special occasions at my grandmother's house meant grillades and grits for breakfast. The tender browned pieces of beef cooked in the fragrantly rich brown sauce filled the house with mouthwatering smells. No one was late to table when the wonderful aroma of this rich, delicious dish wafted up the stairs. The dish must have brought back wonderful memories of her New Orleans childhood, and she enjoyed them every bit as much as we did. While you can cook it on top of the stove in an hour, you can also simmer it in your slow cooker for five to six hours on low. Nowadays we don't just confine this to breakfast; it makes a terrific family dinner as well.

★ TIP: Creole seasoning is a spicy commercial mixture of herbs and seasonings usually found in the spice section of the supermarket.

¼ cup flour

½ teaspoon dried thyme

1½ teaspoons salt, plus more to taste

¾ teaspoon pepper, plus more to taste

6 strips bacon, chopped

2 pounds veal or beef round steak, sliced into strips

2 tablespoons Creole seasoning ★

1 cup diced onion

½ cup diced celery

½ cup sliced green onions (from 7 or 8 onions)

2 teaspoons minced garlic (from 2 medium cloves)

½ cup red wine

1 cup beef stock

1 cup chopped tomato

1 bay leaf

½ teaspoon Worcestershire sauce

¼ cup chopped fresh curly-leaf parsley (4 tablespoons)

4 cups (1 quart) water

1 cup quick grits (not instant)

Pinch cayenne pepper

1 tablespoon butter

1. In a medium bowl, combine the flour, thyme, 1 teaspoon of the salt, and ½ teaspoon of the pepper.

2. Heat a large skillet (not nonstick) over medium-high heat and add the bacon. Cook until the fat is rendered and the bacon is just crispy and brown. With the pan off the heat, use a slotted spoon to remove the bacon and drain on paper towels. Reserve for garnish. Remove and reserve all but approximately 3 tablespoons of the bacon fat.

3. While the bacon is cooking, season the sliced meat with salt, pepper, and Creole seasoning.

4. Return the pan to the heat and dredge the slices of meat in the seasoned flour, coating each piece and shaking off any excess flour. Add the meat slices to the hot pan in batches, and cook until nicely browned on both sides. As slices are browned, remove them from the pan and reserve on a plate.

5. When all the meat has been cooked and set aside, reduce the heat to medium and add a little more bacon fat to the pan, if necessary. Add the onion, celery, and a pinch of salt, stir and cook

(continues on page 136)

until translucent, approximately 5 minutes. Stir in the green onions and garlic and cook 2 minutes more. Add the red wine, scraping the bottom of the skillet to remove all caramelized bits. Stir in the stock, tomato, bay leaf, Worcestershire sauce, and the parsley. Bring to a simmer, and add the reserved meat and any accumulated meat juices to the sauce. ★

Continue to cook, partially covered, until the meat is very tender, 30 to 40 minutes. If the gravy gets too thick, add water to thin slightly, but it should be thick and rich looking.

6. Prepare the grits while the meat is simmering: Bring the water and the remaining ½ teaspoon salt to a boil in a large saucepan over medium-high heat. Add the grits in a slow steady stream, whisking constantly to prevent lumps from forming. Reduce the heat to low and cook, stirring occasionally, until thick and creamy, about the same consistency as soft polenta, about 5 minutes. Season with the remaining ¼ teaspoon pepper, the cayenne pepper, and butter. Cover and reserve.

7. Taste the grillades and add more salt and pepper if desired. Serve warm spooned over soft grits in a shallow bowl, garnished with the reserved bacon.

VARIATION

If introducing grits to your family seems more than you want to cope with—though the flavor and texture are very much the same as polenta—grillades and their accompanying gravy go very well with rice, noodles, polenta, or even garlicky mashed potatoes.

★ **TIP:** For a hands-off **finish**, pour everything into the slow cooker at this point and cook for 5 to 6 hours on low.

Beef Goulash

✓ *MAKE-AHEAD*   ✓ *TAKE-ALONG*   ✓ *READY AND WAITING*

Not just another stew, this delicious slow cooked dish is seasoned with paprika, which adds Hungarian flavor. It's terrific for casual entertaining, though you will find your family will enjoy it any time you prepare it. A bowl of green beans with mushrooms, your favorite salad, and crusty rolls will make the meal complete with minimum effort.

*TIP: For less fuss, pour all ingredients into a slow cooker at this point and cook on low for 6 to 8 hours.

2 pounds stew meat, cut into 1-inch cubes

Salt and freshly ground pepper, to taste

3 tablespoons olive oil

1 medium onion, sliced

1 green bell pepper, halved, seeded, and cut into 1-inch cubes

2 teaspoons minced garlic (from 2 medium cloves)

1 tablespoon paprika, plus more for garnish

1 teaspoon chili powder

1 bay leaf

Pinch cayenne pepper

2 cups water or chicken stock

2 tablespoons tomato sauce

1/3 cup sour cream

1 tablespoon flour mixed with a little cold water, to thicken goulash, if desired

1 pound egg noodles, cooked, seasoned with 2 tablespoons butter and a touch of nutmeg

1. Season the beef cubes with salt and freshly ground pepper.

2. Warm 2 tablespoons of the olive oil in a 4-quart stew pot over medium-high heat. Add the seasoned meat in one layer and cook until lightly browned on all sides. If all of the stew meat will not fit in an even layer, cook the meat in two batches. Do not crowd the pieces of meat or it will stew in its own juices rather than brown. As the beef browns, remove the pieces to a bowl and reserve. When all the meat is cooked and reserved, add the remaining olive oil and reduce the heat to medium.

3. Add the onion, green pepper, and a pinch of salt to the pot and cook until just beginning to soften, 4 to 5 minutes, stirring often. Add the garlic, paprika, chili powder, bay leaf, and cayenne. Cook, stirring continuously, until you can smell the spices. Add the water or stock and tomato sauce and stir well to combine. Return the reserved meat and any accumulated juices to the pot, stir to combine, and bring to a simmer. Reduce the heat to low, cover, and cook at a simmer for about 1½ hours, until the meat is very tender. *

(*continues on page 138*)

4. Stir in the sour cream. Remove the bay leaf and adjust the seasoning with salt and freshly ground pepper.

5. If the sauce is too thin, add a little of the flour/water mixture and bring just to a simmer but do not boil or the sour cream will curdle. The sauce will thicken within 2 minutes of adding the flour. Add more flour/water mixture, if desired. Skim any fat or foam off the surface of the goulash.

6. Serve hot garnished with a sprinkle of paprika along with a bowl of warm buttered egg noodles that have been seasoned with a pinch of nutmeg.

Hands-Off Pasta Sauce

✓ EASY PREPARATION ✓ MAKE-AHEAD ✓ READY AND WAITING

For this family pleaser, you need about 15 minutes of hands-on preparation and then you can return to whatever you were doing. Dinner nearly cooks itself. Freeze half of the sauce in several one-cup containers and you will have dinner in minutes on a no-time-to-cook work night. There are many ways to use this delicious tomato sauce—with pasta, of course—but it is also delicious spooned over roast fish fillets or triangles of fried polenta. Or pour it around browned pork chops, cover, and braise until tender.

2 tablespoons olive oil

1 cup diced onion

Salt, to taste

1/2 teaspoon chopped fresh oregano

1 teaspoon chopped fresh rosemary

1 1/2 teaspoons chopped garlic
(from 2 small cloves)

1 bay leaf

1/4 cup white wine

3/4 cup chicken or vegetable stock

2 cups tomato sauce

3 cups chopped canned tomatoes
with juice

1/4 cup capers, rinsed

1/8 cup pitted chopped Kalamata
olives

1/8 cup chopped fresh Italian
flat-leaf parsley

Parmigiano-Reggiano cheese,
for garnish

1. In a large skillet, warm the olive oil over medium heat. When hot, add the onion, sprinkle with salt, and stir to combine. Cook until soft, 5 to 7 minutes.

2. Add the chopped fresh herbs, garlic, and bay leaf and cook 1 minute. Add the white wine, bring to a boil, and reduce by half. Add the stock, tomato sauce, and chopped tomatoes.

Stir to combine the ingredients, bring to a simmer, and reduce the heat to low. Partially cover and cook 1 1/2 hours. ✱

3. Stir in the capers, olives, and fresh parsley. Season again with salt and pepper if necessary, and serve with your choice of pasta garnished with plenty of grated Parmigiano-Reggiano cheese. ✱

✱ TIP: If you want a truly **no-watch sauce**, pour the combined ingredients into a slow cooker and cook on low for 4 to 6 hours. The end result will be thick and rich.

✱ TIP: **Fusilli, ziti, rigatoni, spaghetti, angel hair, and linguine** are just some of the pasta possibilities that can be used here. While Italians often confine chunky sauces like this to cut pastas with nooks and crannies, and creamy smooth sauces to long pasta, this sauce seems to cross the line— especially here in the U.S. Use whatever pasta you and your children like best.

Fall-off-the-Bone Pork Ribs

✓ MAKE-AHEAD   ✓ TAKE-ALONG   ✓ READY AND WAITING   ✓ SOMETHING SPECIAL

One of the shortcomings of many rib recipes is that the meat ends up dry and tough. Not with this dish—the method of browning the ribs first and finishing them in a slow cooker covered in sauce ensures that the ribs become succulently tender, spicy, and delicious. This is one of my family's favorites. Make these ahead if you like and reheat for dinner the next day.

1 tablespoon paprika

1 tablespoon chili powder

1/4 teaspoon cayenne pepper

1 teaspoon dry mustard

1 teaspoon ground cumin

1/2 teaspoon dried oregano

2 tablespoons kosher salt

1 teaspoon freshly ground pepper

1 rack pork spare ribs, about 4 pounds, or the same weight of baby back ribs, rinsed and dried

1/4 cup apple cider vinegar

1/4 cup packed brown sugar

1/2 cup lemon juice (from 3 to 4 large lemons)

2 cups bottled chili sauce (from two 12-ounce bottles)

2 teaspoons minced fresh curly-leaf parsley

1 teaspoon Dijon mustard

1/4 cup Worcestershire sauce

Salt and freshly ground pepper, to taste

1. In a small bowl, combine the paprika, chili powder, cayenne pepper, dry mustard, cumin, oregano, kosher salt, and freshly ground pepper. Rub this spice mixture generously over both sides of the spare ribs, place in a baking dish, and cover with plastic wrap. Marinate for at least 1 hour at room temperature or, preferably, refrigerate overnight.

2. Preheat the oven to 400°F.

3. Arrange the spare ribs on a rack set in a baking pan and place in the preheated oven. Roast the ribs 15 to 20 minutes, until browned. Turn the ribs over and brown on the other side, 15 minutes more.

4. While the ribs are browning, in a bowl, combine the vinegar, brown sugar, lemon juice, chili sauce, parsley, mustard, and Worcestershire sauce and whisk to combine. Season with salt and freshly ground pepper.

5. Remove the pan from the oven and, when cool enough to handle, cut the ribs into individual serving pieces of 2 or 3 ribs each. Put the ribs in the slow cooker and pour over the sauce mixture, stirring gently to coat them with the sauce. Cover the slow cooker and cook on low for 6 hours or until the meat is falling-off-the-ribs tender.

SERVING SUGGESTION

Serve these ribs hot with your choice of accompaniment such as coleslaw or potato salad, or with lots of hot buttered noodles to catch all the delicious sauce.

Swiss Steak

✓ *MAKE-AHEAD*   ✓ *READY AND WAITING*

I find this very economical and filling dish is just the thing for satisfying teenage hungers, especially when they've been stoked by sports practice after a long day of school. And it is as easy as it is tasty—tender beef slowly simmered in a tomato-based sauce. Don't forget to serve your favorite green vegetable and pass plenty of crusty bread. A fresh fruit cobbler would be an excellent way to finish the meal.

2 pounds boneless top or bottom round steak, cut into eight 4-ounce portions

4 tablespoons flour

1 teaspoon salt, plus more to taste

¼ teaspoon freshly ground pepper, plus more to taste

½ teaspoon paprika

3 tablespoons olive oil

¾ cup diced white onion

½ cup diced green pepper

1 cup canned diced tomatoes

½ cup water or stock

1. Place a large piece of plastic wrap on the counter and put 4 steaks on the plastic wrap, leaving at least 2 inches between each steak. Place another large piece of plastic wrap over the steaks. Firmly pound each steak to an even ½ inch thickness. Remove the pounded steaks and reserve. Repeat with the remaining steaks.

2. Combine the flour, 1 teaspoon salt, ¼ teaspoon pepper, and paprika on a plate. Season each steak with salt and freshly ground pepper. Lightly coat the steaks in the seasoned flour, knocking off any excess.

3. Warm 2 tablespoons of the olive oil in a large skillet over medium-high heat. When the oil is hot, add the prepared steaks, 4 at a time, and cook until browned, 3 to 4 minutes. Turn the steaks over and brown the other side. Remove from the pan and reserve.

4. In the same pan, reduce the heat to medium-low and add the remaining tablespoon of olive oil. Add the onion and green pepper, stirring to combine. Season with salt. Cook until tender, about 5 minutes, being careful not to brown. Add the tomatoes and water or stock, scraping to remove any caramelized bits from the bottom of the pan.

5. Return the seared steaks to the skillet, nestling them into the sauce. Bring to a simmer, cover, and cook over very low heat for 1½ to 2 hours, until the steaks are fork tender.

SERVING SUGGESTION

Serve the steaks and sauce spooned over steamed rice, garlic mashed potatoes, or your favorite pasta.

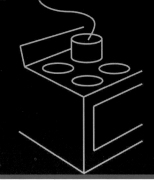

Make Aheads
for the Freezer

If you are making the effort to cook today, why not cook enough for the freezer at the same time? Every time I plan ahead and cook extra, at later meals, I am so glad that I did. You might think at first that most foods won't freeze well. The truth is that many foods freeze very well at one stage of preparation or another. With a bit of planning, freezing meals will give you the opportunity to eat well, even when you don't have time to cook.

Be sure to read the recipe carefully in order to tell if something freezes well. Is there any cream in it? Fresh herbs? Are these dishes that are fully cooked or would it be better to freeze them uncooked? For instance, I make a butternut squash puree and then freeze it. Later, I can finish it with broth and cream once I have thawed the mixture and begin final heating. Add a little fresh sage and I have made a perfect soup from the frozen base. The same puree can become a great side dish just by thawing it, mixing in a little fruity olive oil, heating, and serving.

At my house we never eat an entire pan of lasagna, pot of chili, or casserole of chicken tetrazzini. I freeze the remainder in aluminum loaf pans just large enough for dinner for three. Then, when time is short, I can reheat a delicious main course, add a salad and some bread, and dinner is on the table.

Here are some make and freeze tips:

- Buy disposable aluminum foil trays, arrange enough servings of a dish (such as the enchiladas) for one meal in each, and freeze.

- Have some of the chili or other dish you make in a large quantity for dinner, then freeze the remaining in single one-cup containers to take to work for lunch.

- If space is at a premium in your freezer, spoon or ladle your required portions into heavy resealable plastic bags, seal them, arrange them flat on a cookie sheet, and freeze. Once frozen, the bags can be stacked in a minimum of space.

- Of course, it is imperative to label each container or bag as carefully as you can—so at a later date you don't pull an unlabeled container out of the freezer and have no idea what's inside.

- If you are freezing cookies, breads, or cakes, wrap them first in plastic wrap and then seal them in plastic freezer bags.

- Always thaw what you have made in the container in which you froze to retain as much moisture as possible and to prevent any cross contamination between foods in the refrigerator.

- Always thaw in the refrigerator if the recipe calls for you to thaw before cooking.

The object is to lighten your load on nights when you don't have time to think about cooking, by planning how you can expand a recipe to be used creatively later on. Or perhaps you don't want to think in detail so far in advance. Then just make extra, store the additional servings, and then one day, a few days or weeks after you've made and served the original dish, you will be thrilled to open your freezer to find that you have something delicious there that will inspire you to create something special for dinner.

Corned Beef Hash

✓ *MAKE-AHEAD*　✓ *FREEZER READY*

This was a childhood staple at our house. Once we had enjoyed the traditional boiled corned beef dinner on St. Patrick's Day, the next best meal would be corned beef hash made from the leftovers. It is hearty enough for teenaged appetites, comforting enough for anyone, and it is equally as good for breakfast or brunch as it is for dinner. Best of all—it can be frozen for at least a month, ready to pull out and reheat at the last minute.

3 tablespoons butter

1 cup minced onion

2 cloves garlic, thinly sliced (optional, but good)

2 cups finely chopped cooked corned beef *

2 cups chopped peeled cooked potato (from about 3 medium potatoes)

Salt and freshly ground pepper, to taste (be generous with the pepper)

2 tablespoons chopped fresh curly-leaf parsley

2 tablespoons heavy cream

1. Melt the butter in a deep heavy skillet over medium heat. Add the onion. Cook until tender, about 6 minutes. Stir in the garlic if you are using it and cook 1 minute more.

2. Add the beef and potatoes and season with salt and pepper. Stir in the parsley and heavy cream. Cook over medium-low heat without stirring until the bottom browns and begins to form a crisp crust, about 10 minutes. Turn the mixture carefully and continue to cook for 5 minutes more. Serve hot. *

SERVING SUGGESTION

Serve with ketchup on the side, along with a green salad and crusty bread.

VARIATION

Instead of turning the hash after 10 minutes, make 4 deep indentations in the surface of the hash. Break 1 egg into each hollow. Slide the skillet into a preheated 450°F oven and bake 10 minutes, until the whites are set and the yolks are still liquid. Serve each diner a portion of the hash with the egg on top. This makes a wonderful winter brunch dish.

★ TIP: Corned beef **tends to crumble** when hot. It is much easier to chop or dice the beef while it is still chilled right from the refrigerator.

★ TIP: **Freeze the hash** in plastic containers for later enjoyment. Thaw in the refrigerator, or in the microwave.

Stuffed Flank Steak with Roasted Peppers and Feta Cheese

MAKES 8 SERVINGS

✓ MAKE-AHEAD   ✓ TAKE-ALONG   ✓ FREEZER READY   ✓ SOMETHING SPECIAL

This is the perfect make-ahead meal. While you are at it make twice as much; the recipe is easy to double and you will have enough for an instant party at any time. Just fill the flank steak, tie and sear it, then freeze. Whenever you are ready, thaw it in the refrigerator then roast it in the oven. Serve with a salad and steaming hot rice for the perfect meal.

★ TIP: Substitute canned chopped green chiles for the serrano if time is an issue.

4 cups fresh cleaned spinach leaves with the stems removed (from about 6 ounces)

2 cups crumbled feta cheese (from about 8 ounces)

1/3 cup plain bread crumbs

2 teaspoons dried oregano

2 tablespoons seeded, deveined, minced serrano chile ★

1/3 cup plus 2 tablespoons olive oil

2 butterflied flank steaks (about 2 pounds—have the butcher in your supermarket do this for you)

Salt and freshly ground pepper, to taste

4 jarred roasted red or yellow bell peppers

1. Cook the spinach in a lightly oiled, hot skillet over high heat, until it is just wilted, 2 to 3 minutes. Remove the skillet from the heat and press out any excess moisture from the spinach.

2. Combine the spinach, feta, bread crumbs, oregano, chile, and 1/3 cup olive oil in a food processor or blender and puree. Set the puree aside.

3. Open the steak up like a book, and season it with salt and pepper. Spread 1/4 of the puree over the meat. Place 2 of the roasted peppers over the puree and then spread another 1/4 of the puree over the peppers. Starting at the long side of the meat, roll the steak up. Tie it with kitchen twine every 2 inches. Repeat with the other flank steak.

4. Brush the meat rolls with the 2 tablespoons olive oil. Heat a large skillet on high heat, place the flank steak rolls in the pan, and sear the meat, browning it on all sides. Remove the meat and cool.

5. Wrap the meat tightly in plastic wrap and then in a resealable plastic bag. Freeze.

6. Up to 24 hours before you are ready to use, remove the meat from the freezer and thaw in the refrigerator.

7. Preheat the oven to 375°F. Place the meat in a roasting pan. Roast for 30 minutes for medium rare, or to desired doneness. Cool the meat slightly and then slice into 1/4-inch slices.

SERVING SUGGESTION

Toss your favorite mixed greens in a simple garlic vinaigrette. Mound a small bed of the salad on individual dinner plates and arrange several slices of the stuffed steak on top. Pass your favorite mustard on the side.

Chili Pie

✓ *EASY PREPARATION*   ✓ *MAKE-AHEAD*   ✓ *READY AND WAITING*   ✓ *FREEZER READY*

Make this delicious pie right when you are ready to serve it, or put the ingredients into the slow cooker when you leave for work. Turn it into a casserole or deep-dish pie plate when you get home, pop on the crust, and bake it while you set the table and make a salad. Easy as pie if you use refrigerated pastry. Freeze in disposable pie plates before baking. Bake still frozen, just add 10 to 15 minutes to the baking time.

1 pound ground beef (90% lean)

1 small onion, chopped (about 1 cup)

2 teaspoons minced garlic (from 2 cloves)

Salt and freshly ground pepper, to taste

2 teaspoons ground cumin

1 tablespoon chili powder, or more to taste

Two 14½-ounce cans diced tomatoes with chiles and the juice

One 15-ounce can red kidney beans, drained and well rinsed

1 cup beef broth

¼ cup chopped fresh cilantro

1 refrigerated pie pastry, flattened

Corn meal

6 wedges cheddar cheese, for garnish

Sour cream, for garnish

1. Preheat the oven to 425°F.

2. Brown the beef in a heavy skillet over medium heat, breaking up the chunks, for about 5 minutes. Remove from the skillet and set aside.

3. In the same skillet cook the onion and garlic over medium heat until tender, about 6 minutes. Season with salt and pepper. Stir in the cumin and chili powder. Cook, stirring, for 1 minute.

4. Stir in the tomatoes, reserved beef, and beans. *

5. If you are not cooking this in the slow cooker, lower the heat, add beef broth, cover, and simmer the mixture for 40 minutes. Stir in the cilantro. Cook a few minutes, uncovered, if the mixture is too liquid.

6. Pour the chili into a 9-inch deep-dish pie plate. Cover with the pastry and form a crust at the edges. Cut steam holes in the crust and sprinkle with corn meal. *

7. Bake 30 minutes, until the crust is golden brown. Serve hot, each serving garnished with a wedge of cheddar cheese and a dollop of sour cream.

SERVING SUGGESTION

A salad of sliced onions, oranges, and beets, garnished with more chopped fresh cilantro, goes very well with this pie.

VARIATION

For a different effect, unroll one 8-ounce can refrigerated crescent rolls, separate into the triangles, and arrange them on top of the chili, points meeting at the middle. Crimp the crust at the edges. Bake at 375°F for 20 minutes. Serve hot with sour cream.

✶TIP: At this point you can **spoon the mixture into the slow cooker,** add 1 cup beef broth, and cook on low for 6 to 8 hours. Spoon into a deep-dish pie plate, cover with pastry, and continue with the recipe.

✶TIP: To freeze, wrap the unbaked pastry-covered pie tightly in plastic wrap and then in a resealable freezer bag or aluminum foil. To cook, remove all wrapping and bake directly from the freezer on a baking sheet in a preheated oven for 40 to 45 minutes. If the pastry begins to brown too quickly because of the additional cooking time, gently cover with a sheet of aluminum foil.

Chicken Tetrazzini

✓ *MAKE-AHEAD*   ✓ *READY AND WAITING*   ✓ *FREEZER READY*

This is a great dish—probably the classic way to use leftover chicken or turkey—that can go straight from freezer to oven. The succulent combination of chicken baked with mushrooms and pasta is especially good to have on hand in the freezer as it is a true comfort food. While you are at it, make one for dinner tonight, and another for a night when you need a special dinner dish waiting for you at home.

*TIP: Cook using two 8-inch square freezer-to-oven dishes: serve from one and freeze the other.

*TIP: To freeze, place the mixture in a freezer-to-oven casserole dish, overwrap well, and freeze for up to 3 months. Bake the frozen tetrazzini at 375°F for 1 hour and 10 minutes, until the mixture is lightly browned on top and bubbly.

1/4 cup butter

1 cup seeded, deveined, and chopped red bell pepper

1/4 cup chopped shallot (from 2 cloves)

2 cups sliced button mushrooms (from about 1/2 pound mushrooms)

3 tablespoons flour

2 cups low-salt chicken broth

1/4 cup dry Sherry

1 cup heavy cream

1 teaspoon salt

1 teaspoon freshly ground pepper

1/4 teaspoon ground nutmeg

6 cups cooked chicken, the equivalent of 2 roasted chickens

8 ounces spaghetti, cooked in salted boiling water until just tender, drained

1/2 cup grated Parmigiano-Reggiano cheese

1. Heat the butter in a large fry pan at medium heat. Add the chopped pepper, shallot, and mushrooms to the pan. Cook for 5 minutes until the vegetables are soft.

2. Sprinkle the flour over the vegetable mixture and cook for 2 minutes, stirring constantly until the flour is hot and bubbly.

3. Add the broth and the Sherry, stirring constantly until the mixture has thickened.

4. Add the cream, salt, pepper, and nutmeg to the mixture and cook for 10 minutes over low heat, stirring repeatedly.

5. Preheat the oven to 375°F. Lightly grease a 9- × 13-inch baking dish. ✱

6. Place the cooked chicken and the cooked spaghetti in a large bowl. Pour the sauce over the chicken and pasta. Sprinkle with half of the Parmigiano-Reggiano cheese. Stir gently to combine.

7. Spoon the mixture into the prepared dish and sprinkle with the remaining cheese. Bake at 375°F for 45 minutes. ✱

VARIATION

This is also a wonderful way to use up the rest of the Thanksgiving or Christmas turkey. Simply substitute cooked turkey for the chicken, and even those family members who can't stand another look at the turkey will enjoy every bite.

Chicken Provençal

✓ *MAKE-AHEAD*   ✓ *READY AND WAITING*   ✓ *FREEZER READY*   ✓ *SOMETHING SPECIAL*

The rich flavor of this vegetable-filled dish makes it a good choice for a festive busy-night supper. Use the slow cooker to have it ready when you get home—a party with no fuss. Freeze the other half in plastic freezer containers. Reheat in the oven or microwave.

4 tablespoons olive oil

Salt and freshly ground pepper, to taste

1/2 cup flour

1/4 teaspoon cayenne pepper

2 tablespoons herbes de Provence ✱

3 pounds chicken thighs

1 large onion, thinly sliced

1/2 large green bell pepper, seeded and thinly sliced

2 cloves garlic, thinly sliced

One 14 1/2-ounce can diced tomatoes, with the juice

1/2 cup chicken broth

1/2 cup white wine ✱

1/3 cup black oil-cured olives

1/4 cup chopped fresh curly-leaf parsley

1. Heat 3 tablespoons of the oil in a heavy skillet over medium-high heat. In a large plastic bag combine the salt, pepper, flour, cayenne, and 1 tablespoon of the Herbes de Provence. Toss the chicken thighs in the bag to coat with the flour mixture. Remove the chicken from the bag, knock off any excess flour, and brown the thighs on all sides in the hot oil.

2. Transfer the chicken to a plate and set aside.

3. Add the remaining 1 tablespoon oil to the skillet. Cook the onion and green pepper until soft, about 6 minutes. Add the garlic and cook 2 minutes more. ✱

4. Put the chicken, vegetables, diced tomatoes, broth, wine, and remaining 1 tablespoon herbes de Provence into the slow cooker, season with salt and pepper, and cook on low for 6 to 8 hours. Add the olives and cook 30 minutes more.

5. Stir in the parsley and serve very hot.

Serving Suggestion

Serve on a bed of hot pasta, or garlicky mashed potatoes. Steamed broccoli with lemon butter goes well, too.

✱ TIP: Herbes de Provence is a classical dried herb mix found in most specialty food shops or on one of the herb and spice web sites, such as penzeys.com.

✱ TIP: For a nonalcoholic dish, substitute 1/2 cup more chicken broth.

✱ TIP: At this point the dish can be frozen, or refrigerated several hours or up to overnight. Bring to room temperature for 20 minutes before continuing with the recipe.

Wild Rice and Smoked Turkey Muffins

MAKES 12 MUFFINS

✓ *MAKE-AHEAD*   ✓ *READY AND WAITING*   ✓ *FREEZER READY*

I love to serve this dish. Everyone is so surprised when they find the muffins have turkey in them! Pair them with a favorite salad, a savory bowl of soup, or add them to a brunch menu for an extra savory treat. They are the perfect freezer muffin. Just reheat them wrapped in foil at 375°F for 5 to 6 minutes and serve.

★TIP: Double-wrap the muffins in plastic wrap and seal in airtight refrigerator bags to prevent them from taking on other flavors.

½ cup unsalted butter (1 stick) plus 1 tablespoon for greasing the muffin tins

½ cup chopped shallot (from 4 medium cloves)

1 teaspoon chopped garlic

1 cup cleaned stemmed and chopped shitake mushrooms (from about 4 ounces)

2 cups all-purpose flour

2 teaspoons baking powder

1 teaspoon salt

1 teaspoon freshly ground pepper

¼ teaspoon ground nutmeg

2 large eggs at room temperature

1 cup whole milk

1 cup finely diced smoked turkey

1 cup cooked wild rice

1. Melt the butter in a medium skillet over medium-high heat. Add the shallot and garlic and cook, stirring, until soft, about 4 minutes. Add the mushrooms. Cook the mushrooms until soft, turning often, about 5 minutes.

2. Preheat the oven to 350°F. Grease 12 muffin cups with unsalted butter.

3. Into a large bowl, sift the flour, baking powder, salt, pepper, and nutmeg together. Mix the eggs and milk together in a medium bowl and stir in the sautéed vegetables, turkey, and wild rice. Pour this over the dry ingredients and stir until just blended—the batter will be thick and lumpy.

4. Scoop ¼ cup of batter into each prepared muffin cup. Bake the muffins for 25 minutes or until the muffins are no longer moist in the center or a toothpick inserted in the middle comes out clean. Cool the muffins on a wire rack for 15 minutes before removing them from the tin. Serve warm, or cool completely before freezing. ★

Herbed Meat Lasagna

✓ *MAKE-AHEAD*　✓ *READY AND WAITING*　✓ *FREEZER READY*

Lasagna is an age-old comfort food, always good to serve anytime. It is great to cook straight from the freezer; it is the perfect keep-on-hand-for-a-quick-home-cooked-meal dish. Just buy some aluminum (disposable) bread pans, and make smaller one-meal portions to freeze for a future dinner. Additionally, this lasagna can easily be made vegetarian. Just eliminate the meat and add three cups thinly sliced parboiled squash or carrots in its place.

1½ pounds lean ground beef (95% lean)

3 tablespoons olive oil

1½ cups finely chopped white onion

2 teaspoons chopped garlic (from 2 medium cloves)

2 cups chopped tomatoes (from 2 medium tomatoes)

1 cup tomato sauce

½ cup tomato paste

3 teaspoons dried basil

1 teaspoon salt

½ teaspoon sage

¼ teaspoon freshly ground pepper

¼ teaspoon rosemary

1 teaspoon Tabasco sauce

10 ounces dried lasagna noodles

4 cups grated mozzarella cheese

1 cup grated Parmigiano-Reggiano cheese (from about 4 ounces), plus more for serving

1 pound fresh spinach, well-washed, stemmed, and finely chopped

¾ pound ricotta cheese

1. Brown the beef in a large skillet over medium-high heat. Drain and set aside. Add the olive oil to the pan. Add the onion and cook for 1 minute, then add the garlic. Cook the garlic about 2 minutes. Return the beef to the pan. Add the tomatoes, tomato sauce, tomato paste, basil, salt, sage, pepper, rosemary, and Tabasco. Reduce the heat to low and simmer the sauce at least 30 minutes, until thick and rich.

2. While the sauce is simmering, cook the lasagna until just tender. Drain, rinse under cold water, and drain well again, keeping the noodles separated.

3. Preheat the oven to 375°F. Butter a 9- × 13-inch aluminum foil baking pan.

4. Spread a layer of sauce in the bottom of the prepared pan. Top with half of the lasagna noodles, and one-third of the mozzarella. Sprinkle with one-third of the Parmigiano-Reggiano.

5. In a large bowl, combine the spinach with the ricotta and spread half of this mixture over the cheeses. Top with another layer of sauce, noodles, cheese, and spinach. End with a layer of sauce and cheese. *

6. Preheat the oven to 375°F. Bake the lasagna for 1 hour or until hot and bubbly. Allow the dish to rest for 15 minutes, then cut into large squares and serve. Pass more Parmigiano-Reggiano on the side.

★ TIP: At this point the lasagna can be wrapped in foil, slid into a resealable freezer bag, and frozen for later use. Twenty-four hours before serving the lasagna, remove it from the plastic bag and place it in the refrigerator to begin to thaw, though in a pinch you can bake the lasagna right out of the freezer. Keep it covered with foil for the first hour, then remove the foil and cook until bubbling.

Turkey and Green Chile Enchilada Pie

✓ *MAKE-AHEAD*   ✓ *READY AND WAITING*   ✓ *SOMETHING SPECIAL*

In addition to using cooked turkey, you can make these enchiladas with leftover cooked pork or steak, or just fill them with cheese for an easy main course. It is another wonderful way to use the rest of the turkey from Thanksgiving or Christmas and not have everyone groan about "turkey again?" Serve the enchiladas with refried beans and packaged Mexican-style rice.

12 fresh 6-inch corn tortillas

1 tablespoon butter

One 10-ounce can green chile enchilada sauce

3 cups cooked turkey meat, shredded

Salt and freshly ground pepper, to taste

One 4-ounce can chopped green chiles

2 cups grated Monterey Jack cheese (from 8 ounces)

2 cups grated cheddar cheese (from 8 ounces)

1 head iceberg lettuce, for garnish

1/2 bunch fresh cilantro leaves, chopped

Fresh salsa, for garnish

Sour cream, for garnish

Black olives, for garnish

1. Place the corn tortillas in a buttered pie plate. Cover the plate with plastic wrap and steam them on high in the microwave for 2 minutes.

2. Preheat the oven to 375°F. Butter a 9- × 13-inch glass dish. Pour the enchilada sauce into a shallow bowl. Spread a thin layer of the sauce on the bottom of the glass dish. Dip a tortilla in the sauce and place it on the right half of the glass dish. Place 2 or 3 pieces of turkey on the tortilla and season with salt and pepper. Add some of the chopped green chiles, and some of the cheeses, then top with another tortilla that has been dipped in the sauce.

3. Repeat the layering process until you reach the sixth tortilla. Finish with a layer of sauce and cheese. Make another enchilada pie on the left-hand side of the dish with the remaining ingredients. ✱

4. Bake for 20 minutes or until heated through. Meanwhile, chop the lettuce and combine it with the cilantro in a medium bowl. Remove the enchilada pies from the oven and cut them into wedges to serve. Garnish with the lettuce, salsa, sour cream, and olives.

✱ **TIP: To freeze,** make the pies in disposable aluminum freezer pans, cover tightly with plastic wrap, and then wrap in aluminum foil or seal in airtight freezer bags. To serve, remove the aluminum foil and plastic wrap, recover with foil, and bake still frozen. Increase the baking time by 15 minutes.

One-Dish Meals

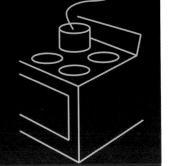

When you're busy and tired and don't want to make a big effort for dinner but want big results, one-dish meals may be just what you need.

You will recognize these modern stews and casseroles as many are updates from long-time family favorites such as Grandma's Baked Spaghetti (page 154) and Red Beans and Rice (page 160). Also in the mix are some new one-dish meals such as Asian Beef Stew (page 156) and Stir-Fried Vegetables with Tofu and Cashews (page 159). Even the new dishes make use of time-tested methods and carry on the tradition of putting everything in one pot.

Nearly all these dishes are perfect for potluck dinners, or for those days when everyone is busy watching the big game or just outside raking up the last of the autumn leaves. One of the nicest things about casseroles is that—like chili and stew—most are even more flavorful the day after they are prepared.

Secrets for easy one-dish meals:

- Put them together ahead of time and bake or finish with little effort.

- When time is pressing, the secret can rest in fully reheating already cooked one-dish meals.

- You can thaw frozen casseroles at room temperature for about 30 minutes before reheating, uncovered, at 300°F to 325°F for another 30 minutes or so.

- Or reheat, right from the freezer, in the microwave, in one-minute intervals on medium, until the center is hot and bubbling.

- Remember, stir the dish several times during the reheating, unless, of course, it is prepared in layers. Take care, though, that whatever method you use to reheat your casseroles, don't overcook them.

In addition to ease of preparation, these savory dishes fill the house with tantalizing aromas and satisfy hungry appetites, all the while leaving little after-dinner cleanup.

Baked Cannelloni with Meatballs

✓ MAKE-AHEAD   ✓ TAKE-ALONG   ✓ READY AND WAITING   ✓ FREEZER READY

Here is one of the ultimate ready-when-you-want-it dinners. Keep the stuffed cannelloni and the meatballs in the freezer, and take them out anytime you want this deliciously filling combination. Add a chopped vegetable salad and garlic bread and you can have company over any time and know there's something wonderful ready to pop in the oven. Or make this one of your special the-whole-family-is-together dinners. If cannelloni pasta is hard to find in your area, substitute jumbo shells.

★ TIP: Use an ice cream scoop to portion the meat mixture. Mold the portion in your hands into firm balls.

MEATBALLS

1 pound ground beef (95% lean)

1 large egg

Salt and pepper, to taste

1/3 cup seasoned bread crumbs

1 small onion, minced (about 1/2 cup minced)

2 teaspoons minced garlic (from 2 cloves)

1 teaspoon dried Italian herbs

2 tablespoons finely chopped fresh Italian flat-leaf parsley

Flour, for dusting meatballs

2 tablespoons oil

CANNELLONI OR SHELLS

12 ounces ricotta cheese (1 1/2 cups)

1 large egg

2 cloves garlic, smashed into a paste with the back of a knife or pressed

1/2 cup chopped fresh curly-leaf parsley

1 cup shredded Parmigiano-Reggiano cheese (from about 4 ounces), plus more, grated, for serving

Salt and pepper, to taste

Cannelloni or jumbo shell pasta, boiled just until softened, 12 to 15 minutes, rinsed in cold water and drained

2 1/2 cups homemade or commercial marinara sauce

1 cup grated mozzarella (from about 4 ounces)

1. Make the meatballs: In a large bowl, combine the ground beef, egg, salt and pepper, bread crumbs, onion, garlic, herbs, and parsley until well mixed. Form the mixture into balls about 1 inch in diameter. ★ Dust the finished meatballs in flour, knocking off any excess.

2. Heat the oil in a large, heavy skillet. Brown the meatballs, a few at a time, on all sides, turning carefully with a spatula. Drain on a rack over absorbent paper towels.

3. Prepare the cannelloni: In a medium bowl, combine the ricotta, egg, garlic, parsley, and Parmigiano-Reggiano cheese. Season well with salt and pepper. Beat with a fork to combine well. With a small spoon, fill the cannelloni tubes or jumbo shells with the cheese mixture. Set aside.

4. Preheat the oven to 350°F.

5. Spoon 1 cup of the marinara sauce into the bottom of a 9- × 13-inch baking or gratin dish. Arrange the filled cannelloni or shells in one layer in the dish, with the meatballs around the edges. Spoon the remaining sauce over the top. Spread 1 cup of the grated mozzarella over the shells. ✱

6. Cover the dish with foil and bake 25 to 30 minutes, until the sauce is bubbling.

7. To serve: Remove the foil and serve with grated Parmigiano-Reggiano cheese on the side.

✱ TIP: For a quick-to-the-table dinner, after the meatballs are browned, arrange them on a baking sheet and freeze them. Once solidly frozen, pack them into a resealable plastic freezer bag. Do the same with the filled cannelloni. When you need a quick dinner, take out as many of each as you need, returning the rest to the freezer. Arrange the frozen pasta and meatballs in an oven-proof dish. Spoon marinara sauce over everything, sprinkle with mozzarella cheese, cover with foil, and bake for 45 minutes until hot and bubbling.

Grandma's Baked Spaghetti

✓ MAKE-AHEAD   ✓ TAKE-ALONG   ✓ READY AND WAITING   ✓ FREEZER READY

Make this dish in advance, refrigerate or freeze it, and then take it out to pop into the oven when you get home from work or are running back-to-back errands, or when unexpected guests mean a larger group for dinner than you expected. This dish fed many a famished appetite after important football games while I was growing up. Add crusty bread and a mixed salad and you are ready for anything.

2 tablespoons olive oil

1 large onion, chopped
(about 1½ cups)

1 large green bell pepper, seeded and
chopped (about 1½ cups)

2 teaspoons minced garlic
(from 2 cloves), or more to taste

1 tablespoon dried Italian herbs

1 pound ground beef (95% lean)

One 6-ounce can tomato paste

One 28-ounce can diced tomatoes,
with juice

One 8-ounce can tomato sauce

1 cup beef broth or red wine

Salt and pepper, to taste

1 pound spaghetti, broken into
large pieces, cooked, and drained

12 slices American cheese

1. Heat the oil in a 4-quart kettle over medium-high heat. Add the onion, pepper, and garlic. Cook, stirring, until the vegetables start to become transparent, about 6 minutes. Stir in the dried herbs. Cook 1 minute.

2. Add the ground beef and cook, breaking up the chunks, until lightly browned, for about 10 minutes. Add the tomato paste, diced tomatoes, tomato sauce, and broth or wine. Season with salt and pepper. Lower the heat and simmer gently for 1 hour.

3. Preheat the oven to 350°F.

4. Add the cooked spaghetti to the kettle with the sauce and stir to combine. Spread the mixture into two 9- × 11-inch baking dishes (if you are going to freeze the spaghetti, use disposable foil pans). Top with the cheese slices. ✱

5. Bake, uncovered, for 25 to 30 minutes, until the cheese is bubbling and lightly browned. Serve very hot. I like to pass a dish of grated Parmigiano-Reggiano cheese for those who like their spaghetti extra cheesy.

✱ TIP: To freeze the dish to serve later: Omit the cheese and wrap tightly in foil or freezer paper. When ready to bake, remove from the freezer, bake, covered with foil, in a preheated oven for 30 minutes, uncover, top with cheese slices, and bake 20 minutes more.

Spicy Scalloped Ham and Potatoes

✓ MAKE-AHEAD   ✓ TAKE-ALONG   ✓ READY AND WAITING   ✓ FREEZER READY

I don't know any better combination than succulent, smoky ham and potatoes baked in a mustard sauce, and it's a favorite with young children, even with the extra kick of chile heat from the jalapeños in the cheese. This dish is delicious served with a salad of endive, avocado, and walnuts. Make plenty, as it freezes well.

2 tablespoons butter, plus more for buttering the baking dish

2 tablespoons flour

Salt and pepper, to taste

2 cups milk

2 tablespoons Dijon mustard

1½ cup grated Monterey Jack cheese with jalapeño (from 6 ounces)

3 large white potatoes, peeled and very thinly sliced

1 medium Vidalia onion, halved and very thinly sliced

2 cups diced smoked ham (about 12 ounces)

3 tablespoons butter, melted

1 cup fresh bread crumbs

1. Preheat the oven to 350°F. Generously butter a medium-sized gratin dish.

2. Melt the 2 tablespoons butter in a heavy saucepan. Stir in the flour, salt, and pepper. Cook for 3 minutes, stirring. Whisk in the milk all at one time. Whisk in the mustard. Cook, stirring, until the sauce is thickened, about 3 minutes. Add the cheese and stir until the cheese melts.

3. In the prepared gratin dish, alternate layers of half the slices of potato, half the onion, and half the ham. Season with salt and pepper. Spoon half the sauce over. Repeat the layers. ✱

4. Cover with foil and bake for 1 hour. Uncover. Combine the melted butter and bread crumbs. Spread the crumbs over the top and bake 20 minutes more until the crumbs are golden.

✱ **TIP:** To freeze the dish to serve later: Wrap the pan with foil and place in the freezer. When you are ready to serve, remove from the freezer and bake, covered, for 1½ hours. Spread with crumbs and bake 20 minutes more.

Asian Beef Stew

✓ MAKE-AHEAD   ✓ FREEZER READY   ✓ SOMETHING SPECIAL

This is a slightly Asian take on a traditional beef stew with the delicious addition of coconut milk. Serve a fruity cabbage slaw on the side to continue the Asian flavor for an easy, festive meal. This stew freezes well, so make it ahead of time and it will be ready to serve on short notice.

2 tablespoons peanut oil, plus a little more

2 pounds chuck steak, cut into 2- × 1-inch strips

1 small onion, sliced

2 teaspoons minced garlic (from 2 cloves)

1 tablespoon minced ginger

2 tablespoons dark brown sugar

One 14-ounce can coconut milk (not sweetened cream)

1/2 cup beef broth, plus more if needed

1 cup small white onions (frozen are fine)

2 medium potatoes, peeled and cubed

Salt and freshly ground pepper, to taste

1/4 cup chopped fresh cilantro

1/4 cup grated coconut, for garnish

1. Heat the oil in a large deep, heavy skillet over medium-high heat. Brown the beef in batches, turning to cook all sides. As each batch is finished, remove it from the skillet and set aside. Add a little more oil to the skillet and then the onion and garlic. Cook, stirring, until tender, about 5 minutes. Stir in the ginger and brown sugar. Cook 1 minute, stirring.

2. Stir in the coconut milk and broth. Return the beef to the skillet. Transfer to a heavy, covered casserole such as Le Creuset or a kettle. ✳

3. Simmer, covered, over low heat for 2 hours, until the beef is very tender. Add a little more beef broth if the sauce becomes very thick.

4. Add the small white onions and the potatoes and season well with salt and pepper. Simmer 30 minutes more (or 1 hour if using the slow cooker). ✳

5. Stir in the cilantro. Cook 5 minutes more. Serve very hot, garnished with grated coconut.

SERVING SUGGESTION

Serve with steamed rice or noodles.

VARIATION

For a dish with a bit of bite, add 1 or 2 dried hot red chiles, such as bird's tongues, at the same time as you add the ginger. Pass hot pepper sauce at the table.

✳ **TIP:** If you are going to use the slow cooker, pour all the ingredients into the cooker and cook on low for 6 hours.

✳ **TIP:** To freeze the dish to serve later: Pour the stew in a freezer container, freeze; when ready to serve, thaw for 24 hours in the refrigerator and then reheat in a double boiler or in the microwave.

Cinnamon-Spiced Chicken Curry

✓ *MAKE-AHEAD*   ✓ *READY AND WAITING*

Cooking for a family often means trying to please many different tastes, but sometimes it seems you cannot satisfy everyone every day. This recipe is especially delicious, pleases almost all palates, and can be a great way to introduce curry to the entire family. It is the perfect one-pot meal. If you are slicing the chicken, cut up some extra and place it in the freezer for the next time you crave this dish. Measure out extra spices and put them together in a labeled plastic bag so that you will be ready to cook on a moment's notice.

1 teaspoon salt

1/2 teaspoon freshly ground pepper

1 tablespoon soy sauce

1/4 teaspoon cayenne pepper

2 boneless skinless chicken breasts, cut into pieces

2 tablespoons olive oil

2 cups finely chopped white onions (from about 2 small onions)

2 cups seeded and chopped fresh tomatoes (from about 4 medium tomatoes)

2 tablespoons seeded and chopped serrano chiles (from about 3 chiles)

1 tablespoon freshly grated ginger

1/2 teaspoon garam masala *

1/2 teaspoon ground cumin

1/8 teaspoon cinnamon, or more to taste

5 whole Tellicherry peppercorns (or other peppercorns if Tellicherry are unavailable)

1 bay leaf *

2 whole cloves, crushed

2 cups uncooked basmati rice

4 cups water

2 cups peas, fresh or frozen

Chopped cilantro, for garnish

Sliced green onion, for garnish

1. In a small bowl, combine the salt, pepper, soy sauce, and cayenne. Add the chicken pieces and marinate while you prepare the vegetables.

2. Heat the olive oil in a medium skillet over medium heat. Add the onions and cook slowly, stirring, until they are golden, about 7 minutes. Add the chicken to the pan, and brown the pieces evenly on all sides.

3. Add the tomatoes, chiles, ginger, garam masala, and cumin. Cover the pan and cook for 15 minutes. Add the cinnamon, peppercorns, bay leaf, cloves, and rice.

4. Stir in the water. Simmer, uncovered, until the water is absorbed, 15 to 20 minutes. Add the peas, remove the mixture from the heat, and let stand 10 minutes. Garnish with cilantro, and chopped green onion.

★ TIP: Garam masala is a common aromatic seasoning frequently used in Indian cooking. You can buy it in specialty food markets, or make your own. The ingredients vary, but often include cumin seeds, peppercorns, cloves, black cardamom pods, and cinnamon, in more or less equally quantities, all ground together.

★ TIP: Leave the **bay leaf** whole during cooking, and be sure to remove it before serving.

Mandarin Orange Turkey Sauté

✓ *MAKE-AHEAD*   ✓ *READY AND WAITING*

These turkey cutlets freeze beautifully and are an excellent addition to your freezer pantry. Keep the mandarin oranges on hand in the pantry for salads or this quick dish.

6 turkey breast cutlets (about 1 pound)

1 teaspoon ground cumin

Salt and freshly ground pepper, to taste

1 tablespoon all-purpose flour

2 tablespoons butter

2 tablespoons olive oil

Two 14-ounce cans mandarin oranges, drained

1 cup chopped green onions (from about 3 bunches)

½ cup chicken broth

⅓ cup orange juice

3 tablespoons chopped Italian flat-leaf parsley, for garnish (optional)

1. Pat the turkey cutlets dry with paper towels. Season with cumin, salt, and pepper. Dust lightly with flour. ✱

2. Melt the butter with the olive oil in a heavy large skillet over high heat. Working in batches, add the turkey cutlets to the skillet and cook, turning once, until cooked through and lightly browned, about 2 minutes per side. Transfer the turkey cutlets to a heated platter after each batch is cooked and cover with foil to keep warm.

3. Add the oranges and green onions to the skillet and sauté until just heated through, about 2 minutes.

4. Using a slotted spoon, arrange the oranges and onions atop the turkey cutlets and keep warm. Add the broth and orange juice to the skillet and boil until reduced to the consistency of heavy cream, about 6 minutes. Season the sauce with salt and pepper; pour over the turkey cutlets. Garnish with parsley, if desired.

SERVING SUGGESTION

Serve with quick couscous or rice pilaf.

✱ TIP: Combine the seasonings and flour in a resealable plastic bag. This makes it easy to dust the turkey with flour and cleanup is a snap. Just drop the cutlets in the bag and shake. You can even make extra bags of seasoned flour for keeping on hand when you need a quick dinner solution. Store the cutlets in the freezer and you will have everything that you need to make this dish in a pinch.

Stir-Fried Vegetables with Tofu and Cashews

MAKES 6 SERVINGS

Tofu will last unopened in the refrigerator for several weeks. That makes it a great item to buy at least once a month. It is extremely nutritious and takes on just about any flavor you put with it. So why not try and "sneak" it in on your family occasionally? Serve this with hot, cooked rice for a more satisfying meal.

2 tablespoons soy sauce

1 tablespoon dry Sherry

1 teaspoon cornstarch

1 package firm tofu, well drained and cut into small squares ✶

3 tablespoons olive oil

1 tablespoon grated fresh ginger ✶

1 cup finely chopped white onion

1 medium red bell pepper, seeded, deveined, and thinly sliced (about 1 cup)

1 pound fresh green beans, trimmed and blanched

1 cup vegetable stock

1/2 teaspoon Asian chili oil

3/4 cup cashews, toasted

Salt and freshly ground pepper, to taste

1. In a bowl, whisk together the soy sauce, Sherry, and cornstarch. Add the tofu and mix to coat.

2. Heat 2 tablespoons of the olive oil in a large skillet over medium-high heat. When the oil is hot, add the ginger.

3. Using a slotted spoon, remove the tofu from the marinade; set the marinade aside. Add the tofu to the pan with the ginger and cook the tofu over high heat until it is golden brown, 4 to 5 minutes. Transfer the tofu to a plate and set it aside.

4. Reduce the heat to medium and add the remaining 1 table-spoon olive oil. Add the onion to the pan and cook, stirring, until soft, about 5 minutes. Add the red bell pepper and cook until soft, 5 minutes more.

5. Return the tofu to the pan and then add the green beans, reserved marinade, stock, and chili oil. Season well with salt and pepper. Stir the mixture constantly until it boils and thickens.

6. Remove the pan from the heat and add the cashews. Transfer to a serving dish. Serve hot.

✶TIP: Tofu is mostly sold in two forms, firm and soft or silken. Firm maintains its shape and can be used in stir-fries and on the grill. Soft is best in sauces and other creamy dishes.

✶TIP: Ginger freezes well. Wrap leftover ginger and freeze for up to 3 months.

Red Beans and Rice

✓ MAKE-AHEAD ✓ TAKE-ALONG ✓ READY AND WAITING ✓ FREEZER READY ✓ SOMETHING SPECIAL

Not your typical rice 'n' beans, this dish is hearty enough for a full meal, or you can accompany it with spicy grilled chorizo or hot Italian sausage for even heartier appetites. After a day of sports, or just an afternoon of snow shoveling or hectic shopping, having this dish ready and waiting will turn exhaustion into elation.

★ TIP: Cajun spices is a commercial mix available in the spice section of your supermarket.

¼ pound (4 ounces) salt pork, well rinsed, cut into ½-inch cubes

1 large onion, chopped (about 1½ cups)

1 large green bell pepper, seeded and chopped (about 1½ cups)

2 large ribs celery, chopped (about 1 cup)

3 teaspoons minced garlic (from 3 medium cloves)

1 teaspoon Cajun spices ★

3 cups dried red kidney beans (from about 1 pound), picked over, soaked overnight, drained, and rinsed

¼ teaspoon crushed red pepper

5 to 6 cups beef broth

Salt, to taste

Hot pepper sauce (such as Tabasco), to taste

¼ cup minced fresh curly-leaf parsley, plus more for garnish

4 cups hot cooked rice

1. Cook the salt pork in a deep skillet over medium-low heat until lightly browned and beginning to render the fat, 5 to 6 minutes. Add the onion, green pepper, celery, garlic, and Cajun spices. Cook, stirring, for 3 minutes.

2. Turn the onion mixture into a slow cooker. Stir in the drained beans and crushed pepper. Add enough beef broth to cover the ingredients by 2 inches, stir once. Cover and cook on low for 6 to 8 hours.

3. Season with the salt, hot pepper sauce, and parsley. Cook 20 minutes more.

4. Ladle some of the red beans into flat soup plates. Spoon ⅓ to ½ cup hot rice in a mound in the center of the beans. Garnish with parsley.

Bountiful Breads

The scent of fresh bread baking filling the house and the sight of the delicious results left on the kitchen counter to be sampled by passersby or served with dinner, would make any family feel loved and well cared for. And, with the convenience of frozen bread dough from the supermarket, your family can enjoy the pleasures of fresh bread often. With it, most of the recipes in this chapter take less than an hour to make, and most of that time you can be tending to other parts of the meal.

When time and energy permit, by all means enjoy the physical and psychological benefits of mixing and kneading your own dough. But virtually all our delicious recipes can be made with frozen bread dough. The key to success is to always have bread dough in the freezer, so be sure to always have it on your shopping list. Whenever you want, thaw some in the refrigerator for 24 to 36 hours and you are ready to go. Most packages provide a quick thaw method, but I suggest you try not to use it as it will change the texture of the dough. Just try to plan ahead.

There are breads in this chapter for every occasion, from the ultimate breakfast treat, Gooey Cinnamon Rolls (page 169), to Stuffed Bread with Green Chiles and Cheddar Cheese (page 162). I've even included a no-yeast quickbread that's fun to make for breakfast or a snack. Virtually all these breads can be baked and then frozen for later use.

No matter whether you use frozen dough or bake it from scratch, bread baking needn't be a daunting experience.

Bread baking tips:

- Look for premade bread dough in the freezer section of the supermarket.

- Don't forget to preheat the oven.

- Yeast dough rises best at 80°F. Cover the bowl with a cloth and put it in a warm corner—on the back of the stove, in the furnace room, or near the warmest radiator, for instance.

- Let bread rise no longer than one to one and a half hours, just until the prints left from poking two fingers into the dough remain in the surface. If the dough overrises before being shaped and baked, the second rise won't have enough yeast left and the bread can collapse. It still tastes fine; it just looks funny.

- Remove finished bread from the pan immediately. You can tell when most loaves are cooked by tapping on the bottom of the loaf with your knuckles or a spoon and listening for a hollow sound.

- If you are not going to eat the bread right away, *always* cool the loaf completely before wrapping it for freezing or storage. Otherwise, the residual heat in the loaf will steam the crust and it will become soggy.

- Now that you are armed with knowledge and recipes, invite the kids into the kitchen for an afternoon of baking and have fun.

Stuffed Bread with Green Chiles and Cheddar Cheese

✓ MAKE-AHEAD   ✓ TAKE-ALONG   ✓ FREEZER READY   ✓ SOMETHING SPECIAL

This recipe will make two beautiful loaves of bread. Make one for dinner tonight, and freeze the other one for later. If you know that your family won't eat a whole loaf, go ahead and freeze it in portions, which makes it easier to thaw. Not only does the stuffed bread go well with a steaming bowl of chili for a quick meal, on its own it can be popped in the oven and warmed through for a quick afternoon snack. For the adults, it pairs nicely with a glass of oaky Chardonnay.

1 tablespoon olive oil

Two 1-pound packages frozen bread dough loaves, thawed

2 cups grated cheddar cheese (from about 8 ounces)

One 4-ounce can diced green chiles

2 teaspoons garlic powder

1/2 teaspoon dried basil

1/2 teaspoon dried oregano

1/2 teaspoon crushed red pepper

Salt and freshly ground pepper, to taste

1 large egg, beaten

1 tablespoon sesame seeds

1. Brush two 11- × 17-inch baking sheets with olive oil. Divide the dough in half. Roll 1 piece of dough out to edges of 1 prepared sheet.

2. Place half the cheese on the dough leaving a 1/2-inch border at the edges. Sprinkle with half the diced green chiles, half the garlic powder, basil, oregano, and crushed red pepper. Season with salt and pepper.

3. Starting at the short end, roll up jellyroll fashion and turn, seam side down, on the baking sheet. Brush with the beaten egg. Using a sharp knife or razor blade, slash the surface of the loaf on an angle. Sprinkle with sesame seeds. Repeat with the second loaf.

4. Preheat the oven to 400°F. Bake 30 to 40 minutes, until golden brown. Cool on wire cooling racks and slice the loaves. This bread freezes well once it is cool.

Tabasco Cheddar Cheese Bread

✓ *MAKE-AHEAD*   ✓ *TAKE-ALONG*   ✓ *FREEZER READY*   ✓ *SOMETHING SPECIAL*

To make this bread, you gently roll the ingredients into the dough, then allow it to rise briefly, creating a lighter final loaf. The great flavor and texture of the bread will make it worth the wait. Toast thin slices and pass them with a glass of good Cabernet Sauvignon or a hearty Zinfandel the next time you invite people over.

2 teaspoons garlic powder

½ teaspoon dried basil

½ teaspoon dried oregano

1 teaspoon Tabasco

2 cups grated cheddar cheese
(from about 8 ounces)

Salt and freshly ground pepper,
to taste

1 tablespoon olive oil

Two 1-pound packages frozen
bread dough loaves, thawed

1 large egg, beaten

1 tablespoon sesame seeds

1. In a medium bowl, combine the garlic powder, basil, oregano, Tabasco, cheese, salt, and pepper.

2. Brush two 11- × 17-inch baking sheets with olive oil. Divide the dough in half. Roll 1 piece of dough out to the edges of 1 prepared sheet.

3. Place half the cheese mixture on the rolled dough leaving a ½-inch border at the edges. Gently roll the ingredients into the dough with a rolling pin.

4. Starting at the short end, roll up jellyroll fashion and turn, seam side down, on the baking sheet. Brush with the egg. Slash deeply crosswise on the upper surface. Sprinkle with the sesame seeds. Repeat as above with the second loaf. Let the loaves rise in a warm place for 15 minutes.

5. Preheat the oven to 400°F. Bake about 30 to 40 minutes, until golden brown. Cool on wire cooling racks and slice the loaves. These loaves freeze well. ∗

∗TIP: To freeze the bread to serve later: Cool the loaves completely, wrap tightly in freezer paper or foil, and seal in heavy freezer bags. Freeze for up to a month.

Olive Tapenade Rolls

✓ *MAKE-AHEAD*   ✓ *TAKE-ALONG*   ✓ *FREEZER READY*   ✓ *SOMETHING SPECIAL*

Gently add tapenade to premade dough for a wonderfully different flavor in this bread. The flavored dough can be shaped into loaves or rolls. Taste your tapenade before you use it. If it seems a bit bland, you may find that you want to sprinkle your rolls with coarse salt before baking for added flavor.

Two 1-pound packages frozen bread dough loaves, thawed

6 ounces premade black olive spread or tapenade ✱

1 teaspoon dried thyme, plus 1/2 teaspoon more for sprinkling on the finished rolls

1/2 teaspoon freshly ground pepper

1/4 cup all-purpose flour, plus 2 tablespoons for the work surface

2 tablespoons cream or milk

1 egg, beaten

1. Place the thawed dough in a mixer fitted with the dough hook attachment, or on a lightly floured work surface. With the machine running, or by hand, add in the olive spread, 1 teaspoon thyme, pepper, and flour in small amounts, kneading well after each addition to incorporated the seasonings completely.

2. If using a dough hook, once the seasonings are incorporated, turn the dough out onto a lightly floured work surface. Cut it into 16 equal pieces and knead the pieces slightly. If you kneaded it by hand, cut the dough into 16 equal pieces. Allow the dough to rest for 5 minutes.

3. Form the dough into tight balls with your hands, cover with a clean cloth, and allow them to rise on the floured surface for 15 minutes.

4. Preheat the oven with the pizza stone inside to 400°F. If you don't have a pizza stone, grease a cookie sheet and transfer the rolls to the cookie sheet.

5. In a small bowl, combine the cream and the beaten egg. Brush lightly over the rolls; sprinkle them with the 1/2 teaspoon thyme.

6. Arrange the rolls on the pizza stone or place the cookie sheet in the oven. Bake about 20 to 30 minutes, until brown and crusty. Remove from the oven and cool on a wire rack—or serve immediately while still hot.

✱ TIP: Try a variety of flavorings, using the same basic technique. Once you have made the rolls with black olive spread, try a commercial sun-dried tomato spread, or a green olive spread—both available in most supermarkets and specialty food shops.

Sun-Dried Tomato and Rosemary Herb Bread

MAKES TWO 1-POUND LOAVES

This is a straight-from-the-pantry bread idea. Keep sun-dried tomatoes packed in olive oil in the cabinet and you will always have the beginnings on hand for this delicious treat. The addition of the dried thyme and rosemary give the basic frozen dough a fantastic new flavor.

1 cup sun-dried tomatoes packed in oil

Two 1-pound packages frozen bread dough loaves, thawed

½ teaspoon dried thyme

½ teaspoon dried rosemary

½ teaspoon freshly ground pepper

¼ cup all-purpose flour

2 teaspoons olive oil

1 egg, beaten

2 tablespoons cream or milk

1. Drain the sun-dried tomatoes on paper towels. Reserve the remaining olive oil in the jar to use as a dipping oil for the bread. Slice the tomatoes into long, thin strips.

2. Place the thawed dough in a mixer fitted with the dough hook attachment, or on a lightly floured work surface. With the machine running, or by hand, knead in the sun-dried tomatoes, thyme, rosemary, and pepper. Add in small amounts, kneading well after each addition.

3. If using a dough hook, once the herbs are mixed into the dough, turn it out onto a lightly floured work surface. Knead the dough to combine any sun-dried tomatoes that may have remained in the bowl.

4. Cut the dough into 2 pieces. Form the dough into 2 tight round

loaves, cover with a clean cloth, and allow them to rise on the floured surface for 15 minutes.

5. Lightly grease a cookie sheet with olive oil. With a rolling pin, gently roll each ball of dough into a 9-inch circle. If the dough shrinks back while you are rolling it, allow the dough to rest for another 10 minutes before continuing. Place the rounds on the cookie sheet.

6. Preheat the oven to 400°F.

7. In a small bowl, combine the beaten egg with the cream. Brush lightly onto the rounds.

8. Set the cookie sheet into the oven, lower the temperature of the oven to 375°F and bake about 40 minutes, until brown and crusty. Remove from the oven and cool on a wire rack.

Poppy Seed Bread Sticks

✓ *MAKE-AHEAD* ✓ *TAKE-ALONG* ✓ *FREEZER READY* ✓ *SOMETHING SPECIAL*

These little bread sticks come together quickly and can be frozen after they have been baked so that you'll have them on hand at a moment's notice. You can flavor them with any seeds that you like. In this recipe, I use poppy seeds, but you could also use sesame, caraway, or even fennel for great variations.

2 teaspoons olive oil

One 1-pound package frozen bread dough, thawed

1/4 cup all-purpose flour

1 egg, beaten

2 tablespoons poppy seeds

Coarse salt (optional)

1. Grease 2 cookie sheets with olive oil.

2. Place the thawed dough on a floured surface. Divide the dough into 10 equal pieces. Let the dough rest 10 minutes.

3. Roll each dough piece between your work surface and the palms of your hands to form a 12-inch-long rope. Arrange 5 ropes on each baking sheet, allowing plenty of space between them. Let the bread sticks rest, covered with a clean towel, for 10 minutes.

4. While the bread sticks are resting, position one rack in the lowest third of the oven and one rack in the center; preheat the oven to 400°F and place a pan of water on the lower rack to provide steam while the bread sticks bake. Brush the bread sticks lightly with the beaten egg. Sprinkle very lightly with the poppy seeds and coarse salt, if desired. Place the baking sheets in the oven, on the rack over the pan of water. Bake 20 to 25 minutes until the bread sticks are shiny, golden, and sound hollow when tapped. ∗

5. Transfer the bread sticks to racks and let cool. ∗

∗**TIP:** The steam from the pan of water in the oven creates a **crustier bread stick**.

∗**TIP:** These bread sticks **can be made ahead**, whenever you have time or the oven is on. Cool completely and wrap tightly in plastic wrap. Wrap with foil and freeze up to 2 weeks. Thaw bread sticks before serving. If you want to serve them warm, wrap the thawed sticks in foil and warm for 15 minutes in a 350°F oven.

Garlic Butter Bread Sticks

✓ *MAKE-AHEAD*   ✓ *TAKE-ALONG*   ✓ *FREEZER READY*

This quick recipe is a twist on the classic garlic bread where individual bread sticks are brushed with garlic butter and baked until crusty. I have made it a million times when I've been in a hurry and have needed to come up with a quick bread to go with pasta or soup. You can use frozen bread dough, but an even quicker solution is to use canned bread stick dough that you can find in the refrigerator section of any supermarket.

1 tablespoon olive oil

One 1-pound package frozen bread dough, thawed, or 1 can of bread stick dough

2 tablespoons all-purpose flour

1/4 cup butter (4 tablespoons, 1/2 stick)

2 teaspoons garlic powder

1 tablespoon lemon juice

1/2 teaspoon salt

1. Brush 2 cookie sheets with the olive oil. If using the frozen white dough, turn the dough out on a floured surface. Divide the dough into 10 equal pieces. Let the dough rest 10 minutes. If you are using the packaged bread stick dough, skip to step 3.

2. Roll each dough piece between your work surface and the palms of your hands into a 12-inch long rope. Arrange 5 ropes on each baking sheet, with plenty of space between each one. Let the bread sticks rise uncovered in a warm draft-free area until puffy and light, about 10 minutes.

3. If you are using the premade refrigerator bread stick dough, remove the dough from the can and separate the bread sticks.

4. Melt the butter in a small saucepan at medium heat. Stir in the garlic powder, lemon juice, and salt.

5. Whichever type of dough you are using, shape the bread sticks

by holding one end in each hand and twisting the dough three times. Place the twisted ropes on a large baking sheet, pressing the ends onto the sheet so they don't unravel.

6. Preheat the oven to 400°F. Brush the bread sticks lightly with the garlic butter. When the oven is preheated, slide the baking sheets onto the racks in the oven. Bake about 30 minutes for the frozen dough or about 12 minutes for the refrigerator bread sticks, until the bread sticks are golden brown.

7. Transfer the bread sticks to racks; cool slightly and serve, warm or hot.

Cranberry Walnut Bread

✓ MAKE-AHEAD   ✓ TAKE-ALONG   ✓ FREEZER READY

Quick breads are a great solution when you don't have time to let dough rise. They go straight from the mixing bowl into the oven and are ready in time for breakfast or an afternoon snack. If you'd prefer muffins to loaves, just fill well-greased cups three-quarters full and cut the baking time down to 10 to 12 minutes.

1 tablespoon butter

1 cup dried cranberries

2 teaspoons grated orange zest

1 cup sugar

2¼ cups all-purpose flour

½ teaspoon salt

1 teaspoon baking powder

½ teaspoon baking soda

3 tablespoons unsalted butter, at room temperature

1 large egg, lightly beaten

½ cup fresh orange juice

½ cup water

1 cup chopped walnuts, toasted

1. Preheat the oven to 325°F. Position a rack in the middle of the oven. Butter one 8½- × 4½-inch loaf pan.

2. Coarsely chop the dried cranberries and place in a small saucepan over low heat. Add the orange zest and ½ cup of the sugar. Heat slowly just to a simmer, stirring to dissolve the sugar. Set aside to cool.

3. In a medium bowl, stir together the flour, salt, baking powder, and baking soda. Set aside.

4. In a separate bowl, combine the unsalted butter and the remaining ½ cup sugar. Beat until light and fluffy, about 3 minutes.

Add the beaten egg. Stir in half of the flour mixture, and then the orange juice and water. Stir in the remaining flour mixture and then the cooled cranberry mixture. Add the walnuts and stir just to combine—the batter will be lumpy. ∗

5. Spoon the batter into the prepared loaf pan. Bake in the preheated oven 55 to 60 minutes, until a toothpick inserted in the center of the loaf comes out clean. ∗

6. Remove the loaf from the oven and cool it in the pan for 5 minutes. Turn out onto a wire rack and cool completely. Slice and serve.

∗ **TIP:** The batter should be **well mixed**, but not overbeaten. Lumps (in the batter itself, not from add-ins like nuts) are fine. If you overbeat the batter the finished loaf will be tough rather than light and crumbly.

∗ **TIP:** Testing bread for **doneness** with a skewer or toothpick is easy. Insert the tester in the center of the loaf or cake and remove. A few crumbs might stick to the tester and that's fine, but there should be no uncooked batter adhering to it. If the center is still uncooked, return the pan to the oven for 10 minutes more and then test again.

Gooey Cinnamon Rolls

✓ *MAKE-AHEAD* ✓ *TAKE-ALONG* ✓ *FREEZER READY* ✓ *SOMETHING SPECIAL*

My grandmother used to make these delicious rolls every time we visited her ranch in Colorado. She labored long over the dough to make it moist and delicious. This recipe has all of the love, caring, and flavor of my grandmother's rolls, but requires much less time in the kitchen—and your family will love it just as much.

Two 1-pound loaves of frozen white bread dough, thawed

2 tablespoons all-purpose flour

3/4 cup butter (1 1/2 sticks), plus 1 tablespoon for greasing the pans

1 1/2 cups packed light brown sugar

3 tablespoon half and half

1 1/2 cups chopped pecans

1/2 cup butter (1 stick), melted

1/2 cup sugar

1/4 cup ground cinnamon

1. Preheat the oven to 350°F. Grease two 9- × 12-inch baking pans.

2. Place 1 of the thawed loaves on a lightly floured surface and roll out into a long rectangle about 12 × 18 inches. Repeat with the other loaf. If the dough shrinks back at the edges and resists rolling, allow it to rest for a few minutes and then continue to roll it into shape.

3. In a large saucepan, melt the ¾ cup butter, add the brown sugar and half and half, and bring the mixture to a simmer. Pour the sauce into two 9- × 12-inch greased pans and sprinkle with the pecans.

4. Brush the dough liberally with the melted butter. In a small bowl, mix together the sugar and cinnamon and sprinkle over the dough.

5. Roll up each rectangle of dough, jellyroll style, from the long side. Trim off the ends and cut each roll into eighteen 1-inch slices with a lightly floured serrated knife. Arrange the rolls, cut side down, in the prepared pans, cover with a clean towel, and let rest for 15 minutes. There should be 18 cinnamon rolls in 6 rows of 3 in each pan.

6. Bake 20 to 25 minutes or until golden. Remove the pans from the oven and immediately invert them onto rimmed cookie sheets. The sauce is very gooey and will stick like glue to the pan if you do not turn the rolls out while it is still hot. Allow the rolls to cool a bit on the cookie sheets, and serve. ✶

✶ TIP: The cinnamon rolls will **freeze well** for up to 3 months if they are tightly wrapped in plastic wrap and then overwrapped in foil. So make one pan for breakfast and freeze one to bring out at a moment's notice. Rewarm in a pan covered with foil.

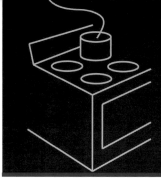

Delectable Desserts

If **you love dessert,** sometimes eating a meal is just a prelude for what you're really in the mood for—even if it is only a homemade cookie or two to accompany a rich, fragrant cup of coffee. If you eat healthfully in general, dessert is a just reward, so why shouldn't you enjoy the simple sweet pleasures of life?

Fresh fruit, tender pastry, caramel, deep dark chocolate: so many ingredients can be combined to create that longed-for sweet finish to the meal. In fact, many of the same ingredients can be used to make desserts as entirely different as pies, candies, cakes, cookies, ice cream, and pastries.

Because just about every kid (or kid-at-heart) loves some kind of dessert, it's often a great lure to getting your children or spouse to help out in the kitchen. Dessert making can be as much fun as dessert eating. Here are some simple tips:

- Bring all ingredients to room temperature before you begin—unless the recipe specifically tells you otherwise, as in ice cream, etc.

- Read the recipe carefully from start to finish—one of the children can read it aloud so that everyone will know what to expect.

- Preheat the oven, if using one, before beginning.

- Use and combine the ingredients exactly as specified in the recipe. This is much more important for desserts and pastries than for savory dishes.

- Measure carefully, especially if you are making pastry.

- Generally bake on the center shelf of the oven.

- If using more than one pan, as in cake layers, don't let them touch each other or the sides or back of the oven, or the finished product will be uneven.

- If the crust or top browns too quickly, gently lay a piece of foil on top of the pan to slow browning and prevent burning. For pies, lightly wrap the entire pie dish in foil, opening only for the last 15 minutes or so of cooking to brown the top and prevent burning the edges.

While a homemade dessert makes any meal festive, don't hesitate to take a shortcut or two if time is lacking. Refrigerated pie crust or cookie dough, a quality cake mix, or a commercial caramel or fudge sauce combined with your own special recipe or touches can save just enough time to mean you can actually make your own dessert tonight.

Spiced Oatmeal Cookies

✓ *MAKE-AHEAD*   ✓ *TAKE-ALONG*

Soft and chewy, chock full of oatmeal and raisins, these cookies make great ice cream sandwiches! Just press a scoop of your favorite flavor between two cookies and enjoy, or better yet, make this a job for the kids—it might leave the kitchen a little messy, but there will be much fun and laughter in the process. Keep plenty of cookies on hand for wholesome snacks and desserts, or pack one in a lunch-box as a treat.

½ cup plus ⅓ cup all-purpose flour

½ teaspoon baking soda

¼ teaspoon salt

¼ teaspoon ground cardamom

¼ teaspoon ground cinnamon

⅛ teaspoon ground allspice

½ cup (1 stick) unsalted butter, at room temperature

¾ cup packed dark brown sugar

1 large egg

1 teaspoon pure vanilla extract

1¼ cups old-fashioned oatmeal ✱

½ cup raisins

1. Preheat the oven to 350°F.

2. In a medium bowl, sift together the flour, baking soda, salt, and spices. Beat the butter until light and fluffy on medium speed in an electric mixer fitted with the paddle attachment, about 3 minutes. Add the brown sugar and beat until the mixture is smooth. Add the egg and vanilla extract and mix just until well combined. Reduce the speed to low and add the flour mixture. ✱

3. Stir until just combined and do not overmix. Fold in the oats and raisins.

4. Drop the dough by table-spoonfuls onto parchment-lined baking sheets, spacing 1½ inches apart. Using moistened finger-tips, flatten the cookies slightly.

5. Bake in the preheated oven for 12 minutes, until the cookies are golden brown. Cool on the baking sheets for 5 minutes and remove to a wire rack.

✱ **TIP:** It is important to **use long-cooking oats** here, not quick-cooking or instant oatmeal.

✱ **TIP:** If your mixer has a **shield**, put it on before adding the flour to avoid having it spun all over the kitchen. Otherwise, turn off the mixer, add the flour mixture, and then turn on very low just until mixed.

Double Chocolate Walnut Cookies

✓ *MAKE-AHEAD*   ✓ *TAKE-ALONG*   ✓ *SOMETHING SPECIAL*

Walnuts and chocolate are excellent companions (their rich flavors are so satisfying, but make sure they're fresh), and the combination makes these double-chocolate cookies a real treat for the chocolate lovers in your family. The cookies freeze extremely well, so bake a double batch and freeze half in an airtight freezer container. Bring them out any time something special is in order.

3 cups bittersweet chocolate chips (from 18 ounces)

4 tablespoons butter (½ stick), at room temperature

¾ cup packed brown sugar

2 large eggs, beaten

1 teaspoon pure vanilla extract

½ cup plus 1 tablespoon all-purpose flour

¼ teaspoon baking powder

1½ cups walnuts, chopped (from about 8 ounces)

1. Preheat the oven to 350°F.

2. Melt 1½ cups of the chocolate chips in a small bowl in the microwave or in the top of a double boiler, stirring until the chips are just melted and the chocolate is smooth. Add the butter and beat until smooth. Add the brown sugar and combine. Beat in the eggs and vanilla and whisk until smooth.

3. Sift together the flour and baking powder on a sheet of waxed paper or parchment. Add to the chocolate mixture and stir with a wooden spoon until just combined. Do not overmix the batter.

4. Fold in the remaining chocolate chips and the walnuts. Refrigerate the dough for 5 minutes.

5. Drop the dough by heaping tablespoons on a parchment-lined baking sheet. Bake in the preheated oven for 10 to 12 minutes. Remove from the oven, cool 5 minutes on the baking sheet, then transfer to a wire rack to cool completely. *

✷ TIP: Your family, like mine, may not be able to resist **eating these while they are still warm.** Be careful, though, because the chocolate chips are extremely hot when they first come out of the oven.

Oatmeal Chocolate Chip Cookies

✓ MAKE-AHEAD   ✓ TAKE-ALONG

These cookies are crisp and somewhat lacy with crunchy oatmeal and soft, gooey chocolate chips—a delightful combination that makes them perfect for that special dessert or snack. These are a bit harder to make than our other cookies, but children love them so much they will often be delighted to help.

1½ cups all-purpose flour

¾ teaspoon baking soda

½ teaspoon salt

⅔ cup (10 tablespoons) unsalted butter, at room temperature

6 tablespoons solid vegetable shortening

¾ cup packed golden brown sugar

¾ cup sugar

2 large eggs

1 teaspoon pure vanilla extract

2 cups old-fashioned oatmeal (not quick-cooking or instant)

1½ cups semisweet chocolate chips (from 9 ounces)

1. Preheat the oven to 350°F.

2. Onto a sheet of waxed or parchment paper, sift together the flour, baking soda, and salt.

3. In a mixer fitted with a paddle attachment, beat together the butter and shortening on medium speed until light and fluffy, stopping once to scrape down the sides of the bowl. Add both sugars and beat until the mixture is smooth.

4. Add the eggs, 1 at a time, incorporating each fully before adding the next one. Add the vanilla extract and mix just until combined. Reduce the speed to low and add the flour mixture. Stir until just combined and do not overmix. Remove the bowl from the mixer and fold in the oatmeal and chocolate chips. Chill the dough for 5 minutes.

5. Drop the dough by heaping tablespoons onto a parchment-lined baking sheet. ✱

6. Bake in the preheated oven for 12 to 13 minutes. Remove from the oven, cool for 5 minutes on the baking sheet, and transfer to a wire rack to cool completely. ✱

✱ **TIP:** The easiest way to form these cookies is with an ice cream scoop. They are available in kitchen stores in various sizes. If the dough tends to stick to the scoop, dip it in flour and shake off any excess before each scooping.

✱ **TIP:** Store the cookies for up to a week in tins rather than plastic boxes. Tins maintain crispness and shape in the cookies better than plastic boxes. Store soft and crisp cookies separately, or the crisp ones will become soggy. You can also wrap these well in foil and freeze them for up to a month.

Peach Cobbler with Pecan Crust

✓ MAKE-AHEAD   ✓ SOMETHING SPECIAL

The batter for this peach cobbler is spread on the bottom of the dish and the peaches are placed on top. While baking, the batter rises up and over the peaches, forming a wonderfully crisp yet cakelike contrast to the peaches.

1 pound ripe peaches (about 4 large), peeled, pitted, and sliced

1½ cups sugar

½ teaspoon ground cinnamon

1 cup all-purpose flour

½ cup chopped pecans (from about 2 ounces)

2 teaspoons baking powder

¼ teaspoon salt

¾ cup milk

6 tablespoons butter (¾ stick)

1. Preheat the oven to 375°F.

2. In a medium bowl, combine the sliced peaches, ¾ cup of the sugar, and the cinnamon. Stir to combine and set aside for 1 hour.

3. In a large bowl, use a whisk to combine the flour, pecans, baking powder, salt, and remaining sugar. Add the milk and whisk until just combined, the batter might be a little lumpy.

4. Melt the butter in a 9-inch oval baking dish in the microwave or oven.

5. Pour the batter over the butter, but do not stir. Spoon the peach mixture on top of the batter and do not stir.

6. Bake in the preheated oven for 40 to 45 minutes, until the crust is puffy and golden brown.

SERVING SUGGESTION

Spoon the hot cobbler into dessert dishes and top with a scoop of vanilla or caramel ice cream.

Spiced Apple, Pear, and Raisin Crumble

✓ *MAKE-AHEAD*   ✓ *TAKE-ALONG*   ✓ *SOMETHING SPECIAL*

Cobblers, buckles, pandowdies, slumps, grunts, crisps, Bettys, crumbles, and roly-polies are all old-fashioned fruit-filled desserts that satisfied our parents and grandparents—whether they were sitting around a campfire or lounging at a table set with silver and fine china—and still make mouths water today. All are combinations of pastry with fruit and sugar. They have the advantage of being quick and easy, no-fuss family dishes that just about everyone will love. This one—cooked fruit topped with a crumble made of sugar, flour, and oats—is especially nice, and the addition of spices and raisins makes it good enough for company.

✱TIP: Use two knives, one in each hand, **to cut up the butter** in the flour. This is an old-fashioned technique, much faster than using just one knife—but not as easy as a pastry blender.

Butter to grease one 9-inch pie plate

1/2 cup sugar

2 tablespoons cornstarch

1/2 teaspoon cinnamon

1/4 teaspoon salt

1/8 teaspoon allspice

2 Fuji or Gala apples, peeled, cored, halved, and sliced 1/4 inch thick

2 Bartlett pears, peeled, cored, halved, and sliced 1/4 inch thick

1 cup raisins, steeped in hot water to soften, drained

1 teaspoon pure vanilla extract

3 tablespoons cold unsalted butter, cut up

1/3 cup firmly packed light brown sugar

1/2 cup old-fashioned oatmeal (not quick-cooking or instant)

1/3 cup all-purpose flour

1. Preheat the oven to 350°F. Butter a 9-inch deep-dish pie plate.

2. In a large bowl, stir together the granulated sugar, cornstarch, cinnamon, salt, and allspice. Add the apples, pears, raisins, and vanilla and stir to combine. Spoon into the prepared pie plate.

3. In a medium bowl, with a pastry blender or two knives cut the butter into the brown sugar until the mixture resembles coarse meal. Add the oats and flour and stir until the butter is completely incorporated and the mixture is evenly crumbly. Sprinkle evenly over the fruit and bake in the preheated oven, 50 minutes to 1 hour, until the filling is bubbly and the topping is golden brown. ✱

SERVING SUGGESTION

A scoop of vanilla ice cream, several spoonfuls of custard sauce, or even just a dollop of heavy or whipped cream makes this dish even better.

Ginger-Pecan Peach Pie

✓ *MAKE-AHEAD*   ✓ *TAKE-ALONG*   ✓ *SOMETHING SPECIAL*

I love to take advantage of fresh fruit at the peak of its season. Peaches are at their best only in the summer, so I serve them every way I can while they are ripe and full of juice—in ice cream, cobblers, and milkshakes; over shortcake biscuits; on breakfast cereal; and, of course, in pies. If you are looking for a pie that's a little more special than the usual, this ginger-flavored version fits the bill.

1¾ pounds peaches, peeled, halved, pitted, and sliced *

⅓ cup packed light brown sugar

Pinch salt

2 tablespoons plus 2 teaspoons packed light brown sugar

1 tablespoon sugar

½ cup pecan halves (from about 3 ounces)

Pinch salt

½ cup all-purpose flour

¼ cup (½ stick) unsalted butter, slightly softened

¾ teaspoon vanilla extract

2 teaspoons cornstarch, sifted

2 teaspoons grated fresh ginger

½ teaspoon lemon zest

1 teaspoon lemon juice

¾ teaspoon ground cinnamon

One 9-inch frozen pie shell or refrigerated pie pastry, defrosted overnight in refrigerator

1. Preheat the oven to 375°F.

2. In a large bowl, combine the peaches, brown sugar, and salt. Gently stir with a rubber spatula or wooden spoon to combine all the ingredients. Set aside for at least 30 minutes and up to 2 hours at room temperature.

3. While the peaches are sitting, prepare the topping. In the bowl of a food processor fitted with the metal blade, combine the brown and white sugars, pecans, and salt. Pulse until the nuts are coarsely chopped. Add the flour, butter, and vanilla and pulse until the mixture is coarse and crumbly. Remove to a bowl and reserve.

4. Drain the peaches in a colander set over a bowl to capture any juices. Pour the saved juice (about ⅔ cup) into a small non-stick saucepan and bring to a simmer over medium-high heat. Simmer without stirring until the juice is reduced by half and is syrupy and golden brown, 4 to 5 minutes.

5. In a large bowl, combine the peaches, cornstarch, ginger, lemon zest, lemon juice, and cinnamon. Gently stir with a rubber spatula or wooden spoon until all traces of cornstarch have disappeared.

6. Pour the reduced syrup over the peaches and stir gently. Pour the peach mixture into the prepared pie crust and sprinkle with the pecan crumb topping. Bake in the preheated oven for 55 minutes to 1 hour, until bubbly and nicely browned. Remove from the oven and cool on a rack until warm.

7. Serve warm or room temperature.

★ TIP: When using fresh **peaches**, peel them with a sharp peeler or blanch in boiling water for 30 seconds to 1 minute, until the skins loosen. Remove from the boiling water and immediately rinse with cold water. The skins will easily peel off of the peaches.

Chocolate Chip Bread Pudding

MAKES 8 SERVINGS

✓ *MAKE-AHEAD*   ✓ *TAKE-ALONG*   ✓ *SOMETHING SPECIAL*

Bread pudding has made an amazing comeback as the ultimate comfort food. A staple dessert in the days when nothing was thrown away, many of us grew up eating it at family dinners. Instead of the usual raisins, try this chocolate chip delight. I haven't yet met a kid who didn't like it.

★ TIP: This mixture can be refrigerated overnight if you like.

Butter to grease one 9-inch baking dish

2 cups half and half

4 whole eggs

2 egg yolks

¼ cup sugar

Pinch salt

1 tablespoon pure vanilla extract

8 cups 1-inch cubed day-old bread (brioche preferred, but white bread will work as well)

1 cup chocolate chips (from 6 ounces)

1. Preheat the oven to 325°F. Butter a 9-inch round or oval baking dish.

2. In a medium bowl, whisk together the half and half, eggs, yolks, sugar, salt, and vanilla.

3. In a large bowl, combine the cubed bread and chocolate chips. Pour the egg mixture over the bread, stirring the bread cubes gently to evenly coat. Let the bread sit at least 1 hour, stirring occasionally, to allow the cubes to absorb the egg mixture. ★

4. Pour the soaked bread into the prepared dish. Bake, approximately 45 minutes to 1 hour, until set and a knife inserted in the center comes out mostly clean. Serve warm.

Serving Suggestion

Whipped cream flavored with a little hot chocolate mix is the perfect topping.

Caramel Banana Shortcake

✓ EASY PREPARATION   ✓ SOMETHING SPECIAL

When company is coming and you are short on time, make this excellent right-from-the-pantry dessert. It looks so elegant and tastes wonderful. It is fine to use the commercial variety of short-cakes. Note: Most of the alcohol from the brandy and rum burns off, so everyone can enjoy it.

8 individual shortcakes, wrapped in foil and warmed in the oven *

4 large bananas

1/3 cup (5 tablespoons) butter

1/3 cup packed dark brown sugar

1/2 teaspoon ground cinnamon

1/8 teaspoon ground cloves

Pinch salt

2 tablespoons rum

2 tablespoons brandy

1 quart vanilla ice cream

1. Warm the shortcakes in a low oven or toaster oven. Peel and slice the bananas in half length-wise. Cut each half into 2-inch pieces.

2. Melt the butter in a large skillet over low heat. Stir in the sugar, cinnamon, cloves, and salt and bring to a simmer. Add the banana pieces to the sauce and cook to heat through, 2 minutes. Add the rum and brandy and ignite with matches or an electric lighter. *

3. Let the flames burn out and stir to combine the sauce.

4. Spoon a scoop of vanilla ice cream on each warmed shortcake and top with caramel bananas.

＊TIP: For a variation on the **texture**, bake frozen buttermilk biscuits, then cool and split to make the shortcakes.

＊TIP: Be sure to **pour all the alcohol into the pan** before lighting it, use a long grill lighter, and stand back from the stove. The alcohol will ignite and flare up, but will die down in a minute or two. Wait until the flame dies before stirring.

Drink to the Good Life

Drinks are often an afterthought at meals but why stick with the same old store-bought sodas and cocktails? There are so many wonderful ideas for drinks with character and distinction, and with minimal effort, you can add any number to your repertoire.

You can give plain old iced tea a kick by adding fruit juice, flavored sodas, or even a dash of rum.

The cocktail hour can be fun, but alcohol doesn't need to be part of the equation. For an all-ages treat, make a batch of the base recipe, add alcohol only for those who want it, and everyone can enjoy themselves while relaxing together after the activities or stresses of the day.

Drinks (and a snack) can tide you over when sitting down for a meal is not possible. When breakfast or lunch is on-the-run, think smoothies. They are both nourishing and portable. Keep the essential ingredients on hand and the blender out on the countertop for extra-fast preparation. Cups with lids and fat straws make them easy to carry on the school bus or in the car.

When the kids come in cold and wet from playing in the snow, give them a big mug of frothy hot chocolate and the day becomes just a bit brighter for everyone. Turn any occasion into something special by including one of our fun drinks.

Teas with Zing

✓ *EASY PREPARATION*　　✓ *MAKE-AHEAD*　　✓ *SOMETHING SPECIAL*

Hot weather will have you thirsting after tall glasses of cold iced tea, but don't just settle for plain tea. Add your favorite fruit juices, fruit sodas, fruit purees, or fruit syrups and create your own signature drink, or just follow our simple suggestions. Keep a pitcher in the refrigerator and you will have an instant quencher ready any time of day or night.

1 orange, well-washed and halved

1/2 medium well-washed lemon

8 orange and spice tea bags, steeped in 6 cups boiling water ✶

1/2 cup sugar

1/2 cup dark rum (optional), or use 1/2 cup more fresh orange juice

Ice cubes

8 mint sprigs, for garnish

8 orange slices, for garnish

1. Squeeze the whole orange and lemon half into the steeping tea and drop into the pitcher. Stir in the sugar until it dissolves. Chill for several hours. ✶

2. Remove the tea bags and fruit from the chilled tea and stir in the rum, if using.

3. Fill glasses with ice cubes and pour in the tea. Garnish with mint sprigs and orange slices.

✶**TIP:** You can also **use any** other **fruity, spiced tea** that you enjoy to make this fun, chilled beverage. If you want a family treat, try one or more of the decaffeinated varieties.

✶**TIP: Try different fruit juices** in place of the orange and lemon. Cranberry, raspberry, white grape, mango, or peach nectar, or even pineapple juice are all perfect for adding to tea. Add whole fresh strawberries for garnish if you like.

Peach Bellinis

✓ *EASY PREPARATION*   ✓ *SOMETHING SPECIAL*

This delicious summer drink originated in Venice at the famous Harry's Bar. It seems to have been named in honor of Giovanni Bellini, the Italian artist, but today the Bellini is famous all by itself. In Italy, Bellinis are made with Prosecco, a slightly sweet sparkling wine, but any sparkling wine or even lemon/lime soda make great substitutes. Since you make these one at a time, add wine to the adults' glasses and soda for the children.

★**TIP:** Yellow peaches are available through much of the year, but check the quality. If it's not summer, the peaches are likely imported so be sure they look and smell fresh. The original drink was made with white peaches, which are available for just a very short time each summer.

3 cups chopped fresh or frozen peaches, thawed ★

1 tablespoon powdered sugar

1/2 cup bottled peach nectar

8 Champagne flutes, rims rubbed with lemon and dipped into sugar

One 750 ml bottle Champagne or 24 ounces 7UP™, well chilled

1. In a blender or food processor, combine the peaches, sugar, and nectar. Puree until very smooth. Chill several hours. Stir well or shake before using.

2. Fill the prepared glasses halfway with peach puree and slowly pour in the Champagne or 7UP.

Cosmopolitans

✓ EASY PREPARATION   ✓ SOMETHING SPECIAL

The Cosmopolitan—a mix of cranberry juice, vodka, and lime—has been all the rage for years and its popularity doesn't seem to be abating. In fact, many restaurants and bars are becoming very creative with their own versions. And you can, too. While vodka is certainly a classic part of the drink, you can substitute seltzer or club soda for the vodka and enjoy a delicious nonalcoholic version with the kids if it's your preference. Make a pitcher of the alcohol-free blend to serve the next time you have a back-yard lunch with neighborhood families or serve a shaker full of the original when the gang gathers for drinks. Also, if you use fun glasses, everyone will enjoy the drink—with or without alcohol.

2½ cups cranberry juice, chilled

½ cup orange juice, chilled

2 tablespoons Rose's Lime Juice *

6 ounces vodka or soda water

Ice cubes

6 chilled martini glasses

6 lime wedges, for garnish

1. In a large pitcher, combine the cranberry juice, orange juice, and Rose's Lime Juice. Stir in the vodka or soda water.

2. Fill a large cocktail shaker three-quarters full of ice cubes. Pour in the juice mixture to cover the ice. Firmly fit the lid onto the shaker and shake vigorously, about 15 to 30 seconds. *

3. Remove the cap from the lid, pour into the chilled martini glasses, and garnish with the lime wedges. Serve immediately. *

＊TIP: Rose's Lime Juice is a commercial, nonalcoholic, sweetened, concentrated lime juice. It is an integral part of many refreshing nonalcoholic drinks, as well as cocktails like gimlets and flavored margaritas.

＊TIP: When using soda water instead of vodka, don't shake the mixture; simply stir to mix well. If you shake the soda, you risk blowing the top off the shaker and splashing the drink everywhere.

＊TIP: If you prefer, pour the nonalcoholic juice mixture over ice in tall glasses. Make another pitcher to keep in the refrigerator for refills.

Virgin Mango Margaritas

✓ *EASY PREPARATION* ✓ *SOMETHING SPECIAL*

Jimmy Buffett may have made "margarita" a household word, but the libation has been around for quite a while. Cointreau, lime juice, and tequila are featured in the original, but today margaritas come in every shape and size. They can be frozen, served over ice, or drunk straight up, and any fruit can be the central ingredient. Equally delicious when alcohol-free, these fruit-filled drinks have the advantage of leaving you clear-headed and refreshed.

3½ cups bottled mango juice

⅓ cup fresh lime juice
(from 3 or 4 large limes)

1 cup sweet and sour mix ✱

6 mint leaves

2 cups crushed ice

1 mango, peeled, cut into ¼-inch cubes, frozen ✱

8 margarita glasses, rims rubbed with lime and dipped lightly into sugar

1. Place all the ingredients except the mango cubes in the jar of a blender and pulse until just blended and smooth.

2. Place 3 to 5 cubes of frozen mango in each prepared glass and fill with the blended margarita mixture. Serve immediately.

✱ TIP: Sweet and sour mix is a bottled combination of lemon and lime juices, sugar syrup, and in some cases egg white to make the final drink frothy. It is available in the drinks section of most supermarkets.

✱ TIP: You can prepare the mango in advance: Spread the mango cubes on a baking sheet and freeze until hard, several hours. Transfer the frozen fruit to resealable freezer bags and store in the freezer until needed.

Juicy Fruit Cooler

✓ *EASY PREPARATION*   ✓ *SOMETHING SPECIAL*

Fruit coolers can be fun and flavorful ways to offer fruit. Use any seasonal fruit for variety. For fun, dip the rims of the glasses in lime juice, and then in red or blue decorating sugar. Garnish these with a strawberry or a piece of fruit on each glass.

✱ TIP: For added fruit taste, use a fruit-flavored seltzer.

2 cups fresh strawberries, blueberries, or blackberries

2 large ripe bananas

3/4 cup cranberry or grape juice

6 ice cubes

2 teaspoons honey

2 cups seltzer water or club soda ✱

1. Clean and trim the berries.

2. Peel the bananas and break them into chunks.

3. Place the berries and chunks of bananas into a blender, then add the juice and the ice cubes. Add the honey, for a slightly sweet flavor, and then put the lid on the blender. Blend on high until the mixture is smooth.

4. Divide the mixture among 6 tall chilled glasses. Fill with seltzer water and serve.

Frozen Fruit Yogurt Smoothies

✓ *EASY PREPARATION*   ✓ *SOMETHING SPECIAL*

Smoothies are good any time of day. They make an excellent breakfast drink, midmorning pick-me-up, lunch on the run, or even an after-school snack. They are also wonderfully satisfying for tempting lagging appetites, especially those of older relatives who have lost interest in many other foods.

✱ TIP: These **smoothies can be refrigerated** for up to 4 hours.

4 cups frozen fruit, such as strawberries, raspberries, peaches, blueberries, thawed

1 banana, sliced

1 cup orange juice

1/2 cup milk

1 1/2 cups vanilla yogurt

2 tablespoons honey

1 teaspoon pure vanilla extract

8 whole fresh strawberries, split from the tip of the berry, halfway up to the stem

1. Combine the thawed frozen fruit, banana, orange juice, milk, yogurt, honey, and vanilla extract in a blender and puree until smooth. If the smoothies are thicker than you prefer, thin with a little extra orange juice or water.

2. Serve in 8-ounce glasses with a fresh strawberry slipped onto the rim of each glass. ✱

DRINK TO THE GOOD LIFE   185

Fruit Sparklers with Fresh Mint

✓ *EASY PREPARATION*   ✓ *SOMETHING SPECIAL*

Those hot summer days that kill normal appetites are perfect for these delicious fruit refreshers. Make up a pitcher of the base and keep it refrigerated to bring out whenever there's a need for something cool and thirst-quenching.

1 cup fresh or frozen raspberries, thawed

1 cup fresh or frozen blueberries, thawed

1/3 cup cranberry juice

1 tablespoon plus 1 teaspoon powdered sugar

8 Champagne flutes or other fancy glasses

One 750 ml bottle Champagne or 24 ounces sparkling water, well chilled

8 large mint leaves, rinsed and very well dried, for garnish

16 raspberries, for garnish

1. Combine the raspberries, blueberries, cranberry juice, and powdered sugar in a blender and puree until smooth. *

2. Pour approximately ¼ cup puree into each flute and fill with Champagne or sparkling water. Garnish each flute with a mint leaf and 2 raspberries. Serve immediately.

*TIP: If a smoother, seed-free puree is preferred, the mixture can be pushed through a mesh strainer, solids discarded. Reserve the puree in the refrigerator.

Frothy Marshmallow Hot Chocolate

✓ *EASY PREPARATION*   ✓ *SOMETHING SPECIAL*

There is never a bad time for a mug of hot chocolate—and a hot chocolate that leaves you with a frothy moustache is even more fun. Why not start a new rainy day tradition at your house and welcome everyone home with this delicious mood lifter? Gather around the kitchen table and swap stories—you'll end up laughing together and ready to tackle whatever you need to do.

4 cups milk

½ cup marshmallow cream

4 packets or ¾ cup hot chocolate mix

4 chocolate-covered candy sticks or candy canes, for garnish *

Mini marshmallows, for garnish

Cocoa powder, for garnish

1. Heat the milk to a scald in a small saucepan over medium heat or in the microwave. *

2. Stir in the marshmallow cream and the hot chocolate mix. Pour the mixture into a blender; cover with the lid and a kitchen towel to keep it from leaking. Pulse the hot mixture 5 to 6 times, to allow some of the steam to escape, then blend on a low speed for 30 seconds.

3. Pour the frothy hot chocolate into mugs and garnish each cup with a candy stick. Top with a few mini marshmallows and a dusting of cocoa powder.

✷ TIP: These **candy sticks** are available in hard mint flavor or with several varieties of hard fruit centers such as orange and raspberry, which are dipped or covered in dark chocolate.

✷ TIP: **Scalding milk** has become unnecessary due to modern pasteurization, but the temperature the milk reaches when scalded is exactly what you want for this hot drink. As milk heats on the stove, tiny bubbles begin to appear around the edges of the pan. If you watch and remove the milk or cream from the heat at this "scald stage" you won't have it boiling over everywhere.

Lip-Smacking Snacks

When you're working hard—or playing hard—having a snack between meals helps get you through the day. Americans are often so active, we love—or even need—to nibble throughout the day. There are a lot of temptations available in stores—but why not create them in your own kitchen? It's often easy to overindulge in fattening snacks such as chips or cookies, so the key to healthy snacking is to provide an energy boost that isn't simply empty calories. When you make what you snack on yourself, you have more control over the flavor and nutrition.

Sweets are important, but should be an occasional treat rather than a daily event. Most days it's a good idea to stick to fresh vegetables, fresh fruit, yogurt, cheese and bread, or fruit-rich smoothies.

Tips for snacking:

- Keep snacks organized. Always keep the ingredients for your favorite snacks on hand in the same place in the pantry, ready to bring out whenever the need arises. In fact, if your family has snacks on a regular basis, you might also keep some ingredients prepped in the refrigerator for quick assembly.

- Serve them at specific times rather than allowing kids to nibble at will.

- Remember that a snack isn't a meal but a pick-me-up, so keep portions small.

- Whether or not you enlist the aid of the children when you are making snacks for a few or for a crowd, be sure to include items that are both easy to prepare and satisfying to eat.

- Avoid a snack rut. Try to vary snack foods, alternating fruit one day with something more savory the next.

- Create individual portions of packaged snacks in single-serving-sized plastic bags or containers for those times when only a snack cake or a handful of corn chips will satisfy. Most of us will stop with one portion, but might overindulge if faced with the whole package.

Some of the dishes in this chapter, like the tostadas and the quesadillas, are tasty, filling snacks but, especially for kids, if you add soup or salad, they can also serve as a satisfying lunch or dinner.

Vegetables and Ranch Dipping Sauce

✓ *EASY PREPARATION*   ✓ *MAKE-AHEAD*

Finding creative ways to serve vegetables is always a challenge. Try this inventive and delicious dipping sauce and you will never go back to prepackaged dressing again. Each time you make this, add a new vegetable for your family to try. Kids will try lots of new things if they can dip them in a tasty sauce. Bread sticks and cheese sticks can round out the perfect snack.

½ cup plain unflavored yogurt

½ cup buttermilk

½ cup mayonnaise

1 teaspoon garlic powder

1 teaspoon dried dill

1 teaspoon freshly ground pepper

2 teaspoons prepared mustard (Dijon is a fine choice, or use your favorite)

1 teaspoon lemon juice

2 cups baby carrots

2 cups fresh cleaned and trimmed green beans *

2 cups celery sticks (from about 6 large ribs)

In a small bowl, beat together the yogurt, buttermilk, mayonnaise, garlic powder, dill, pepper, mustard, and lemon juice. Chill for several hours. Serve with a plate of carrots, green beans, and celery sticks. *

*TIP: Blanch green beans in boiling water for a minute or two and then refresh in cold water for crunchy, dippable, bright green beans.

*TIP: When you are **trying new dippers**, don't forget cucumber sticks, sticks of fresh green and red bell pepper, tomato wedges, raw asparagus spears, blanched sugar snap peas, wedges of fresh fennel, and even spears of raw zucchini.

Cream Cheese and Nut Sandwiches on Cinnamon Raisin Bread

✓ *EASY PREPARATION*   ✓ *MAKE-AHEAD*   ✓ *TAKE-ALONG*

Some years ago, the Chock full o'Nuts coffee shop chain in New York, sold thousands of these sandwiches every day, along with steaming bowls of the day's special soup, to bankers, secretaries, messengers, shoppers—anyone who stepped up to the counter. It was inexpensive, popular, and nourishing—and worth keeping the tradition alive.

8 ounces cream cheese, softened (low-fat is fine)

3/4 cup chopped toasted pecans or walnuts (from about 3 ounces)

1 1/2 teaspoons cinnamon

2 tablespoons honey

8 slices cinnamon-raisin coffee bread, commercial or homemade, or even our Cranberry Walnut Bread (page 168)

1. In a small bowl, whip together the cream cheese, nuts, cinnamon, and honey.

2. Lay out 4 slices of bread. Spread each slice thickly with the cream cheese mixture. Top each with another slice of bread. Cut off the crusts if you like. Cut each sandwich into quarters. ✱

SERVING SUGGESTION

For lunch, serve with a steaming bowl of our Rotisserie Chicken and Wild Rice Soup (page 38), and watch your children gobble every bit.

✱ **TIP:** These sandwiches keep very well for up to **24 hours.** Wrap them tightly in plastic wrap or aluminum foil, refrigerate overnight, and pop into bag lunches for a special school treat.

Sloppy Joe Tostadas

✓ *MAKE-AHEAD*   ✓ *READY AND WAITING*

Who doesn't enjoy delicious, warm comfort food every now and then? Sloppy Joes are a great dish to make as a family because just about everyone loves them. The classic is served on a soft burger bun that soaks up all the luscious juices; this version puts a Tex-Mex accent on an old favorite. Let the kids chop the onion and green pepper under your supervision, then they can put together the final tostadas to serve the family. One of these makes a perfect after-school snack; two are an easy main course for dinner along with salad and fruit. The mixture freezes well, so any leftovers can be put in the freezer for another time.

★ TIP: Tostadas are 6- or 8-inch corn tortillas that have been fried flat, not folded like taco shells. You can top a tostada with almost anything you like. They are available in boxes in most supermarkets.

1 pound lean ground beef (95% lean)

1 cup chopped white onion

1/2 cup chopped green bell pepper

1 teaspoon garlic powder

4 teaspoons ground cumin

1/4 teaspoon dried oregano

1/4 teaspoon paprika

1 teaspoon salt

1 teaspoon freshly ground pepper

1 tablespoon mild chili powder, or more to taste

One 14 1/2-ounce can of tomatoes

2 tablespoons tomato paste

Eight 6- or 8-inch premade tostadas ★

1/2 cup grated cheddar cheese (from 2 ounces)

1. Brown the ground beef in a medium-sized skillet on medium-high heat until it is cooked through, about 10 minutes. Add the onion and the bell pepper. Cook, stirring, until the onion and green pepper are soft, about 8 minutes more.

2. Add the garlic powder, cumin, oregano, paprika, salt, pepper, and chili powder to the pan. Gently stir it into the beef mixture.

3. Add the tomatoes and tomato paste to the pan and stir them in gently. Cook for 20 minutes, stirring occasionally, until very thick.

The mixture can be refrigerated at this point for up to 2 days and reheated in the microwave when ready to serve.

4. Once the beef mixture is hot, carefully spoon it onto the tostada shells. Sprinkle with cheese and serve.

SERVING SUGGESTION

If you like, pass plates of sliced tomato and avocado, thinly sliced sweet onion, and a bowl of sour cream for folks to add at will.

Pigs in a Blanket

✓ *EASY PREPARATION*   ✓ *MAKE-AHEAD*

These little wrapped gems can be made with several different ingredients. Start with a premade dough and fill it with all sorts of fun things. Cheese sticks, chicken fingers, and fish sticks are all good choices—kids can use their imaginations to think of more. A child of any age can help make these delicious treats.

1 can (8 count) crescent roll dough

1 pound hot dogs, turkey, beef, or pork

4 slices American cheese, cut in half

2 teaspoons yellow mustard

1 egg, beaten

1. Preheat the oven to 375°F. Separate the crescent roll dough along the perforations into 8 triangles.

2. Cut each hot dog carefully three-quarters of the way through lengthwise. Place half a slice of cheese into the slit of each hot dog.

3. Spread mustard on each triangle of crescent dough.

4. Wrap each hot dog in a triangle of dough, starting with the long end and rolling toward the tip.

5. Place the wrapped hot dogs on a cookie sheet. Repeat with all of the hot dogs. Brush each filled triangle with the beaten egg glaze.

6. Bake for 15 minutes, or until the dough is golden brown and the hot dog is cooked through.

VARIATIONS

These little wrappers provide you with the opportunity to be creative. Add pizza ingredients, such as pepperoni, pizza sauce, and cheese. Substitute turkey and cheese. Or, gather your favorite vegetables and wrap them up, too!

Cheesy Quesadillas

MAKES 4 QUESADILLAS

✓ EASY PREPARATION   ✓ MAKE-AHEAD   ✓ TAKE-ALONG

I always keep cheddar cheese, flour tortillas, and shredded cooked chicken on hand so I can quickly satisfy my son's craving for his favorite snack. You will want to keep your favorites in the refrigerator, too. Tortillas freeze just fine; just place a piece of parchment paper in between each one so they won't stick together, wrap them in freezer paper, and freeze.

Eight 12-inch flour tortillas

4 cups grated cheddar cheese

1 cup grated Monterey Jack cheese (from about 4 ounces)

½ teaspoon ground cumin

½ teaspoon ground oregano

½ teaspoon salt

¼ teaspoon chili powder

2 tablespoons butter

½ cup tomato salsa (optional)

Guacamole (homemade or good quality commercial), for garnish

Sour cream, for garnish

1. Place 4 tortillas on the cutting board.

2. Top each tortilla with 1 cup of cheddar cheese and ¼ cup Monterey Jack cheese.

3. In a small bowl, combine the cumin, oregano, salt, and chili powder. Sprinkle the spice mixture over the cheese.

4. Spoon on a little salsa, if desired, and then top each tortilla with another tortilla.

5. In a medium skillet, melt ½ tablespoon butter over medium-high heat. Place 1 filled quesadilla in the pan once the butter is hot and bubbly. Cook, turning once, until the cheese is melted and the tortilla is golden brown on both sides. Repeat with the remaining tortillas. *

6. Serve with more salsa, guacamole, and sour cream for garnish.

✱TIP: If your child—like my son, Matthew, used to—wants to make these on his own, he or she can **heat them in the microwave.** Until he was older, cooking them "in a pan" as he called it (on the stove), was something that we only did when we were cooking together.

Frozen Fruit Ice Pops

✓ *EASY PREPARATION*   ✓ *MAKE-AHEAD*   ✓ *SOMETHING SPECIAL*

Icy fruit pops are flavorful snacks anytime but are particularly refreshing on hot summer days—and you can make them in many delicious flavors to please a crowd. These are a great way to sneak yogurt and fruit into your kids' diets, and can be made up to two months ahead. So, stock up on fruit and yogurt, prepare a whole bunch, and make room in your freezer!

1 cup apple or orange juice

1 cup fresh ripe strawberries, peaches, or bananas, cut into pieces

1 cup vanilla yogurt

1 tablespoon honey

9 wooden craft sticks

Two 6-count ice pop molds, or nine 3-ounce paper cups ✱

1. In a blender, combine the juice, fruit, yogurt, and honey. Blend until smooth.

2. Divide the mixture evenly among ice pop molds or paper cups and freeze for 24 hours. ✱

3. Gently unmold the ice pops by placing the molds in warm water for a minute. Then loosen the ice pop gently from the cup. Or, if using paper cups, simply tear them away from the frozen treat.

✱**TIP:** You can make your own ice pop molds with 3-ounce (or 5-ounce) paper cups. Fill the cups with the mixture and place them on a cookie sheet. Cover all the cups tightly with a single piece of plastic wrap and carefully poke a hole with a knife in the middle of the plastic wrap on each cup. Place the craft sticks through the hole in the plastic wrap. The plastic wrap will help the sticks stand up straight until the ice pop is set.

✱**TIP:** Keep these frozen treats on hand for longer than 24 hours and up to 4 days by unmolding the fully frozen pops, wrapping them individually in plastic wrap, and storing in a hard plastic freezer box.

Peanut Butter and Jelly No-Bake Nuggets

✓ *EASY PREPARATION*   ✓ *NO COOKING NEEDED*   ✓ *SOMETHING SPECIAL*

All kids love to make candy. Even the youngest cook can whip up these little treats—each with a surprise center. Let them make these for a special snack, when they have invited a friend to play.

¼ cup (½ stick) butter, softened

½ cup peanut butter

1¼ cups confectioners' sugar

25 small fruit jelly beans, such as Jelly Belly®

½ cup sugar cookie crumbs (from about 2 large cookies) ✳

1. In a medium bowl, cream the butter and peanut butter. Stir in the sugar until the mixture is about the texture of modeling clay. Refrigerate 1 hour.

2. Form teaspoons of the mixture into balls, inserting one jelly bean into the center of each.

3. Roll finished balls in cookie crumbs.

4. Arrange the nuggets on a cookie sheet and chill for 1 to 2 hours before serving.

✳ TIP: To make the cookie **crumbs,** break up the cookies and whirl the pieces in a food processor.

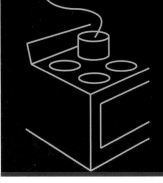

Cooking with Kids

Having young children join you in the kitchen to help make their own dinner or snacks creates the perfect opportunity to teach them techniques and food and kitchen safety in a fun way. All they will think about is getting in on the action and the yummy results.

When working in the kitchen with you, kids will learn more than just how to follow a recipe—they will start to know their way around the kitchen. They will learn to recognize foods when they are whole and uncooked, and to appreciate the ingredients and how to handle them. They will learn about cutting, mixing, and baking and how to be careful around hot ovens, scalding liquids, and sharp knives. With frequent exposure to food and cooking comes familiarity and, after that, confidence.

Tips for cooking with kids:

- First and always—all cooks, no matter their age, should wash their hands thoroughly with soap and water before beginning.

- Start with simple recipes that require little preparation, such as English Muffin Pizzas (page 197), or Peanut Butter–Chocolate Bananas on a Stick (page 201), or recipes in which ingredients are simply assembled before cooking or may not even need to be cooked. Children as young as three can work with you if they can be set up at the counter on a sturdy chair or stool, even if their hands need adult guiding the first few times. The thrill of accomplishment they feel will be obvious.

- Move on to slightly more complicated recipes that involve more advanced techniques. Highly supervised cutting is next, teaching a respect for the sharpness of knives and other cutting instruments. All the same safety rules that I discuss for adults (in the book's introduction) apply to children, especially regarding keeping knives in plain sight but out of reach at all times.

- Using the microwave, the toaster oven, or the stovetop with an adult nearby should be the next step. But rules should be firm and invariable—these appliances must be used only with supervision.

- Baking may well be the first category of cooking that children can accomplish by themselves from start to finish—even if an adult must be on hand the first few times to remove the hot pans from the oven.

- Make the same recipe together more than once. As when reading the same bedtime story over and over, the repetition gives children an understanding of the cooking process from beginning to end, as well as the confidence to ultimately make something entirely on their own. It won't take much to convince them a simple dish has become their specialty and children love to be the best at something.

Once they have mastered the recipes in this chapter, they can move on to other dishes in the book, concentrating on the foods they enjoy eating most. With kids in the kitchen, the key is to remain relaxed, focusing on the enjoyment you are sharing. The results are well worth the time and effort.

English Muffin Pizzas

✓ *EASY PREPARATION*   ✓ *MAKE-AHEAD*

When I was young, I loved pizza. My mom could not keep enough pizza dough on hand to satisfy my ongoing craving. So I became very creative to satisfy my hunger. From crackers to bread, almost anything I could find in the kitchen became a crust for pizza topping. One day, without anything but English muffins in the freezer, I made this for my brother and me; it became an instant favorite for us. Your kids will love making these, too, and if you keep the ingredients on hand it can be an anytime treat.

4 English muffins, split in half

2 cups pizza sauce (available in all supermarkets)

2 cups grated mozzarella cheese (from about 8 ounces)

½ cup grated Parmigiano-Reggiano cheese (from about 2 ounces)

½ pound sliced pepperoni

1. Preheat the oven to 400°F.

2. Arrange the eight English muffin halves on a cookie sheet.

3. Top each muffin half with ¼ cup pizza sauce. Top each half with ¼ cup mozzarella cheese and 2 tablespoons of Parmigiano-Reggiano cheese. Finish each pizza with pepperoni slices. Place the cookie sheet in the preheated oven.

4. Bake for 10 to 15 minutes until the cheese melts and the sauce is heated through. Serve while still hot.

Mini Meat Loaves

✓ MAKE-AHEAD   ✓ READY AND WAITING   ✓ SOMETHING SPECIAL

These tiny meat loaves are made in muffin tins and turn out perfectly time after time. One makes a snack; count on two per person for a quick dinner. Serve them hot with macaroni and cheese or mashed potatoes, and keep leftovers in the refrigerator to slice for a quick meat loaf sandwich.

1 cup chopped white onion

2 pounds lean ground beef
(at least 95% lean)

1 cup Italian seasoned bread crumbs

1 teaspoon salt

2 teaspoons yellow mustard

1 teaspoon Worcestershire sauce

1/2 teaspoon freshly ground pepper

1/4 cup ketchup, plus 1/2 cup
for topping

2 large eggs

1. Preheat the oven to 350°F.

2. Combine the onion with the ground beef in a medium bowl.

3. Add in the bread crumbs, salt, mustard, Worcestershire sauce, pepper, and 1/4 cup ketchup.

4. Break the eggs into a small bowl and beat them lightly. Pour the eggs over the meat and gently toss the mixture with two forks until the ingredients are well combined.

5. With your hands, divide the meat into 12 equal balls and press them into a 12-muffin pan. Spread the 1/2 cup topping ketchup over the tops of the meat loaves. *

6. Bake the meat loaves in the preheated oven for 20 minutes. Cool on a wire cooling rack for 10 minutes, turn out, and serve. *

★ TIP: Even very young kids love to help form the little loaves. Just be sure they wash their hands thoroughly with soap and water both just before and after they help.

★ TIP: The meat loaves are done when the interiors reach 160°F with an instant-read thermometer. Just check it by removing the pan from the oven (if kids are doing most of the baking, adults should step in here), and sticking in the thermometer. If it hasn't reached 160°F, return the pan to the oven and bake a little longer.

Chicken Nuggets and Homestyle Fries

✓ *EASY PREPARATION*   ✓ *MAKE-AHEAD*   ✓ *SOMETHING SPECIAL*

Kids just love chicken nuggets—it seems universal. Even though fast-food versions are readily available, it's always better to have them eat and even help make them at home. With only a little supervision even the newest young cook can prepare this favorite snack. This easy recipe bakes both the chicken and fries at the same time.

1 cup Italian-seasoned bread crumbs

2 tablespoons vegetable oil

1 teaspoon salt

1 teaspoon paprika

1 teaspoon dried thyme

1/2 teaspoon freshly ground pepper

1/2 pound chicken breast, cut into 2-inch squares

2 russet potatoes, well washed, unpeeled, cut into thin wedges

1. Preheat the oven to 400°F.

2. Combine the bread crumbs and oil in a large plastic bag. Add the salt, paprika, thyme, and pepper.

3. Fill a small bowl with warm water. Line a cookie sheet with aluminum foil.

4. One at a time, dip each piece of chicken into the water and then drop it into the bag with the bread crumbs. Shake well to remove excess crumbs. Repeat with the potatoes.

5. Pat the bread crumbs onto the chicken pieces and on the potato wedges to coat completely, then place each piece on the cookie sheet, leaving space between each one.

6. Bake on the cookie sheet in the preheated oven for 15 to 20 minutes, until crisp and lightly browned. Serve with ketchup or barbecue sauce.

S'mores in a Blanket

✓ MAKE-AHEAD   ✓ SOMETHING SPECIAL

If you were ever a Girl or Boy Scout and loved spending chilly nights around a campfire combining graham crackers, chocolate squares, and charred marshmallows for an evening treat, these are for you. With the croissant crust, these are sophisticated, yet so down to earth the kids will want them for dessert. The flavors are the same as the old favorite, and the ready-to-use refrigerated dough is easy enough for everyone to use. Make them up ahead of time, and pop them into the oven minutes before you want to serve them.

One 8-ounce can refrigerated quick crescent rolls

½ cup mini marshmallows

½ cup milk chocolate chips

4 cinnamon graham crackers, crumbled into pieces, or 16 mini honey graham bear crackers

2 tablespoons butter, melted

1. Preheat the oven to 375°F.

2. Open the crescent rolls and separate into 8 triangles.

3. In a large bowl, mix together the marshmallows, chocolate chips, and graham cracker pieces.

4. Place a large spoonful of the mixture on the wide end of 1 dough triangle. Fold in the edges and roll up toward the tip, pressing the edges together to seal. Dip the rolls in melted butter, coating one side. Press the roll, buttered side down, into an ungreased muffin cup. Repeat with the remaining dough triangles.

5. Bake 12 to 15 minutes until golden brown.

6. Serve hot, but be sure to warn lucky eaters that the inside will be very hot as the mini marshmallow melts into a sweet cream in the middle.

Peanut Butter–Chocolate Bananas on a Stick

MAKES 6 SERVINGS

These healthy snacks are perfect for dessert. Children love to participate in all the steps, especially squeezing the bananas—just don't let them become overenthusiastic or they will end up with mashed banana.

✱ TIP: Serve these the same day they are made, as they will become soggy if kept any longer.

3 large ripe bananas, peeled, cut in half across

6 tablespoons smooth or chunky peanut butter

6 flat ice pop sticks

8 ounces semisweet chocolate chips, melted

1. Fill a small shoe box or 1-quart disposable plastic refrigerator box with dried beans or rice. The extra weight this provides keeps the box from upsetting once the banana sticks are set into it. Use a knife to cut 6 slits in the lid, just large enough to poke an ice pop stick through. Tape the lid to the box. Set aside.

2. Gently press down on or squeeze each banana half, moving from tip to cut end. The banana will separate into 3 long equal-length triangular sections. Spread the 2 inner sides of one section with peanut butter. Place an ice pop stick on side coated with the peanut butter, leaving about 2 inches of the stick extended beyond the cut edge, and re-form the three triangular sections of each banana half, pressing gently so it sticks together and looks a lot like a corn dog. Repeat with remaining banana halves.

3. Holding the stick, carefully dip each banana "pop" in the melted chocolate, coating at least two-thirds of the length of the banana half.

4. Gently push each stick end into one of the slits cut in the top of the shoe box or plastic food storage box, and chill the bananas for 20 minutes, or until the chocolate sets. ✱

Quick and Easy Cinnamon Pull-Apart Loaf

✓ *EASY PREPARATION*   ✓ *MAKE-AHEAD*   ✓ *TAKE-ALONG*   ✓ *SOMETHING SPECIAL*

Using refrigerated dough makes this fun loaf as easy as any quick bread, and it adds a special touch to any weekend brunch. Kids love the way the loaf pulls into individual pieces, and they will be eager to learn how to make it. The only step they may need help with is removing the pan from the oven when baked. I also like to cool the loaf and then slice it with a bread knife into thick slices, to toast and enjoy with a cup of freshly brewed coffee or frothy hot chocolate.

½ cup (1 stick) butter, melted

1 cup sugar

1½ teaspoons ground cinnamon

½ teaspoon ground ginger

Two 1-pound loaves frozen bread dough, thawed

1. Preheat the oven to 350°F.

2. With a pastry brush, generously grease a 10-cup bundt or tube pan with melted butter.

3. In a flat bowl or soup plate, stir together the sugar, cinnamon, and ginger until well mixed. Pour the remaining melted butter into another flat bowl or soup plate.

4. Divide the thawed bread dough into 24 pieces and form into balls with your palms. Roll each ball in the melted butter and then in the sugar mixture. Layer the sugar-covered dough in the prepared pan. Press the dough balls lightly in place. *

5. Sprinkle 2 tablespoons of the remaining sugar mixture over the top of the loaf.

6. Cover the pan with a towel and let rise about 30 minutes or until doubled in bulk.

7. Bake 30 to 35 minutes. Cool on a rack for 5 minutes, and then turn out onto a plate. Cool 10 minutes before serving.

＊TIP: To prevent air pockets, arrange the dough balls in layers in the prepared pan, alternating slightly so that each ball sits on top of the space between the two balls beneath it. As the loaf rises it will fill in the spaces so there will be few air pockets.

Chocolate Chip Cookie Pizza

✓ *MAKE-AHEAD*   ✓ *TAKE-ALONG*

For years I have gone to Old Chicago Pizza in Boulder, Colorado, and the meal is never complete, especially for my son, without a chocolate chip pizza. This is my homemade version of that wonderful treat. Serve warm with ice cream, and if you've ever tried theirs, I think you will agree that this is the next best thing; if you've never been to Old Chicago Pizza, you and your kids will still be glad you have this recipe.

1¼ cups all-purpose flour

½ teaspoon baking soda

½ teaspoon sea salt

½ cup unsalted butter,
at room temperature

½ teaspoon pure vanilla extract
(I prefer Madagascar vanilla for
the intense flavor) ✱

¼ cup plus 2 tablespoons sugar

¼ cup plus 2 tablespoons dark
brown sugar

1 large egg, room temperature

1¼ cups chocolate chips
(from about 7½ ounces)

1. Preheat the oven to 375°F.

2. In a small bowl, combine the flour, baking soda, and salt.

3. In a large bowl, cream together the butter, vanilla, and sugars using a wooden spoon. Add the egg and stir until combined. Add the flour in 3 parts to the butter mixture, incorporating each addition thoroughly. Stir in the chocolate chips.

4. Spread the dough with your fingers from edge to edge in a greased pizza pan or 9-inch pie plate.

5. Bake in the oven for 20 minutes or until golden brown and slightly firm.

6. Cool on a wire cooling rack. While still warm, cut into wedges and serve with vanilla ice cream.

✱TIP: Right now, vanilla is extremely expensive, but **do not substitute artificial vanilla flavoring** for the real thing. If Madagascar vanilla is out of your budget range, use another pure vanilla extract.

Chocolate Chip–Toffee Mini Muffins

✓ MAKE-AHEAD   ✓ TAKE-ALONG

Children love these little gems not just for breakfast—by themselves or with cinnamon cream cheese—but as a snack at any time. You can also cut them in half, add a scoop of vanilla ice cream, and you have dessert for everyone.

Butter to grease 30 mini muffin cups

2 cups all-purpose flour

1 cup sugar

1 teaspoon baking powder

1 teaspoon ground cinnamon

Pinch salt

2/3 cup mini chocolate chips

1/3 cup toffee chips *

2 large eggs, lightly beaten

1 cup buttermilk

1/4 cup (1/2 stick) butter, melted and cooled

1. Preheat the oven to 375°F.

2. Generously grease the bottom and sides of 30 mini muffin cups. In a medium bowl, stir together the flour, sugar, baking powder, cinnamon, salt, chocolate chips, and toffee chips.

3. In another medium bowl, beat together the eggs, buttermilk, and butter. Pour the mixture over the dry ingredients. Stir just until moist; the batter should be full of lumps.

4. Fill prepared muffin cups two-thirds full. Bake 12 to 15 minutes. Set the pan on a wire rack and cool 2 to 3 minutes. Turn out onto a plate.

SERVING SUGGESTION

Roll hot muffins in 1 cup granulated sugar as soon as they are turned out of the pan.

✱ TIP: For a chocolate alternative, **toffee chips** are available in bags in the baking section of many supermarkets. You can also find other flavored chips like white chocolate, peanut butter, even mini candy-covered bits that can be substituted for chocolate chips in many recipes. They are a delicious addition to many baked goods. Try adding them to your favorite chocolate chip or oatmeal cookie recipe.

Index

A

Alcoholic drinks
  Cosmopolitans, 182
  Fruit Sparklers with Fresh
    Mint, 186
  Peach Bellinis, 181
  Teas with Zing, 180
American cheese
  Baked Spaghetti, 154
  Pigs in a Blanket, 192
Appetizers, 20–32
  Crispy Fried Tortilla
    Chips, 29
  Crispy No-Fry Tortilla
    Chips, 28
  Crusty Pizza Rolls with
    Tomato Dipping Sauce,
    30–31
  Deep-Fried Cheese Bites
    with Curry Mayonnaise,
    25–26
  Grilled Vegetable
    Quesadillas, 32

  Herbed Cheddar Cheese
    Spirals, 24
  Hot and Spicy Spinach Crab
    Dip, 21
  Jalapeño Poppers with Chili
    Mayonnaise, 22–23
  Layered Cheese–Avocado
    Bean Dip, 27
Apples, Spiced Apple, Pear,
  and Raisin Crumble, 175
Apricot-Glazed Chicken with
  Sweet Apricot Stuffing, 85
Asian Beef Stew, 156
Asian Broiled Salmon Salad,
  48
Asian Dressing, 116
Avocado, Layered Cheese–
  Avocado Bean Dip, 27

B

Baked Cannelloni with
  Meatballs, 152–153
Baked Onions, 126

Baked Spaghetti, 154
Baked Whole Snapper with
  Tomato Tartare, 72–73
Bananas
  Caramel Banana Shortcake,
    178
  Frozen Fruit Ice Pops, 194
  Frozen Fruit Yogurt
    Smoothies, 185
  Juicy Fruit Cooler, 184
  Peanut Butter–Chocolate
    Bananas on a Stick, 201
Barbecue Ranch Dressing,
  44–45
Beans
  Chili Pie, 145
  Grilled Chicken Salad with
    Black Beans and Barbecue
    Ranch Dressing, 44–45
  Mom's Beef and Beer Chili,
    40
  New England Baked Beans,
    132

  Red Beans and Rice, 160
  Turkey-Chipotle Chili, 86
  Vegetable and Bean
    Soup, 36
Beans, refried, Layered
  Cheese–Avocado Bean Dip,
  27
Beef
  Asian Beef Stew, 156
  Baked Spaghetti, 154
  Beef Goulash, 137–138
  Bollito Misto with Green
    Sauce, 108109
  Broiled New York Strip
    Steaks with Baby
    Greens, 46
  Chili Pie, 145
  Classic Beef Stroganoff on
    Buttered Noodles, 102
  Corned Beef Dinner, 131
  Corned Beef Hash, 143
  Cumin-Crusted Chuck
    Roast, 101

Beef (*continued*)
    Grillades and Grits, 135–136
    Herbed Meat Lasagna, 149
    Jerked Roast Filet of Beef
        with Coconut Rice, 103–104
    Meatballs, 152
    Mini Meat Loaves, 198
    Mom's Beef and Beer Chili,
        40
    Ropa Vieja, 133–134
    Sloppy Joe Tostadas, 191
    Stuffed Flank Steak with
        Roasted Peppers and Feta
        Cheese, 144
    Swiss Steak, 141
Beef leftovers
    Beef Enchilada Pie, 117
    Hearty Salad with Asian
        Dressing, 116
    Irish Stew, 114
    Lentils with Shredded Beef
        and Feta Cheese, 120
    Roasted Beef or Lamb with
        Gnocchi and Sherry
        Cream Sauce, 115
    Stuffed Eggplant Mediter-
        ranean, 118
Beer, Mom's Beef and Beer
    Chili, 40
Blackberries, Juicy Fruit
    Cooler, 184
Blueberries
    Frozen Fruit Yogurt
        Smoothies, 185

    Fruit Sparklers with Fresh
        Mint, 186
    Juicy Fruit Cooler, 184
Bollito Misto with Green
    Sauce, 108–109
Braised Turkey Breast with
    Olives, 87
Bread pudding, Chocolate
    Chip Bread Pudding, 177
Breads
    Cranberry Walnut Bread,
        168
    Garlic Butter Bread Sticks,
        167
    Gooey Cinnamon Rolls, 169
    Olive Tapenade Rolls, 164
    Poppy Seed Bread Sticks,
        166
    Quick and Easy Cinnamon
        Pull-Apart Loaf, 202
    Stuffed Bread with Green
        Chiles and Cheddar
        Cheese, 162
    Sun-Dried Tomato and
        Rosemary Herb Bread,
        165
    Tabasco Cheddar Cheese
        Bread, 163
Broccoli, Orzo with Vegetables
    and Herbs, 123
Broiled New York Strip Steaks
    with Baby Greens, 46
Bulgur wheat, Roasted
    Tomatoes and Bulgur, 129

Butter Leaf Salad with Glazed
    Scallops, 51

C

Cabbage
    Corned Beef Dinner, 131
    Vegetable and Bean
        Soup, 36
    See also Napa cabbage
Cake, Caramel Banana
    Shortcake, 178
Candies, Peanut Butter and
    Jelly No-Bake Nuggets, 195
Cannelloni with Meatballs,
    152–153
Caramel Banana Shortcake,
    178
Carrots, Vegetables and Ranch
    Dipping Sauce, 189
Cashews, Stir-Fried
    Vegetables with Tofu
    and Cashews, 159
Celery, Vegetables and Ranch
    Dipping Sauce, 189
Cheddar cheese
    Cheesy Potato Soup, 35
    Cheesy Quesadillas, 193
    Chicken, Cheese, and
        Portobello Quesadillas, 96
    Chicken Enchiladas with
        Tomatillo Sauce, 97–98
    Deep-Fried Cheese Bites
        with Curry Mayonnaise,
        25–26

    Herbed Cheddar Cheese
        Spirals, 24
    Layered Cheese–Avocado
        Bean Dip, 27
    Pork or Beef Enchilada Pie,
        117
    Potato and Onion Omelets,
        62–63
    Sloppy Joe Tostadas, 191
    Stuffed Bread with Green
        Chiles and Cheddar
        Cheese, 162
    Tabasco Cheddar Cheese
        Bread, 163
    Turkey and Green Chile
        Enchilada Pie, 150
Cheese. *See* American cheese;
    Cheddar cheese; Feta cheese;
    Gouda cheese, smoked;
    Gruyère cheese; Monterey
    Jack cheese; Mozzarella
    cheese; Parmigiano-
    Reggiano cheese; Ricotta
    cheese
Cheese and Vegetable
    Enchiladas, 124
Cheesy Potato Soup, 35
Cheesy Quesadillas, 193
Chicken
    Apricot-Glazed Chicken
        with Sweet Apricot
        Stuffing, 85
    Bollito Misto with Green
        Sauce, 108–109

Chicken with Feta Cheese and Tomatoes, 82

Chicken Nuggets with Homestyle Fries, 199

Chicken Provençal, 147

Chicken and Rice—with Variations, 80–81

Chicken Tetrazzini, 146

Chunky Sour Cream and Basil Chicken Salad, 43

Cinnamon-Spiced Chicken Curry, 157

Classic Roasted Chicken, 78

Grilled Chicken Salad with Black Beans and Barbecue Ranch Dressing, 44–45

Rotisserie Chicken and Matzo Ball Soup, 39

Rotisserie Chicken and Wild Rice Soup, 38

Spicy Chicken Curry with Side Dishes, 83–84

Chicken leftovers
Chicken, Cheese, and Portobello Quesadillas, 96

Chicken Enchiladas with Tomatillo Sauce, 97–98

Chicken Fried Rice, 95

Chicken and Yogurt Pitas, 89

Creamed Chicken and Mushrooms on Toast, 93

Herbed Chicken Patties, 90

Old-Fashioned Chicken and Dumplings, 91–92

Quick and Easy Chicken Pot Pie, 94

Chickpeas
Curried Turkey with Herbed Couscous, 99

Lamb and Brown Rice Salad, 119

Children. See Kids, cooking with

Chiles. See Chipotle chiles; Green Chiles; Serrano chiles

Chili
Chili Pie, 145

Mom's Beef and Beer Chili, 40

Turkey-Chipotle Chili, 86

Chili Mayonnaise, 22

Chipotle chiles, Turkey-Chipotle Chili, 86

Chocolate
Chocolate Chip Bread Pudding, 177

Chocolate Chip Cookie Pizza, 203

Chocolate Chip-Toffee Mini Muffins, 204

Double Chocolate Walnut Cookies, 172

Frothy Marshmallow Hot Chocolate, 187

Oatmeal Chocolate Chip Cookies, 173

Peanut Butter–Chocolate Bananas on a Stick, 201

S'mores in a Blanket, 200

Chunky Sour Cream and Basil Chicken Salad, 43

Cinnamon Pull-Apart Loaf, 202

Cinnamon Rolls, Gooey, 169

Cinnamon-Spiced Chicken Curry, 157

Cobbler, Peach Cobbler with Pecan Crust, 174

Coconut milk
Asian Beef Stew, 156

Coconut Rice, 104

Shrimp and Coconut Soup, 41

Spicy Chicken Curry with Side Dishes, 83–84

Cookies
Chocolate Chip Cookie Pizza, 203

Double Chocolate Walnut, 172

Oatmeal Chocolate Chip, 173

Spiced Oatmeal, 171

Cooking
with children. See Kids, cooking with

with family, 5–7

fitting into schedule, 4–5

Corned Beef Dinner, 131

Corned Beef Hash, 143

Cornmeal-Crusted Trout, 71

Cosmopolitans, 182

Couscous, Curried Turkey with Herbed Couscous, 99

Crabmeat, Hot and Spicy Spinach Crab Dip, 21

Cranberry Walnut Bread, 168

Cream Cheese and Egg Frittata, 58

Cream Cheese and Nut Sandwiches on Cinnamon Raisin Bread, 190

Creamed Chicken and Mushrooms on Toast, 93

Creamy Roasted Tomato Soup, 34

Crispy Fried Tortilla Chips, 29

Crispy No-Fry Tortilla Chips, 28

Croissant French Toast, 64

Crumble, Spiced Apple, Pear, and Raisin Crumble, 175

Cumin-Crusted Chuck Roast, 101

Curry dishes
Cinnamon-Spiced Chicken Curry, 157

Curried Turkey with Herbed Couscous, 99

Curry Mayonnaise, 26

Spicy Chicken Curry with Side Dishes, 83–84

D

Deep-Fried Cheese Bites with Curry Mayonnaise, 25–26

Desserts
Caramel Banana Shortcake, 178

Desserts (*continued*)
  Chocolate Chip Bread
    Pudding, 177
  Chocolate Chip Cookie
    Pizza, 203
  Ginger-Pecan Peach Pie,
    176
  Peach Cobbler with Pecan
    Crust, 174
  S'mores in a Blanket, 200
  Spiced Apple, Pear, and
    Raisin Crumble, 175
  See also Cookies
Dipping sauces
  Chili Mayonnaise, 22
  Curry Mayonnaise, 26
  Ranch Dipping Sauce, 189
  Tomato Dipping Sauce, 31
Dips
  Hot and Spicy Spinach Crab
    Dip, 21
  Layered Cheese–Avocado
    Bean Dip, 27
Double Chocolate Walnut
  Cookies, 172
Dressings
  Asian, 116
  Barbecue Ranch, 44–45
Drinks
  Frothy Marshmallow Hot
    Chocolate, 187
  Frozen Fruit Yogurt
    Smoothies, 185
  Juicy Fruit Cooler, 184

Virgin Mango Margaritas, 183
  See also Alcoholic drinks
Dumplings
  basic recipe, 92
  Old-Fashioned Chicken and
    Dumplings, 91–92

E

Eggplant
  Grilled Vegetable
    Quesadillas, 32
  Oven Ratatouille, 127
  Stuffed Eggplant Mediter-
    ranean, 118
  See also Japanese eggplant
Eggs
  Cream Cheese and Egg
    Frittata, 58
  Croissant French Toast, 64
  Mediterranean Egg Cups, 59
  Potato and Onion Omelets,
    62–63
  Salmon and Chive
    Scrambled Eggs, 53
  Santa Fe Mini Tortes, 60–61
  Tomato and Ham Quiche,
    54–55
  Vegetable Strata, 56–57
Enchiladas
  Cheese and Vegetable
    Enchiladas, 124
  Chicken Enchiladas with
    Tomatillo Sauce, 97–98
  Pork or Beef Enchilada Pie,
    117

Turkey and Green Chile
    Enchilada Pie, 150
English Muffin Pizzas, 197

F

Fall-off-the-Bone Pork Ribs,
  140
Fennel, Mediterranean Egg
  Cups, 59
Feta cheese
  Chicken with Feta Cheese
    and Tomatoes, 82
  Lentils with Shredded Beef
    and Feta Cheese, 120
  Stuffed Flank Steak with
    Roasted Peppers and Feta
    Cheese, 144
  Vegetable Strata, 56–57
Fish and shellfish
  Asian Broiled Salmon
    Salad, 48
  Baked Whole Snapper with
    Tomato Tartare, 72–73
  Butter Leaf Salad with
    Glazed Scallops, 51
  Cornmeal-Crusted
    Trout, 71
  Fish Stew, 74–75
  Grilled Salmon Fillets with
    Lime Butter Baste, 66
  Mediterranean Seared Tuna
    Salad, 49
  Ratatouille-Stuffed Tilapia
    Fillets, 67–68

Shrimp and Pesto Pasta
    Salad, 50
  Shrimp, Sausage, and
    Vegetable Stew, 76
  Spiced Dover Sole Fillets
    with Creamed Spinach, 69
  Tuna Steaks with Olive
    Tapenade, 70
Freezer make-aheads
  Chicken Provençal, 147
  Chicken Tetrazzini, 146
  Chili Pie, 145
  Corned Beef Hash, 143
  make and freeze tips, 142
  Stuffed Flank Steak with
    Roasted Peppers and Feta
    Cheese, 144
  Turkey and Green Chile
    Enchilada Pie, 150
  Wild Rice and Smoked
    Turkey Muffins, 148
French toast, Croissant French
  Toast, 64
Frittata, Cream Cheese and
  Egg Frittata, 58
Frothy Marshmallow Hot
  Chocolate, 187
Frozen Fruit Ice Pops, 194
Frozen Fruit Yogurt Smoothies,
  185
Fruit. *See* specific types
  of fruit
Fruit Sparklers with Fresh
  Mint, 186

G

Garlic Butter Bread Sticks, 167

Ginger-Pecan Peach Pie, 176

Gnocchi, Roasted Beef or Lamb with Gnocchi and Sherry Cream Sauce, 115

Gouda cheese, smoked, Cheese and Vegetable Enchiladas, 124

Green beans
Stir-Fried Vegetables with Tofu and Cashews, 159
Vegetables and Ranch Dipping Sauce, 189

Green chiles
Chicken and Rice—with Variations, 80–81
Grilled Vegetable Quesadillas, 32
Layered Cheese–Avocado Bean Dip, 27
Pork or Beef Enchilada Pie, 117
Santa Fe Mini Tortes, 60–61
Stuffed Bread with Green Chiles and Cheddar Cheese, 162
Turkey and Green Chile Enchilada Pie, 150

Green Sauce, 109

Grillades and Grits, 135–136

Grilled Chicken Salad with Black Beans and Barbecue Ranch Dressing, 44–45

Grilled Lamb Chops with Mandarin Orange Salad, 47

Grilled Salmon Fillets with Lime Butter Baste, 66

Grilled Vegetable Quesadillas, 32

Grits, Grillades and Grits, 135–136

Gruyère cheese, Tomato and Ham Quiche, 54–55

H

Halibut fillet, Fish Stew, 74–75

Ham
Spicy Scalloped Ham and Potatoes, 155
Tomato and Ham Quiche, 54–55
Vegetable and Bean Soup, 36

Hearty Salad with Asian Dressing, 116

Herb-Crusted Lamb Chops, 107

Herbed Cheddar Cheese Spirals, 24

Herbed Chicken Patties, 90

Herbed Meat Lasagna, 149

Homestyle Fries, 199

Honey Kiwi Salsa, 106

Hot dogs, Pigs in a Blanket, 192

Hot and Spicy Spinach Crab Dip, 21

I

Ice pops, Frozen Fruit, 194

Irish Stew, 114

J

Jalapeño Poppers with Chili Mayonnaise, 22–23

Japanese eggplant, Ratatouille-Stuffed Tilapia Fillets, 67–68

Jerked Roast Filet of Beef with Coconut Rice, 103–104

Juicy Fruit Cooler, 184

K

Kids, cooking with
Chicken Nuggets and Homestyle Fries, 199
Chocolate Chip Cookie Pizza, 203
Chocolate Chip-Toffee Mini Muffins, 204
English Muffin Pizzas, 197
Mini Meat Loaves, 198
Peanut Butter–Chocolate Bananas on a Stick, 201
Quick and Easy Cinnamon Pull-Apart Loaf, 202
S'mores in a Blanket, 200

Kitchen
equipment, 14–16
fresh foods, buying guide, 17–18
pantry, organizing, 9–11

safety guidelines, 18–20

staples, listing of, 11–14

Kiwifruit, Honey Kiwi Salsa, 106

L

Lamb
Grilled Lamb Chops with Mandarin Orange Salad, 47
Hearty Salad with Asian Dressing, 116
Herb-Crusted Lamb Chops, 107
Wine and Rosemary Marinated Leg of Lamb, 105

Lamb leftovers
Hearty Salad with Asian Dressing, 116
Irish Stew, 114
Lamb and Brown Rice Salad, 119
Roasted Beef or Lamb with Gnocchi and Sherry Cream Sauce, 115
Stuffed Eggplant Mediterranean, 118

Lasagna, Herbed Meat Lasagna, 149

Layered Cheese–Avocado Bean Dip, 27

Leftovers. *See* Beef leftovers; Chicken leftovers; Pork leftovers; Turkey leftovers

Lentils with Shredded Beef and Feta Cheese, 120

M

Make-ahead meals. *See* Freezer make-aheads
Mandarin oranges
    Grilled Lamb Chops with Mandarin Orange Salad, 47
    Mandarin Orange Turkey Sauté, 158
Mangoes
    Asian Broiled Salmon Salad, 48
    Virgin Mango Margaritas, 183
Marshmallow
    Marshmallow Hot Chocolate, 187
    S'mores in a Blanket, 200
Matzo balls, Rotisserie Chicken and Matzo Ball Soup, 39
Mayonnaise. *See* Dipping sauces
Meatballs, 152
Meat loaf, Mini Meat Loaves, 198
Mediterranean Egg Cups, 59
Mediterranean Seared Tuna Salad, 49
Mini Meat Loaves, 198
Mixed Vegetables and Quinoa, 122

Mom's Beef and Beer Chili, 40
Monkfish, Fish Stew, 74–75
Monterey Jack cheese
    Cheesy Quesadillas, 193
    Chicken, Cheese, and Portobello Quesadillas, 96
    Chicken Enchiladas with Tomatillo Sauce, 97–98
    Grilled Vegetable Quesadillas, 32
    Layered Cheese–Avocado Bean Dip, 27
    Pork or Beef Enchilada Pie, 117
    Santa Fe Mini Tortes, 60–61
    Spicy Scalloped Ham and Potatoes, 155
    Turkey and Green Chile Enchilada Pie, 150
Mozzarella cheese
    Baked Cannelloni with Meatballs, 152–153
    Crusty Pizza Rolls with Tomato Dipping Sauce, 30–31
    English Muffin Pizzas, 197
    Herbed Meat Lasagna, 149
Muffins
    Chocolate Chip-Toffee Mini Muffins, 204
    Wild Rice and Smoked Turkey Muffins, 148
Mushrooms
    Chicken, Cheese, and Portobello Quesadillas, 96

Chicken Tetrazzini, 146
Creamed Chicken and Mushrooms on Toast, 93
Hearty Salad with Asian Dressing, 116
Veal Scallops with Onions and Mushrooms, 110
Wild Rice and Smoked Turkey Muffins, 148
Mussels, Fish Stew, 74–75
Mustard-Crusted Pork Roast, 111

N

Napa cabbage, Asian Broiled Salmon Salad, 48
New England Baked Beans, 132

O

Oatmeal cookies
    Oatmeal Chocolate Chip Cookies, 173
    Spiced Oatmeal Cookies, 171
Old-Fashioned Chicken and Dumplings, 91–92
Olive tapenade
    Olive Tapenade Rolls, 164
    Tuna Steaks with Olive Tapenade, 70
Omelets, Potato and Onion Omelets, 62–63

One-dish meals
    Asian Beef Stew, 156
    Baked Cannelloni with Meatballs, 152–153
    Baked Spaghetti, 154
    Cinnamon-Spiced Chicken Curry, 157
    Mandarin Orange Turkey Sauté, 158
    Red Beans and Rice, 160
    Spicy Scalloped Ham and Potatoes, 155
    Stir-Fried Vegetables with Tofu and Cashews, 159
Onions
    Baked Onions, 126
    Potato and Onion Omelets, 62–63
    Pumpkin and Onion Casserole, 128
    Roasted Onions and Potatoes, 125
Orzo with Vegetables and Herbs, 123
Oven Ratatouille, 127

P

Parmigiano-Reggiano cheese
    Baked Cannelloni with Meatballs, 152–153
    Baked Onions, 126
    Chicken Tetrazzini, 146
    Cream Cheese and Egg Frittata, 58

Deep-Fried Cheese Bites
with Curry Mayonnaise,
25–26
English Muffin Pizzas, 197
Herbed Cheddar Cheese
Spirals, 24
Herbed Meat Lasagna, 149
Hot and Spicy Spinach Crab
Dip, 21
Jalapeño Poppers with Chili
Mayonnaise, 22–23
Tomato and Ham Quiche,
54–55
Pasta
Baked Cannelloni with
Meatballs, 152–153
Baked Spaghetti, 154
Herbed Meat Lasagna, 149
Shrimp and Pesto Pasta
Salad, 50
Pasta sauce, Hands-Off Pasta
Sauce, 139
Peaches
Frozen Fruit Ice Pops, 194
Frozen Fruit Yogurt
Smoothies, 185
Ginger-Pecan Peach Pie, 176
Peach Bellinis, 181
Peach Cobbler with Pecan
Crust, 174
Peanut butter
Peanut Butter–Chocolate
Bananas on a Stick, 201

Peanut Butter and Jelly
No-Bake Nuggets, 195
Spicy Peanut Soup, 37
Pears, Spiced Apple, Pear, and
Raisin Crumble, 175
Pecans
Cream Cheese and Nut
Sandwiches on Cinnamon
Raisin Bread, 190
Ginger-Pecan Peach Pie, 176
Peach Cobbler with Pecan
Crust, 174
Peppers, bell
Oven Ratatouille, 127
Stir-Fried Vegetables with
Tofu and Cashews, 159
Peppers, roasted, Stuffed
Flank Steak with Roasted
Peppers and Feta Cheese,
144
Pesto, Shrimp and Pesto Pasta
Salad, 50
Phyllo pastry, Crusty Pizza
Rolls with Tomato Dipping
Sauce, 30–31
Pies, Ginger-Pecan Peach Pie,
176
Pies, main dish
Chili Pie, 145
Pork or Beef Enchilada Pie,
117
Quick and Easy Chicken Pot
Pie, 94

Turkey and Green Chile
Enchilada Pie, 150
Pigs in a Blanket, 192
Pitas, Chicken and Yogurt
Pitas, 89
Pizza
Chocolate Chip Cookie
Pizza, 203
English Muffin Pizzas, 197
Pizza Rolls with Tomato
Dipping Sauce, 30–31
Poppy Seed Bread Sticks, 166
Pork
Fall-off-the-Bone Pork Ribs,
140
Hearty Salad with Asian
Dressing, 116
Mustard-Crusted Pork
Roast, 111
Pork leftovers
Hearty Salad with Asian
Dressing, 116
Pork Enchilada Pie, 117
Spicy Pork Casserole, 113
Stuffed Eggplant Mediter-
ranean, 118
Portobello mushrooms,
Chicken, Cheese, and
Portobello Quesadillas, 96
Potatoes
Cheesy Potato Soup, 35
Homestyle Fries, 199
Potato and Onion Omelets,
62–63

Roasted Onions and
Potatoes, 125
Spicy Scalloped Ham and
Potatoes, 155
Vegetable and Bean
Soup, 36
Pot pies, Quick and Easy
Chicken Pot Pie, 94
Poultry
carving guidelines, 79
See also Chicken; Turkey
Pumpkin and Onion
Casserole, 128

Q
Quesadillas
Cheesy Quesadillas, 193
Chicken, Cheese, and
Portobello Quesadillas, 96
Quiche, Tomato and Ham
Quiche, 54–55
Quick and Easy Chicken Pot
Pie, 94
Quinoa, Mixed Vegetables and
Quinoa, 122

R
Ranch Dipping Sauce, 189
Raspberries
Frozen Fruit Yogurt
Smoothies, 185
Fruit Sparklers with Fresh
Mint, 186

Ratatouille-Stuffed Tilapia
Fillets, 67–68
Red Beans and Rice, 160
Red snapper, Baked Whole
Snapper with Tomato
Tartare, 72–73
Rice
Chicken Fried Rice, 95
Chicken and Rice—with
Variations, 80–81
Coconut Rice, 104
Lamb and Brown Rice
Salad, 119
Red Beans and Rice, 160
Spicy Chicken Curry with
Side Dishes, 83–84
Rice noodles, Shrimp and
Coconut Soup, 41
Rice, wild. *See* Wild rice
Ricotta cheese
Baked Cannelloni with
Meatballs, 152–153
Herbed Meat Lasagna, 149
Roasted Chicken, Classic, 78
Roasted Onions and Potatoes,
125
Roasted Tomatoes and Bulgur,
129
Rolls
Crusty Pizza Rolls with
Tomato Dipping Sauce,
30–31
Gooey Cinnamon Rolls, 169
Olive Tapenade Rolls, 164

Ropa Vieja, 133–134
Rotisserie Chicken and Matzo
Ball Soup, 39
Rotisserie Chicken and Wild
Rice Soup, 38
Rubs, Jerk Rub, 103

S

Salads
Asian Broiled Salmon
Salad, 48
Broiled New York Strip
Steaks with Baby
Greens, 46
Butter Leaf Salad with
Glazed Scallops, 51
Chunky Sour Cream and
Basil Chicken Salad, 43
Grilled Chicken Salad
with Black Beans and
Barbecue Ranch Dress-
ing, 44–45
Grilled Lamb Chops
with Mandarin Orange
Salad, 47
Hearty Salad with Asian
Dressing, 116
Lamb and Brown Rice
Salad, 119
Mediterranean Seared Tuna
Salad, 49
Shrimp and Pesto Pasta
Salad, 50

Salmon
Asian Broiled Salmon
Salad, 48
Grilled Salmon Fillets with
Lime Butter Baste, 66
Salmon, smoked, Salmon and
Chive Scrambled Eggs, 53
Salsa, Honey Kiwi Salsa, 106
Sandwiches
Chicken and Yogurt
Pitas, 89
Cream Cheese and Nut
Sandwiches on Cinnamon
Raisin Bread, 190
Santa Fe Mini Tortes, 60–61
Sauces
Green Sauce, 109
Hands-Off Pasta Sauce, 139
Tomatillo Sauce, 97
See also Dipping sauces
Sausage
Bollito Misto with Green
Sauce, 108–109
Shrimp, Sausage, and
Vegetable Stew, 76
Scallops
Butter Leaf Salad with
Glazed Scallops, 51
Fish Stew, 74–75
Serrano chiles, Cinnamon-
Spiced Chicken Curry, 157
Shellfish. *See* Fish and
shellfish

Shitake mushrooms, Wild
Rice and Smoked Turkey
Muffins, 148
Shortcake, Caramel Banana
Shortcake, 178
Shrimp
Fish Stew, 74–75
Shrimp and Coconut
Soup, 41
Shrimp and Pesto Pasta
Salad, 50
Shrimp, Sausage, and
Vegetable Stew, 76
Sloppy Joe Tostadas, 191
Slow-cooked foods
Beef Goulash, 137–138
Corned Beef Dinner, 131
Cumin-Crusted Chuck
Roast, 101
Fall-off-the-Bone Pork Ribs,
140
Grillades and Grits,
135–136
Hands-Off Pasta Sauce,
139
Herbed Meat Lasagna, 149
New England Baked Beans,
132
Ropa Vieja, 133–134
Swiss Steak, 141
Smoothies, Frozen Fruit
Yogurt Smoothies, 185
S'mores in a Blanket, 200

Snacks
    Cheesy Quesadillas, 193
    Chocolate Chip-Toffee Mini
        Muffins, 204
    Cream Cheese and Nut
        Sandwiches on Cinnamon
        Raisin Bread, 190
    English Muffin Pizzas,
        197
    Frozen Fruit Ice Pops, 194
    Peanut Butter–Chocolate
        Bananas on a Stick, 201
    Peanut Butter and Jelly
        No-Bake Nuggets, 195
    Pigs in a Blanket, 192
    Sloppy Joe Tostadas, 191
    Vegetables and Ranch
        Dipping Sauce, 189
Sole fillets, Spiced Dover Sole
    Fillets with Creamed
    Spinach, 69
Soups
    Cheesy Potato Soup, 35
    Creamy Roasted Tomato
        Soup, 34
    Rotisserie Chicken and
        Matzo Ball Soup, 39
    Rotisserie Chicken and Wild
        Rice Soup, 38
    Shrimp and Coconut
        Soup, 41
    Spicy Peanut Soup, 37
    Vegetable and Bean
        Soup, 36

Spaghetti
    Baked, 154
    Chicken Tetrazzini, 146
Spiced Apple, Pear, and Raisin
    Crumble, 175
Spiced Dover Sole Fillets with
    Creamed Spinach, 69
Spiced Oatmeal Cookies, 171
Spicy Chicken Curry with Side
    Dishes, 83–84
Spicy Peanut Soup, 37
Spicy Pork Casserole, 113
Spicy Scalloped Ham and
    Potatoes, 155
Spinach
    Herbed Meat Lasagna, 149
    Hot and Spicy Spinach Crab
        Dip, 21
    Mediterranean Egg Cups, 59
    Spiced Dover Sole Fillets
        with Creamed Spinach, 69
Stews
    Asian Beef Stew, 156
    Beef Goulash, 137–138
    Fish Stew, 74–75
    Irish Stew, 114
    Shrimp, Sausage, and
        Vegetable Stew, 76
Stir-Fried Vegetables with Tofu
    and Cashews, 159
Strawberries
    Frozen Fruit Ice Pops, 194
    Frozen Fruit Yogurt
        Smoothies, 185
    Juicy Fruit Cooler, 184

Stuffed Bread with Green
    Chiles and Cheddar Cheese,
    162
Stuffed Eggplant Mediter-
    ranean, 118
Stuffed Flank Steak with
    Roasted Peppers and Feta
    Cheese, 144
Stuffing, Sweet Apricot
    Stuffing, 85
Sun-Dried Tomato and
    Rosemary Herb Bread, 165
Swiss Steak, 141

T

Tabasco Cheddar Cheese
    Bread, 163
Talapia fillets, Ratatouille-
    Stuffed Tilapia Fillets,
    67–68
Teas with Zing, 180
Toffee, Chocolate Chip-Toffee
    Mini Muffins, 204
Tofu, Stir-Fried Vegetables
    with Tofu and Cashews,
    159
Tomatillos, Chicken Enchi-
    ladas with Tomatillo Sauce,
    97–98
Tomatoes
    Chicken with Feta Cheese
        and Tomatoes, 82
    Creamy Roasted Tomato
        Soup, 34

Hands-Off Pasta Sauce,
    139
Orzo with Vegetables and
    Herbs, 123
Oven Ratatouille, 127
Roasted Tomatoes and
    Bulgur, 129
Tomato Dipping Sauce, 31
Tomato and Ham Quiche,
    54–55
Tomatoes, sun-dried, Sun-Dried
    Tomato and Rosemary Herb
    Bread, 165
Tomato Tartare, 72
Tortes, Santa Fe Mini Tortes,
    60–61
Tortillas
    Cheese and Vegetable
        Enchiladas, 124
    Cheesy Quesadillas, 193
    Chicken Enchiladas with
        Tomatillo Sauce, 97–98
    Crispy Fried Tortilla
        Chips, 29
    Crispy No-Fry Tortilla
        Chips, 28
    Grilled Vegetable Quesadil-
        las, 32
    Santa Fe Mini Tortes,
        60–61
    Turkey and Green Chile
        Enchilada Pie, 150
Tostadas, Sloppy Joe Tostadas,
    191

Trout, Cornmeal-Crusted
Trout, 71
Tuna
Mediterranean Seared Tuna
Salad, 49
Tuna Steaks with Olive
Tapenade, 70
Turkey
Braised Turkey Breast with
Olives, 87
Mandarin Orange Turkey
Sauté, 158
Turkey-Chipotle Chili, 86
Turkey and Green Chile
Enchilada Pie, 150
Wild Rice and Smoked
Turkey Muffins, 148
Turkey-Chipotle Chili, 86
Turkey leftovers, Curried
Turkey with Herbed
Couscous, 99

V

Veal
Bollito Misto with Green
Sauce, 108–109
Grillades and Grits, 135–136
Veal Scallops with Onions
and Mushrooms, 110
Vegetables
Baked Onions, 126
Cheese and Vegetable
Enchiladas, 124
Mixed Vegetables and
Quinoa, 122
Orzo with Vegetables and
Herbs, 123
Oven Ratatouille, 127
Pumpkin and Onion
Casserole, 128
Roasted Onions and
Potatoes, 125
Roasted Tomatoes and
Bulgur, 129

Stir-Fried Vegetables with
Tofu and Cashews, 159
Vegetable and Bean Soup, 36
Vegetables and Ranch
Dipping Sauce, 189
Vegetable Strata, 56–57
See also individual types of
vegetables
Virgin Mango Margaritas,
183

W

Walnuts
Cranberry Walnut Bread, 168
Cream Cheese and Nut
Sandwiches on Cinnamon
Raisin Bread, 190
Double Chocolate Walnut
Cookies, 172
Wild rice
Rotisserie Chicken and Wild
Rice Soup, 38

Wild Rice and Smoked
Turkey Muffins, 148
Wine and Rosemary
Marinated Leg of Lamb, 105

Y

Yogurt
Chicken and Yogurt
Pitas, 89
Frozen Fruit Ice Pops, 194
Frozen Fruit Yogurt
Smoothies, 185
Ranch Dipping Sauce, 189

Z

Zucchini
Grilled Vegetable Quesadil-
las, 32
Oven Ratatouille, 127
Ratatouille-Stuffed Tilapia
Fillets, 67–68
Vegetable Strata, 56–57

PANTRY CHECKLIST

Here is a list of foods and flavorings to have on hand—in the cupboard, refrigerator, and freezer. Cut or copy the list and post it in your kitchen or take it with you when you go to the market. It will help you always have what you need and make food shopping more efficient.

Dried Herbs and Spices

- ❏ Allspice
- ❏ Basil
- ❏ Bay leaves
- ❏ Cayenne pepper (ground red chile pepper)
- ❏ Chili powder (preferably a pure chili powder such as ancho or pasilla)
- ❏ Cinnamon, ground
- ❏ Crushed red pepper
- ❏ Cumin, ground
- ❏ Curry powder (several strengths, if you like)
- ❏ Garlic powder
- ❏ Ginger, ground and crystallized
- ❏ Mustard, dried powder
- ❏ Nutmeg, whole
- ❏ Old Bay Seasoning (spicy seasoning mix with great pepper flavor)
- ❏ Onion powder
- ❏ Oregano
- ❏ Paprika, sweet Hungarian
- ❏ Peppercorns, black and white (and a grinder)
- ❏ Poppy seeds
- ❏ Rosemary
- ❏ Sage
- ❏ Salt (if possible, sea salt, ground and coarse)
- ❏ Seasoned pepper (such as Mrs. Dash, for quick effective seasoning of everyday foods)
- ❏ Sesame seeds
- ❏ Tarragon
- ❏ Thyme

Other Seasonings and Flavorings

- ❏ Anchovy fillets in olive oil
- ❏ Baking powder, double acting
- ❏ Baking soda
- ❏ Beans, white, great northern, and black, in cans and dried
- ❏ Bouillon, cubes and powder (to use in a pinch if you have no broth or stock)
- ❏ Brandy
- ❏ Bread crumbs, unseasoned and panko (Japanese bread crumbs)
- ❏ Chicken broth, low-sodium, canned or boxed
- ❏ Chocolate, unsweetened and semisweet morsels
- ❏ Cocoa, unsweetened baking
- ❏ Cornmeal, yellow
- ❏ Cornstarch
- ❏ Flour, unbleached all-purpose
- ❏ Honey
- ❏ Horseradish, jarred
- ❏ Jam, seedless apricot, raspberry, or other favorite
- ❏ Ketchup
- ❏ Mandarin oranges, canned
- ❏ Mustard, Dijon, yellow, and your favorite flavored varieties
- ❏ Oil, olive (regular and extra-virgin), vegetable, peanut, Asian sesame, and walnut
- ❏ Olives
- ❏ Peanut butter, chunky and/or creamy
- ❏ Pineapple chunks, canned
- ❏ Roasted red bell peppers, jarred
- ❏ Sherry, dry

- ❏ Soy sauce, light and, if you like, a low-sodium one as well
- ❏ Sugar, granulated white and dark brown
- ❏ Tabasco sauce
- ❏ Tomatoes, whole plum, diced, tomato paste, tomato puree, and sun-dried
- ❏ Vanilla extract, pure
- ❏ Vinegar, white wine, red wine, cider, rice wine, and balsamic
- ❏ Wine, at least Chardonnay and Cabernet (not the commercial product sold as cooking wine)
- ❏ Worcestershire sauce
- ❏ Yeast, dry active

Pasta and Grains

- ❏ Arborio rice (for risotto)
- ❏ Bulgur
- ❏ Couscous
- ❏ Lentils
- ❏ Cut pastas (small shells and other shapes)
- ❏ Thin pastas (linguine, spaghettini, or angel hair)
- ❏ Rice, white long-grain, basmati, and brown

Fresh Basics

- ❏ Butter, unsalted—or salted if you prefer—except for baking
- ❏ Cheddar cheese
- ❏ Eggs, grade A large (unless otherwise noted, all recipes call for large eggs)
- ❏ Garlic, fresh cloves, or finely chopped in oil (to use in a pinch)
- ❏ Goat cheese, or another soft cheese such as ricotta or cream cheese
- ❏ Lemons
- ❏ Margarine
- ❏ Mayonnaise
- ❏ Milk, whole and fat-free
- ❏ Parmigiano-Reggiano cheese
- ❏ Yogurt, plain nonfat

Freezer Basics

- ❏ Berries of all kinds
- ❏ Bread, sourdough, ciabatta, and whole wheat
- ❏ Bread dough, store-bought (to make pizzas, breads, and crusts)
- ❏ Chicken, shredded and cubed
- ❏ Chocolate wafers and graham cracker crumbs
- ❏ Corn, yellow and/or white kernels
- ❏ Green beans, preferably the small haricot verts, or extra-thin beans that you can buy flash-frozen
- ❏ Nuts and seeds, pecans, almonds, pine nuts, poppy seeds, and sesame seeds (stored in the freezer they will last twice as long)
- ❏ Peaches
- ❏ Peas
- ❏ Pesto, store-bought or homemade
- ❏ Pie crusts, store-bought, folded or rolled, not prefitted into pans
- ❏ Tomato sauce
- ❏ Tortillas, corn and flour
- ❏ Vanilla ice cream

Premade Mixes and Other Items

- ❏ Barbecue rubs (Storebought are OK as long as they are not high in salt or sugar, they Make your own and store for up to 6 months.)
- ❏ Barbecue sauce,1 or 2 really good commercial ones (for quick grills)
- ❏ Bread mixes
- ❏ Brownie mixes and cake mixes
- ❏ Chutneys, tapenades, and specialty jams
- ❏ Crackers (Try low-fat and lower-sodium)
- ❏ Granola

Metric Conversion Guide

Weight

U.S. Units	Canadian Metric	Australian Metric
1 ounce	30 grams	30 grams
2 ounces	55 grams	60 grams
3 ounces	85 grams	90 grams
4 ounces (¼ pound)	115 grams	125 grams
8 ounces (½ pound)	225 grams	225 grams
16 ounces (1 pound)	455 grams	500 grams (½ kilogram)

Volume

U.S. Units	Canadian Metric	Australian Metric
¼ teaspoon	1 mL	1 ml
½ teaspoon	2 mL	2 ml
1 teaspoon	5 mL	5 ml
1 tablespoon	15 mL	20 ml
¼ cup	50 mL	60 ml
⅓ cup	75 mL	80 ml
½ cup	125 mL	125 ml
⅔ cup	150 mL	170 ml
¾ cup	175 mL	190 ml
1 cup	250 mL	250 ml
1 quart	1 liter	1 liter
2 quarts	2 liters	2 liters
3 quarts	3 liters	3 liters
4 quarts	4 liters	4 liters

Note: The recipes in this cookbook have not been developed or tested using metric measures.

Temperatures

Fahrenheit	Celsius
32°	0°
212°	100°
250°	120°
275°	140°
300°	150°
325°	160°
350°	180°
375°	190°
400°	200°
425°	220°
450°	230°
475°	240°
500°	260°

Measurements

Inches	Centimeters
1	2.5
2	5.0
3	7.5
4	10.0
5	12.5
6	15.0
7	17.5
8	20.5
9	23.0
10	25.5
11	28.0
12	30.5